"Angelica Harris adds another chapter to her own oeuvre of courage, love, and redemption with *Living with Rage: A Quest for Solace*. The highest form of spiritual alchemy is to transform one's own psychic pain into healing for others. Th~~i~~~~s~~ ~~is~~ what Harris has spent her adult life ~~do~~~~ing~~ ~~and~~ ~~touched~~ upon with this painful, honest, an~~d~~ ~~moving~~ ~~recounting~~ ~~of~~ her own horrifying adolescent ex~~perience.~~ ~~She~~ ~~lets~~ ~~us~~ know that no matter how difficult t~~he~~ ~~circumstance,~~ we (like her) can make it through, hea~~l~~ ~~and~~ ~~learn~~ to give love to others, where once there was only pain. Thank you, Angelica!"

—TOM BLOCK, FOUNDING PRODUCER
AMNESTY INTERNATIONAL HUMAN RIGHTS ART FESTIVAL

"What an inspiration Angelica is! This is an honest and candid memoir, a book that will have you in tears but will also have you cheering for the strong and successful woman sharing her story to make a difference in the lives of others. This book is a gift!"

—JENNIFER GERONIMO, SPEAKER/AUTHOR MANAGER
LIFE ENLIGHTENMENT

"*Living With Rage: A Quest For Solace* is a beacon in the darkness for those struggling to emerge from their own abusive situations. When I asked a family member about my own childhood abuse, I was told, 'Just forget it—it's not part of who you are now.' I was shocked at this dismissive attitude. It is and will always be a part of me, because it makes me want to show the world that I HAVE survived and thrived despite it! Thank you, Angelica Harris, for pouring out your heart to show this positivity to the millions of other survivors. And God bless the millions of poor souls who weren't lucky enough to survive their abuse. Let this book be a prayer for them."

—PATRICIA GATT, *QUEENS CHRONICLE*

"In one snapshot of an afternoon moment, *Living with Rage: A Quest for Solace,* gives the reader the history of a teenager caught in physical and verbal abuse. The young girl's desire to save her parent is tangled with self-preservation. There are no answers to be found in this web, and the reader immediately understands the reason for Angelica Harris's quest. They want her to find the solace she deserves. This is a novel for those who know the experience and those who can't comprehend the world of domestic violence."

—JEANNE MCELVANEY, AUTHOR OF *SPIRIT UNBROKEN: ABBY'S STORY* AND "SEXUAL ABUSE INSIGHTS" BLOG AT GOTOSPIRIT.COM

"The inspiring life of Angelica Harris, which she generously shares with others, brings truth to the issues of abuse and offers hope to all who read her book."

—LELA ALBERT, FOUNDER, RESTORING HIS PEOPLE MINISTRIES

LIVING
WITH
RAGE

A QUEST FOR SOLACE

ANGELICA HARRIS

LIVING WITH RAGE: A QUEST FOR SOLACE

Writers of the Round Table Press
1670 Valencia Way
Mundelein, IL 60060

Writers of the Round Table Press and logo are trademarks of
Round Table Companies and Writers of the Round Table Inc.

Publisher: Corey Michael Blake
Executive Editor: Katie Gutierrez Painter
Production Manager: Erin Cohen
Digital Distribution: David C. Cohen
Cover Design: Nathan Brown
Interior Design/Layout, Back Cover: Sunny DiMartino
Proofreading: Rita Hess
Last Looks: Mary Laine
Promotional Materials: Kristin Westberg
Social Networking: Mary Laine & Kristin Westberg

Printed in Canada

First Edition: December 2011
10   9   8   7   6   5   4   3   2   1

Library of Congress Cataloging-in-Publication Data
Harris, Angelica
Living with Rage: A Quest for Solace / Angelica Harris.—1st ed. p. cm.
ISBN 978-1-61066-018-1
Library of Congress Control Number: 2011938509
1. Biography Women. 2. Family & Relationships, Abuse. I. Title.

TABLE OF CONTENTS

ACKNOWLEDGEMENTS

Eleanor Roosevelt said: "No one can make you inferior without your consent."

Consent is a big word. When you are a child and someone violates you or beats you senseless, the only word whose meaning you know is fear. But fear is what keeps the pain buried, and the only way to release it is to get help. I have received help from many sources, and that is how I have granted myself consent to share my story.

To my family—my husband, John, and our children, Andrea and John—I am truly grateful to you for allowing me to bring our lives to the page. Most families do not have an author for a spouse or mother—at least not one who writes about their private lives—but you all selflessly and with pride allowed me to share this story. I cannot count how many hours at the dinner table we spoke about this book, mapping out the journey together. You are all my inspiration in life, and I thank God every day for each of you! Thank you—you do not know how much I truly love you.

To my daughter, Andrea—you are the woman I wanted to be at your age, yet could not be because I did not know myself. You have been there to listen to me, to understand what my life has been, and you were the person who kept telling me that my book was so important it had to be written. I have been truly blessed to have you in my life. Thank you, my dear daughter, my girl—I love you!

To my social worker, Emily Kelman-Bravo, at the Tourette Syndrome Association, for the countless hours I have spent in your chair. It was there that I unleashed the monsters of the past—Emily, thank you so very much. And to Evan Michaels, social worker with the program, you helped guide my son and my husband through many hard times, and helped keep my husband and me together through the challenges—thank you!

I want to thank my friend and publisher Corey Michael Blake. It was you who long ago read the words of my character, Arianna Lawrence, in my *Excalibur* book series and told me that Arianna would just be the stepping stone to where my path truly lies. You listened to me vent about my past, and you are the one who told me that my readers were asking questions about whether

Arianna's abuses were really my own. I was hesitant to write the tales of my real life, but you assured me that if I had the courage to write it, you would be there to help me. Thank you for keeping your promise!

To Katie Gutierrez Painter, the young and energized editor and writer whom Corey sent to guide me through every step of this journey. After a time, I found the words I had put in Arianna's mouth coming from mine. Katie, you have been a support team all your own, explaining that this book would not be one of slander or melodrama, but one of truth through my eyes. To date, you are making sure all my i's are dotted and t's crossed so that I can bring *Living With Rage: A Quest for Solace* to the person holding it now. For this, I have to say: Katie, thank you from the bottom of my heart. You were there to listen to my fears about writing my memoir, calm my tears as my life unfolded on the page, and share in my absolute joy as I saw the fruits of my labor come to fruition.

To Jennifer Geronimo, my producer with Life Enlightenment. You gave me the idea to start a Blog Talk Radio show, and through you, I have found so many people who have been through my journey. You helped me connect with Amnesty International, IVAT (The Institute on Violence, Abuse, and Trauma), and the many groups for domestic violence and sexual assault that I share conversations with each day. Jennifer, I thank you for your assistance, your friendship, your belief in me, and your love.

To my Kiwanis Club in Glendale—you showed me the true spirit of community. You helped me understand how to take my business and awareness of my work to another level, to watch it grow through community. It is with your help that my Excalibur Reading Program is now reachable to so many children and families in our area.

To my friend, Pat Gatt, who kept encouraging me to move forward with my reading program when the chips were down, who kept telling me to "write it down!" You said that my courage to write this book would help people know there is a light at the end of the tunnel—Pat, I love you like a sister!

To *Queens Parent Magazine* and Ellen Klein for helping to spread the word about my Excalibur Reading Program—thank you!

To the rest of my publishing team—Nathan Brown, who designed my book cover (one word, man: brilliant); and Kristen Westberg and Erin Cohen, for their invaluable support and advice on everything Angelica Harris, Inc. and Excalibur Reading Program. You are my success team. Thank you!

They say God does not give us more than we can handle. There were days I wondered how much more could I handle and whether there really was a God. Thank you to my pastor, Father John Fullum, for assuring me that God knew what I was born to do. This gave me the strength and courage to weather every storm with love and without guile.

Thank you, my Lord and Savior Jesus Christ—it is You whom I give this book to.

And to all those who suffer the loneliness and pain of all trials and tribulations—there is a light at the end of the tunnel. Just look for it!

—Angelica Harris

INTRODUCTION:
A DAUGHTER'S IMPEDANCE

Impedance: an electrical resistance. A measure of opposition. It is a term that could describe my life since I was a young girl. I was a caregiver, a provider, a housekeeper, an honor student. I was a child who did not move without her parents' approval, who sacrificed her happiness and dreams for the sake of family. Those sacrifices opposed the forward motion of my life. They stripped me of an identity, forcing me to spend decades searching for one as an actress, a hairdresser, a mother, a wife, an author, and an entrepreneur. Who was I, besides my parents' daughter? Besides the girl, then young woman, who was abused and who kept that abuse a secret?

Just when I began to put pen to paper about my life, my father passed away after a two-year struggle. I found that mourning him—and the anger I harbored over his death—was keeping me from moving forward on this book; my mother, too, is gone, and we do not speak ill of the dead. But then, what do we do with our rage when someone who hurt us dies—do we bury it and go on?

NO.

Rage does not disappear when it is buried; under dirt, it grows. It intensifies. But if we talk about our emotions—let them out, let them go, and try to find forgiveness—then we can break the patterns of impedance.

My parents and I had a complicated relationship whose different layers I am still trying to untangle and understand. I loved my family, but their constant demands twisted my love into a weapon against me. I was always angry, and that anger built a boundary to my success at an early age. That anger has remained with me for years. Now, at this time in my life, I am telling my story with the belief that voicing my rage will tame it and bring the justice it craves.

Ten days before my dad died, I held him in my arms and told him to go to my mother and to God. All I wanted was for us both to be set free—he from illness, and me from the constant worries about him. His passing, like my mother's, did not set me free; neither would putting my story in a box.

So it is with great respect for my own worth that I give you my story of survival against domestic violence and sexual assault. It is the story I was almost ready to bury with my father.

If you find parts of your life within this book, know that you have a voice. You *can* find freedom and self-empowerment. We *can* undo the damage and surge forward … unimpeded.

PROLOGUE:
A MOTHER'S MADNESS

In my hand: two tickets to the Elvis Presley concert at Madison Square Garden. I had purchased the tickets with hard-earned money from my job as a checker in a supermarket. I couldn't wait to go, and I fantasized about the show as I walked home from the bus stop. I had loved Elvis Presley for ten years, ever since seeing him on "The Ed Sullivan Show" and "The Johnny Carson Show" when I was six. I owned many of his records, and seeing him in person was my greatest wish.

On 61st Street and 44th Avenue in Woodside, I walked up the steps of my house and let myself in. It wasn't until I was heading down the long beige hallway that I realized my mother was home.

"Where have you been?" she asked me as I strolled into the living room. Her face was expressionless and pale. Her eyes looked past me and straight at the wall. I knew this look.

"I had rehearsal for the play," I said.

"You didn't tell me."

"Mom, I told you in school yesterday, remember?"

"No, you did not!" she yelled.

"You were sitting by Mr. Ryan's office taking hall passes from the kids who were going to the student union meeting—remember?"

My mother was a small woman: five feet two inches tall, one hundred and thirty-five pounds. She had a mild olive complexion and dark Italian eyes, and by the time she was forty years old, she had snow-white hair and never thought to color it. At her size and stature, she shouldn't have been threatening, but her moods transformed her into someone terrifying.

"Where were you?" she yelled again.

"At rehearsal!"

"You're lying!"

My mother walked around the coffee table toward me, with the wide-eyed glare she always wore just before she blew. I stepped back, but her hand flew at me. The strike caught my right eye, and I put a hand to my face. My eye felt as though it was on fire.

"I'm not lying, Mom! I was at rehearsal!"

My heart was pounding as I tried to move out of harm's way, and Mom came at me again, ramming her hand against my back.

"Call Ms. Klausman and ask her!" I screamed.

My mother's cheeks were reddening. I knew I had to move, but where? I began to run out of the living room and toward the kitchen, but she was steps behind me: "Tell me the truth!"

I knew where this fight was going and ran to my room, desperately trying to close the door before my mother's temper got out of hand. It was too late. *Whack!* With the sting of Dad's belt on my back, I fell onto my bed. Mom whipped me more times than I could count. The pain seared into my chest. Dazed, I tried to ward off the belt, taking a pillow from my bed and shielding myself beneath it. Finally, after what felt like forever but was only a few minutes, I managed to roll off my bed and rise to my feet. I hunched my shoulders, feeling as though a dull knife were running between my shoulder blades. Tears streamed down my cheeks.

"Go ahead—cry!" Mom screamed. "Cry like a baby!"

I tried to suck up the tears, but I was hurting all over. I had been telling Mom the truth, but the truth was not what her manic mind wanted to hear.

I made it past her out of my room, but she followed me to the kitchen, blocking my exit back to the living room and out the front door.

"I needed you to go to the store." Her face was red, and she brushed her hair away from her brow.

"I told you that I would go to the store and do the laundry when I got home. I'll do it, I promise."

"You don't love me."

"What do you mean, Mom? I do love you!"

"Then why ... are you ... lying?" Her voice swelled, erupted. The window was open, and I knew the neighbors could hear her.

I wanted to drop to my knees and cry, beg forgiveness, but for what? I was a good kid. I went to school, earned honor status, worked part-time in a supermarket, did my chores, and went to church on Sundays. What else did she want from me?

She stood before me, and I wished I could jump out the window and into the yard. The belt was in her hand and she was swishing it at her side.

When I moved, she whipped the belt across the refrigerator door, catching me sharply on the arm. I pushed forward, dashing across the room, but she snapped the belt against my back. Finally, I shoved her aside and yanked the belt from her hand.

Mom's face was frozen in that glare she had when she could hear nothing but her own voice. "You disrespect your mother—give me the belt!"

My back, arm, and leg were searing with pain. I threw the belt in the direction of my younger brother's room—Adam wasn't home—and tried to maneuver around the kitchen table. That was when I heard the sound of metal rattling in the kitchen drawer.

"Go ahead," my mother said. "Kill me. You don't love me."

My mother was pushing the kitchen butcher knife against her throat. I stood stock still, staring, my heartbeat pulsing through my whole body.

"Mom, please," I said. "Put that thing down."

"You want me dead. Don't you?" Mom was leaning against the kitchen counter. Her body and hands were shaking as badly as mine were. Her eyes were like a cat's, pupils fixed and dilated. The knife shook like a steel feather in her hand, and I was afraid she would really do it.

I took a small step forward, and Mom thrust the knife toward me. *What do I do?* I thought desperately. *God, help me, please. If you love me, God, help me.*

My mouth was dry as sand, and my hands were ice cold. My stomach tightened to the small of my back. I didn't know whether I should run or stay: could she kill me or herself?

"Okay, you're right," I said. "I lied. I went to Pop's for pizza and forgot the time."

I thought the lie might calm her down, but she yelled, "I knew you didn't love me!" and lunged at me, knife in hand.

I backed up against the kitchen wall, holding my back firm as my legs began to give out from under me. My hands were as cold as if they'd been dipped in the icebox for an hour. I looked at my mother, and an inexplicable calm began to run down my back, through the pain. I began to beg her, "Mom, I'm sorry. I do love you. I was a bad girl. I'm sorry. Please put down the knife."

She looked at me, her eyes enraged, glaring so hard I thought we were both going to die. Then again came the wave of calm across my back, and I moved toward her.

"You don't love me." Again she put the knife to her throat. "You never did."

As I came to her, she thrust the knife at me, and I wedged a kitchen chair between us. I was sweating and felt as though I was going to break. I wanted to run, but I was afraid that when I got back she'd be dead.

"Mom, please," I begged again.

There were tears in her raging eyes. I had to stay.

I reached for the chair, and it distracted her. She dropped her knife-holding hand down to her side. I saw my chance and lunged toward her, slapping the knife from her fingers. It fell to the floor.

She looked at me, dazed.

I kicked the knife under the cabinet, then grabbed my mother and held her. I held her so hard I could feel her shaking in my arms.

"Please, I love you so much, Mommy—I'm sorry!"

She shoved me away, and before I could manage to move backwards, she smacked me across the face. Her hand was hot and stung my tear-drenched cheek. My face was on fire.

"You don't love me!" she screamed. "You never did."

Finally, I found the strength to run out of the kitchen, through the living room, and out the front door.

Mom followed me, yelling all sorts of obscenities, as I ran down the block. I ran up 61st Street, hot with embarrassment as my neighbors watched my mother screaming at me. She called me names that no child should hear from her own mother. I felt like a criminal.

That day was the last of my adolescence. That was the day Angelica the girl died and Angelica became an adult—forever.

PART I

CHILDHOOD
UNDER
SIEGE

CHAPTER 1:
A NEW
HABIT

When I was four years old, my parents bought our first house. They had been married seven years and saving hard to become home-owners.

Grandpa—stout and broad, an older version of my father—was sitting on Dad's red club chair the day my parents came home with the keys. Grandma was reclining on the gray couch across the room. My younger brother, Adam, and I played on the floor, over the gray carpet with pretty red roses and green leaves patterned throughout. The walls were cream-colored, and beautiful red velvet curtains hung over the windows. Pictures of my mother's family hung on the walls. Her parents had died before I was born, but if I looked up from the floor, the whole family history beamed down at me.

Mom and Dad walked into the room, smiling, and Grandpa rose from his chair.

"Well?" Grandpa said in his deep voice. "Is it yours?"

"Finished the paperwork today!" Dad jingled some keys, and Grandma and Grandpa hugged my parents tightly.

"Proud of you, son," said Grandpa, holding back tears.

Most of my parents' family owned their own homes, and my Uncle Pat, Dad's younger brother, had wanted Dad to purchase land near him in Hol-brook, New York. Dad worked in Long Island City for a company called Legion Utensils and preferred to be near his job, so the house was in Wood-side, Queens.

Grandma and Grandpa went with us to see the house that day. My brother and I sat on their laps in the back of the car.

"Did they clean up for you as promised?" asked Grandpa.

"They did to a point," said Mom, looking over her shoulder.

"The house needs a lot of work," said Dad.

"Mom, where are we going?" I asked.

"To see our new house."

"New house?"

"Yes, Angelica, our new house."

"I like our old house."

"Never mind, just be quiet while Dad is driving," Mom said.

Grandma gave me a kiss on the cheek, and I looked out the window.

At the time, in the spring of 1961, Queens Boulevard in Woodside was tree-lined. I had always loved trees—the taller, the greener, and the higher a tree climbed to the sky, the better. When we arrived at 44th Avenue, there was a six-story high-rise on the corner and one right across the street from the house Dad pointed out as ours. I looked at the high-rises and immediately disliked them. Where were the trees and flowers that I was so used to?

Still, from the outside, I liked the house itself. It was brick-front with brown shingles and a metal gate. We climbed up four steps that led to the brown entry door and into a tiled vestibule. When Dad opened the door, I noticed a staircase and instantly rushed toward it.

"Sweetheart, we live down here," Dad said.

The hall we all walked down was a putrid gray that led to a dark brown door at the end. Dad unlocked the door, which led into a narrow room and to the kitchen in the back of the house. The kitchen had two white metal cabinets on one wall and a washing machine on the other. We walked through what was to be the living room, and that was when I began to cringe: the walls were dark gray and had so many holes it looked as though someone had taken a hammer to them. Adam, who was almost two years old, put his fingers in some of the holes and pulled out dried plaster, which went all over the floor. Mom gave Dad a recriminating look and took a tissue out of her purse to clean my brother's hand.

"We'll get these walls fixed, V, once we move in," Dad said to Mom.

In the next few weeks, Dad and Grandpa plastered the holes and white washed some of the walls, but to me the house remained spooky. It felt angry, like when Mom got mad at Adam and me for not cleaning up our toys. The sounds of the house scared me; the heat coming up sounded like a gun going off.

After we moved in, I had a recurring nightmare about houses—walking through dark rooms with plates, clothes, and broken glass all over the floors. Sometimes the rooms in my dream would change or the darkness give way by a hint of light coming from a hall or open window, but the feeling of fear remained. I would wake up crying in the middle of the night, begging my parents to take me back to our old house in Maspeth.

It took me a year to get used to the house, with its cracking and creaking floors and the banging sounds the furnace made when the heat came on. Adam and I still shared a room, but this one was considerably larger. Dad had painted it the same yellow as our old room, with the same pink and blue borders, and Mom and Dad took us to choose our linoleum for the floor. The one we decided on had a fantasy design with the fairy tale characters of Cinderella, Tom Thumb, Humpty Dumpty, and others on it. Adam and I had fun, playing in our room amongst our toys, jumping up and down on our beds. Mom didn't always like when we did that, but Dad laughed a lot. I loved Dad's laugh; it was always so jolly, just like Santa Claus.

We had a spacious backyard that was surrounded by the walls from the six-story Winston Apartment complex next door and the back of the garage from the houses on the other block. I never really got used to those walls; they made me feel like a caged animal. I missed my trees from the house in Maspeth. However, a great big maple tree grew behind the garage. I could not see its trunk, but when I went into my yard, I loved looking at its leaves and branches that grew high above my head.

Adam and I had our very own swing set that Santa brought to us for Christmas that year. My brother and I climbed on those metal bars as though we were trapeze artists. We had the greatest of times in our yard, playing in the soil. We made mud pies and tracked dirt throughout the basement, up the steps, and right into Mom's clean house. Mom would scream bloody hell at us, then take one look at our dirty faces and clothes and laugh her head off. We must have been a sight, but Mom loved that it was good healthy fun. She used to hug us both, then give us baths, a cold glass of Ovaltine, and some animal crackers before dinner. We were our mother's little king and queen in those days. She would wrap me in my soft fluffy towel as she dried me, cradling me in her arms. She told me she loved me and kissed me on the cheek. In Mom's arms, I owned the whole world. Her face was radiant when she held me, her deep brown almond-shaped eyes lit up with joy, her laughter billowing.

Things began changing when it was time for me to start grade school. I wanted to stay at Public School 11, where I'd gone to kindergarten, but Mom insisted that I get a Catholic education and registered me at St. Sebastian's School for first grade.

It was the first day in my new school, and I had a nun as a teacher. When Sister Anne walked into the class, dressed in her full black habit, I wanted to run. Where the heck was her body? Did she *have* a body? Why was she wearing a big black and silver cross hanging from a rope tied to her waist? It looked like the one hanging on the altar in church. I had seen the sisters in church before but had never been that close to one. Sister Anne had a distinct aura about her, and to me it was not a kind one. Behind that white band around her forehead and the black veil that covered her head and hair was a hard expression. She stood behind her desk and began to take roll call of her new students. Her voice was just as hard as her expression, and my stomach began to tighten.

That afternoon, Mom and Adam were waiting for me outside, amid the group of moms and their younger kids. Mom greeted me with a big hug and kiss, which I returned before leaning down and giving Adam a hug and kiss in his carriage. We walked home with some of the mothers and the kids in my class who lived near us.

That evening, I told Mom, "I don't like Sister Anne. She scared me today."

Mom sifted through the paperwork that Sister had given her and Dad to fill out and sign.

I tugged at my mother's sleeve. "Mommy, do I have to go back to that school tomorrow?"

Mom kept rummaging through the papers.

"Mommy!"

Mom's brows pinched. She glared at me. It was an expression I had never seen before. She continued to fill out the papers as I stood waiting for an answer. Finally, she looked directly at me, squinting.

"You will learn to like St. Sebastian's," she said.

She took my books out of my school bag, read my homework list, and set my books before me. "Do your homework," she said, and that was that.

Mom was very religious. We said prayers before bed and grace before dinner every night. There were many days when Mom would sit on the chair in the quiet of the living room and say her rosary by herself. Mom had a public school education but belonged to more religious organizations and groups than I could count. Her social life revolved around church settings. She held office and was a respected community leader in church, and this followed her to every parish she belonged to. Dad had been happy with me staying at Public School 11, but Mom was adamant about my going to Catholic school and got her way.

That night, after Mom dismissed my fears about Sister Anne, I went into my room and sat on the floor, leaning up against my bed. I took my dolls and stuffed animals and sat them all around me, as though they could shield me from sadness. I had a brown stuffed dog that I would cuddle with, and I held imagined conversations with him—with all of my stuffed animals—often.

"Hi, Brownie." I cried on his shoulder. "Mommy is mad at me."

Brownie snuggled up to my ear and whispered, "Why?"

"'Cause I don't like Sister Anne."

Brownie held tight near my neck and wrapped his long fluffy tail around my shoulder.

"Angelica, don't cry," said my doll, Chatty Cathy. "I'm here for you."

I pulled Chatty Cathy near me and placed her on my lap. Brownie and Chatty Cathy cuddled with me, and I lay down on the floor, sobbing on Brownie's furry back.

"Sister Anne looks like a monster," I said. "I can't go back to school tomorrow."

Brownie pushed his back close to my face, and I fluffed him around me.

"Why does Mommy not listen to me? I feel like she doesn't like me anymore." I yawned, and the next thing I knew my father was picking me up from the floor and placing me on my bed. He kissed me and said goodnight, and I quickly fell asleep.

A few weeks later, I still felt the same about Sister Anne. There was something about this woman in black that, deep in my stomach, gave me knots.

I had always been one of those kids who needed to use the bathroom more than just before I left for school in the morning and during mid-morning snack break, when we had a small box of milk and some cookies. It was always me asking Mom to go home while she was talking with her friends, because I had to use the bathroom. I've also always been temperature sensitive, and on a rainy and damp spring day, every single window was wide open in our classroom; Sister Anne loved having the windows open. I was six years old and freezing. The dampness hit my back and chilled me to the bone, instantly making me need to use the bathroom.

Sister Anne was in the front of the room, writing the alphabet on the blackboard. When she turned to face the class, I raised my hand.

"Yes, Angelica, what is it?" she asked.

"Can I go to the bathroom, please?"

"No, you may not," she said. "Write your letters in your book."

I picked up my pencil and began to write my letters, but my legs began to shake. I raised my hand again.

"Angelica, what do you want now?" Sister asked, annoyed.

"Please, Sister, I need to go to the bathroom."

"I said no before, and it is no now." She turned her back to me and wrote on the board again, then sat down at her desk.

My classmates began to laugh under their breath, and all I could think of was running out the door, across the hall, and into the girls' room. I tried to hold it, but my stomach started to hurt badly and again I lifted my hand.

Sister shot up from her desk, the heels of her shoes pounding the floor. She came and stood over me. "Angelica, I said no!" she yelled. "You will wait until you go home." Then she picked up my pencil and tapped me on the cheek with it.

I began to cry, flushed with embarrassment. Crying did not help; it just made me shake more and I could feel myself begin to lose control. I refused to wet myself, so when Sister went back to the board to write another letter, I ran out of the room and to the bathroom. I sat there, peeing, crying, and shaking at the same time. I was scared of what Sister would do.

A minute later, I heard footsteps in the bathroom and saw Sister's black shoes and the hem of her black habit from under the stall door. I wanted to crawl beneath the side of the stall and run, but where?

I wiped myself, picked up my underpants, and adjusted my uniform.

"Angelica, get out of there and back to class!" Sister yelled, her voice echoing on the porcelain tile walls. I did not respond.

She yelled again and this time reached under the stall and grabbed my ankles. I screamed and knew I had nowhere to go. I unlocked the door and she pushed it open, grabbed me by my ear, and dragged me back to class.

"Look, class," she declared, tugging at me. "This is a disobedient girl!"

Then she forced me to stand by her desk. I tried hard not to cry, but the tears rolled down my cheeks. My classmates looked as frightened as I was. Sister sat next to me, placed me over her lap, and spanked me hard, over and over, all the while telling the class how awful a child I was. When she was done, she put me in the corner and told me to stay there until the end of the school day.

Every part of my body hurt. My legs were shaking, and I wanted to throw up. With my back turned to the class, I heard Sister teach. Then, what felt like hours later, the bell finally rang, and it was time to go home.

Sister allowed me to pack my school bag, and I took my sweater out of the cloakroom. We lined up, and some of the other students either stared at me or laughed quietly. Their snickering made me feel as though I really had been that bad girl Sister described. My real friends came up from behind me, and my friend Donna—a sweet girl with flowing sunset red hair and green eyes—whispered in my ear, "Are you okay?"

I looked at her with fear in my gut.

Sure enough, Sister came near me and pulled at my sweater. "Shut up!" she yelled. She stood by me as we walked down the steps and out the door.

Waiting on 58th Street, as always, were my mother and Adam. Sister called my mom from across the street and Mom came over. Sister dismissed the rest of the class.

"Mrs. Marquise," Sister said once the four of us were alone, "do you not teach your daughter manners at home?"

Mom's face was stunned. "Of course! I don't understand, Sister. I try to teach my children how to behave all the time."

Sister folded her arms, and they disappeared under her big black sleeves. "Well, little Miss Angelica here disobeyed me today."

Mom looked questioningly at me, then back at Sister. "What happened?"

"Angelica went to the lavatory without my permission."

"Mommy, please," I said, "I need to tell you what happened."

"She did what?" Mom asked Sister.

"Mommy, please." I pulled on my mother's jacket. "I asked Sister—"

"You should punish her tonight, Mrs. Marquise." Sister's stare made me want to crawl under a parked car. "She just picked herself up from her desk after I said no and went to the lavatory."

With more and more agitation, Mom tapped her foot on the ground, right next to my brother's carriage wheels.

"Mom—"

"Be quiet," Mom said. "Sister is speaking."

"But Mom!"

"Quiet!" Mom shouted. She put her finger over my mouth. "It won't happen again, Sister," she added curtly.

Sister walked across the street, and Mom grabbed my shoulder and held tight. I could feel her fingers dig into my skin. She began to pull me down the block, where my friends and their moms were waiting.

"Mommy, please, I asked Sister three times—"

Mom held up her hand. "Be quiet!" A few seconds later she started yelling at me, right there on the sidewalk in front of my friends, her friends, and the whole school.

"Angelica's mommy, it wasn't her fault!" said my friend Francis, her green eyes wide.

"Virginia, listen to her," said Maureen, Donna's mother and my mother's longtime friend. She spoke with an enchanting Irish brogue. "Donna said—"

"I don't care what Donna said," Mom interrupted. "Angelica disobeyed Sister."

"But Angelica's mommy—" cried Francis again.

Mom pulled me away from my friends, and we walked home alone and in silence.

We'd barely walked through our front door when I tried again. "Mommy, please listen to me. I asked Sister—" But Mom just walked into her room without a word. She emerged a few moments later, grabbed my arm, and *whack!* I felt the sting of something hit me on my butt, and my little body quivered like a feather on a windy day. I screamed and began to cry. When I turned and looked at my mother, she had that vague expression again, and I saw my father's brown belt in her hand. She swung it again at me, and I tried to move away, but it slapped hard against my thigh. My leg felt scalded. I squatted down on the floor, and Mom stood over me and said nothing. My body ached, first from Sister's beating and now my mother's.

Mom had spanked my brother and me before, either for not cleaning up or not behaving, but to take my dad's belt ... that was the first time. It hurt, but it probably shocked me more.

Mom left the room, and I jumped when she returned a few minutes later. I was still squatting on the floor.

"If Sister says no, then you listen to her. Do you hear me?" Mom said.

It was hard to reconcile the woman who had just beaten me with the loving mother I had always known, and I could not understand why she would choose to believe Sister over her own friends or me. It wasn't until much later that I began to understand: my mother was becoming a religious fanatic.

CHAPTER 2:
TRAGEDY
IN THE
HEART

I was the third grandchild of Mea, as everyone called my grandmother, and Grandpa Salvatore, who both emigrated from Italy. My grandmother was born in Rome and Grandpa in Sicily. They both came from large families and were married very young: my grandmother was fifteen and Grandpa twenty when they became husband and wife. By the time Grandma was twenty, she had four children, and she and Grandpa went on to have eight more; four died from childhood illnesses, and instead of mourning them, Grandma and Grandpa adopted four more children and gave them a loving home.

I loved going to my grandparents' house. Grandma made me feel like a princess, and Grandpa sat me on his lap and taught me Italian songs, even though Dad did not like us to speak Italian in the house. He'd served in the United States Army and often said, "After all, we are Americans. Not foreigners." But Grandpa and Grandma spoke fluent Italian and Grandpa was hell-bent on teaching me Italian through song.

The day after Sister Anne and Mom spanked me, my family went to my grandparents' house for dinner. The house always smelled like spaghetti sauce and meatballs and Grandma's famous coffee-can bread. Right away, Grandpa picked me up and sat me on his lap. He kissed my cheek and gave me his magical bear hug, whispering in my ear, "What song do we sing?"

I smiled. "'Marina,' Grandpa!"

Mom had gone into the kitchen and came back with plates in her hands to set the table. Dad was sitting across from Grandpa, showing my little brother a deck of cards and teaching him the card game War. Adam was laughing as he watched Dad shuffle the deck.

Grandpa counted, *"Uno, due, tre,"* and we sang the song from his part of Italy. "Ah, *Marina, Marina, Mari—ne, ti voglio al piu presto sposar!"* He was smiling as we sang, and we swayed back and forth in the chair. When I sang with my grandpa, the house was filled with magic.

"Marina, Marina, Mari—na, ti voglio al piu presto sposar!" I sang with joy and laughter in my voice.

"O mia bella mora, no non mi lsciare, non mi devi rovinare, oh, no, no, no, no, no!" he wailed.

"Oh, no, no, no, no!" I wailed back, and he hugged me with all his might as he counted down with his fingers. *"Uno, due, tre,"* and together we shouted, "Oh, no, no, no, no—no!"

Grandma came from the kitchen, leaned on a chair holding her wooden spoon, and conducted the two of us in song. Then she joined her voice with ours as we sang, *"O mia bella mora, no non mi lsciare, non mi devi rovinare, oh, no, no, no, no, no!"*

Grandpa gave me a great big wet kiss and put me down. I bowed like a star, and he applauded while Dad laughed his head off. The laughter was contagious as my brother chimed in, and the actress in me shone through as I could not help but sing again, "Oh, no no!"

Grandpa rose from his chair and picked me up, wrapping me in his arms and dancing me around in a circle. The room spun before Grandpa sat down with me again in his chair at the head of the table. I began to slip from Grandpa's lap, and he grabbed my leg to secure me. That was when my red dress rolled up my leg and Grandpa saw the black and blue belt mark stretching across my thigh.

He looked at the welt and at me, and I put my head down in shame. The magic was gone from our singing, and I thought I was in trouble. He smiled, but it was a smile of pity, and he shook his head back and forth. He looked at my father, who had still been playing cards with Adam across the table. Dad was quiet, just as he always was when he was trying to figure things out. Mom came near the two of us, putting a plate setting in front of Grandpa, and I flinched. Grandpa held me close, as though he were protecting me from Mom. He coughed and had one word to say, which he yelled toward my mother: *"Disgrazia!"*

When Mom left the room, silently, Grandpa called Dad over to look at the bruise. I wanted to cry but was afraid Mom would hit me again, so I kept quiet in Grandpa's protection. Dad told his father that this was the first time he had seen the wound, which was the truth. But if I expected him to do anything about it, I would be disappointed. His gig was avoidance, as I would slowly learn.

CHAPTER 3:
HUMILIATION
BY
BIRTHDAY

B y the time I was entering adolescence, I couldn't help but wonder what had happened to my mother. She used to be a beautiful, nurturing woman who brought to her children a table of love, who succored us in a warm and caring environment that held no boundaries. As a child, I'd thought of her like Superman: nothing could damage the atmosphere that she sheltered us with so unconditionally. Mom was the best, and she always made sure that we had the finest that she and my dad could afford. If we lacked material things, there was never an absence of love or spiritual guidance.

Adam and I had been brought up to be devout Catholics. Mom and Dad were profound in their beliefs, and that gave us structure. Their example showed that we were loved not only by them, but also by our God and Jesus Christ. So where had it all gone wrong? How had a woman who had been perfect in the eyes and minds of her children developed such a monstrous alter ego? Had it begun the first time she hit me with the belt? The next? I didn't know. But by the time I was turning thirteen, I was sure of one thing: she'd changed, and I was afraid it was for good.

It was midterms at school, and my birthday was just around the corner. I was about to be a teenager—finally—and according to the church I was about to be confirmed and a soldier of Christ. An adult.

I was excited and begged my mother for a birthday party. She told me that I could have some friends over as long as I did all my chores and took care of my brother.

Do all my chores, I thought. I laughed inside. What if I didn't pick up that spec of dust? She'd cancel my birthday party? Yes, she would, I knew. Because, though Mom was a natural, fair leader when it came to being president or chairperson for one of her organizations or an event she was running, at home she was a tyrant. I was in her fault line, so I'd do what I needed to do in order to have my party.

"Hi, doll," Mom said, a few days before my party was supposed to happen.

"Hi, Mom." I moved toward her as she was washing dishes and kissed her on the cheek.

"I need you to clean the bathroom for me."

"But it's midterm week," I said. "I have homework and a history test tomorrow."

"Maureen and Theresa are coming over later to talk about the rosary dinner for Father Curran," Mom said. "I need to get my report ready. Clean the bathroom."

I stood by the washing machine, my stomach in knots. If I retaliated, there would go my party, and it was at the end of the week. But I needed to study. "Mom, please. Can't the bathroom wait?"

"No."

"But Mom!"

"Don't 'But Mom' me, young lady. If you want your party, you will get it done now."

With that odd glare, Mom picked up her portable typewriter and banged it on the table. My heart skipped a beat. Before I knew it, Mom's fingers were flying on the keyboard, and it was as if I'd disappeared.

Damn, I thought. She'd been home all day. Why was I coming home to do her chores?

This was nothing new. I was used to standing by my bedroom door, which was right off the kitchen, and watching her type. I knew I had to study and do my homework, but if I ignored her demands, it would be the belt. In this case, I knew she would take my party from me, so I went into the bathroom and started cleaning.

Soon it was suppertime, and Mom took the typewriter and her papers and put them on the coffee table in the living room. I was in my room, finally studying for my history test.

"Angelica, set the table!" Mom yelled across the house.

Mom's words were like sandpaper rubbing the back of my neck. My hands clenched tightly around my history textbook. It hadn't even been twenty minutes since I'd sat on my bed to get my work done. I could not stand it anymore. I was an honor student and wanted to go to a great high school. If I didn't keep my grades up, that would not happen.

But, again, I knew better than to argue and went to set the table. Dad came home, took a quick shower, and we ate dinner. As soon as I cleaned off the table, Mom took her typewriter and papers and started getting things ready for her meeting while I washed and my brother dried the dishes, helping me put them back in the cabinets.

Mom's friends arrived, and I went in my room to get some homework done while she had her meeting. I had barely gotten my history review questions and math homework done when Mom called, "Angelica, please get the coffee and cake ready."

I was fuming. "Why can't Adam help out?"

"He's having trouble with spelling and needs to study."

I knew that was true, but my brother could spare a few minutes and do the task.

After Mom's friends left, all I wanted was to go in my room, put on my pajamas, and study. I closed the door for some quiet, as my brother had the radio on in his room next to mine and my parents were watching television.

"What are you doing in here?" Mom swung open the door without knocking.

"I'm studying for midterms," I said through a yawn.

"You can't spend some time with your father and me?"

"Mom, I have to study!" I pulled a piece of paper from under my book; it was the layout of the pages I needed to study for my exam.

"What are you hiding from me?" Mom yelled.

"Mom, what hiding? This is my test sheet for midterms."

Mom grabbed the sheet from my hands. "Why did I not see this?"

"It's from my teacher. You didn't have to see it, and I need that to study." I rose from bed and went to take it from her, but she pulled away.

"What are you hiding?" she repeated.

"I'm not hiding anything. Mom, give it back—please!"

My mother held the paper in her hand. Then my father walked through the kitchen and to the doorway of my bedroom.

"What's going on?" Dad asked.

"She's hiding something from us!" Mom said.

Dad looked at me questioningly.

"Dad, look," I pleaded, "I did everything Mom told me to do, including making cake and coffee for her friends, and now I need to study. I closed the door for quiet, not because I'm hiding something."

I reached for the paper in my mother's hand, and Mom went to slap me. Swiftly, Dad slipped his body between Mom and me.

"Virginia, what was that about?" Dad asked, aggravated. "What gives?"

"She's hiding something—I know it!"

Finally, I lost it, screaming, "Mom, go ahead and look for yourself—I am not hiding anything!"

The clock on my desk said that it was eleven p.m., and all I wanted was to study. But I watched as Mom ransacked my bed, pulling off the sheets and the covers only to find a mattress, and when that did not satisfy her, she went to my school bag and my purse, dumping everything out and messing up my room.

Dad tried to stop her, but she pushed him away.

"For crying out loud, V," he said, "leave it alone!"

"You always believe her," Mom spat. "Not your own wife."

"Enough is enough. All I want is peace in this house!" Dad looked at me again and then Mom. "Got me?" Then he turned and went back to watch television. I wanted to cry but held it in my gut. If I cried, there would be more hell to pay.

Mom pointed at me. "I know you are hiding something. I'll find it."

She left my room in a state of mayhem. Then my brother walked in, half-asleep; Mom and I had woken him up with our yelling. He looked at the mess on the floor and knelt to help pick it up.

"Go back to sleep, Adam," I said tiredly.

I was afraid that Mom would hit him because of me. It had happened before. When Mom was mad at one of us, we knew to take cover because once she hit one, the other was not far behind. By the time I was thirteen and Adam eleven, we knew when to duck and cover our own asses lest we both be beaten.

"No, I can help," Adam said.

"Adam, please go back to bed. I can do this," I whispered, afraid she would come in and slap him. I put my body over the mess and begged, "Get back to your room before Mom takes the spoon out. Now!"

With Mom, I got hit with the belt and Adam with the wooden spoon. In the end, we both wore the marks of our punishments, and my mention of the spoon was enough to make him to pull away. With unshed tears in his eyes, he put my wallet on the bed and returned to his room.

It was after midnight when my parents and brother finally went to sleep. I stayed up, doing my homework with a flashlight to keep Mom at bay.

That Friday—the day of my party—Sister handed back our religion tests. I had studied for my history test, as well as for science and English, but had not devoted much effort to religion. There were two reasons for this. One: it was pushed down my gullet so much that it was boring. Two: I'd been so busy with Mom's chores that week that I had not had time to study all that I needed to. Still, I gasped when I got the test back. I'd failed.

I sat at my desk looking at my friends, who would be at my house in a few hours for my party. I knew they wouldn't say anything about grades, if for no other reason than Mom had also invited *their* moms. (I couldn't have a whole party just for me—that would be insane!) None of us were perfect in school, and if our moms were around, we avoided the mention of academics at all costs. That was the rule.

That day, I came home from school, took off my uniform, and immediately joined Mom in preparing the house for my party. We put balloons and party streamers in the living room and spread a cute birthday tablecloth that Mom had purchased at the discount store on the kitchen table. We set paper plates, napkins, and cups on the table, and Mom called the pizza parlor around the corner and ordered two large pies and soda for six o'clock.

My friends came dolled up in party dresses, we had some noshes and soda, and then we settled into my room to play Monopoly, listen to The Beatles, and talk about our crushes on David Cassidy, Paul McCartney, and other rock stars.

When the pizza man came, we all gathered around the kitchen table. Mom's friend Theresa distributed the slices, and we talked and ate and had a great time. Afterward, Mom cleaned up with her friends while we girls went outside, where we jumped rope and took turns riding our bikes up and down the block.

A little while later, Mom called us back in for cake. Mom had ordered the cake from Woodside Bakery, and it was my favorite: white sheet cake with whipped cream icing and pretty pink sugar roses. It read, "Happy 13th Birthday Angelica." My friends and their moms sang "Happy Birthday" to me, and then I cut my cake and Mom gave everyone a piece. When we finished, we went back in my room to continue playing Monopoly while Mom and her friends socialized in the kitchen over coffee.

Then everything began to crumble.

My mother walked into my room, her face red. I was sitting on my bed looking at my friends, and—though I couldn't explain why—a knot formed in my stomach.

Mom yanked me off the bed. "So what did you get on your religion test this week?" she demanded.

My six friends wore identical flabbergasted expressions.

I bowed my head, and Mom yelled again, "Well, what did you get?"

I stared at the beige rug in my room.

Mom grabbed me by the shoulders and shook me. My friend Francis gasped and backed toward the window. I could see she wanted to say something but was afraid.

I took a deep breath and said, "I got a sixty."

Mom grabbed me and dragged me to the corner of my room, where she spanked me and told me to stay there.

"Mom, please!" I begged. " I did the chores you asked me to do, and when I went to study, I feel asleep. Please don't do this in front of my friends!"

"Virginia, come on, let it go. It's her birthday," said Mom's friend Theresa.

"She lied to me, and I don't like liars!" Mom yelled. I turned to see what was going on, and Mom yelled, "Did I say you could move from that corner?"

"No," I said, and my friends and their moms looked at me with pity.

"I am sorry I brought it up," said Maureen, mom's friend from her church societies.

"*You're* sorry? *Angelica* should be sorry for lying to me."

If I could, I would have killed myself right there, standing in the corner of my room near the radiator and the high rise, where the window lent to me being able to see my friends as they stood outside my bedroom door gawking at me. Francis, also thirteen but little for her age, put her fingers to her mouth. I think she was crying for me. I could hear Mom's friends coming to my defense.

"Come on, Virginia, you didn't fail a test when you were a kid?" It was Theresa.

"Yeah, I did, but I didn't lie about it to my mother."

"Virginia, I knew your mother," said Theresa, who had known my mother since girlhood. "She was strict and you were not the perfect kid. None of us were perfect."

"Mrs. Marquise, please let Angelica come out," Francis managed, almost inaudibly.

"No, she lied to me!" Mom said stubbornly.

My friends and their moms surrounded me with support, but my mother was not giving in. It was my birthday party, and that was my initiation to becoming a teenager: humiliation.

CHAPTER 4:
A CONFIRMED
ADULT

After my birthday party, I could not look at my friends for a while. I had been humiliated in front of them and felt worthless. The whole idea of a party had been tainted for me, so when May came and I received my confirmation, I felt no excitement when Mom wanted to hold another party. Instead, I spent that day scared out of my wits, wondering whether, if something went wrong, she would take it out on me again. All I did know, even at that age, was that the party wasn't for me; it was for her. I was her daughter, which meant that my success was a reflection on *her*. Even if she was proud of me—which I knew she was—*that* was what she wanted to show off to people: her excellent parenting, of which I was the direct result. And if I called the quality of that parenting into question, I paid the price—royally.

I had to stop getting in Mom's way.

The solution came when my brother went to summer camp, abandoning his paper route. After unsuccessfully trying to find a part-time job after school, I decided to take over for him.

Dad was happy that I took the job, but Mom was anything but pleased. I was a girl, after all, and should not be allowed to do boy things. A paper route was a boy's job, and Mom hated the idea of her friends seeing me on my bike with the *Long Island Press* paper sack hanging on the back of it.

Every day before I left home to pick up the papers, Mom either yelled or found something for me to do to make me late: it was either do the breakfast dishes or make the beds, fold the clothes she'd just brought in from the clothesline or take up the iron, or perhaps one of the rooms needed dusting and vacuuming. More than the paper route being a boy's job, I later realized, she was upset because it took me away from home, away from being her personal housemaid. I found myself cringing with anger every day as I came home. This anger became a chronic thorn at my side, and I needed to get out from under it.

I may have only been thirteen, but I had to be cunning to do what I wanted. So I got up in the morning, did my chores—even asking Mom if she needed anything else—and then, when all was done, I jumped on my bike and rode fast to pick up the papers and happily deliver them. That summer I became an entrepreneur: I not only delivered papers for my brother's route, but I was taking on new orders and growing my own little business.

When the fall semester began, I realized that it was going to be difficult to wake up even earlier and deliver papers before school. So I began to hunt for a new job. After all, Dad was always telling my brother and me that we needed to earn our keep.

After school and on weekends, I took to the streets of Woodside and Roosevelt Avenue. Like a detective searching for clues, I searched for a job. I scoured every store window for a Help Wanted sign and took my dad's suggestion of looking in the classifieds. Anytime I saw an opportunity, I went and filled out an application.

Finally, on my way home from school one day, I saw a sign on the window of our neighborhood pharmacy. It said, Cashier Wanted Inquire Within. I knew Mr. Zarchy, the owner, because my parents shopped in his store, so I went inside and asked him about the job. He interviewed and hired me on the spot.

I began my job a week later, earning a dollar and fifty cents an hour. To me, that money was gold, and I worked hard for it. I felt like a queen when Mr. Zarchy placed my first paycheck in my hand. I looked down at the number: thirty-five dollars and fifty cents, and it was all mine! I couldn't wait to get home and show my parents.

Dad was home early from work when I walked in the door that Friday evening. He was sitting at the table with his coffee, fixing my brother's roller skates.

"Hi, doll," Dad said, grinning. "How was work?"

I placed my purse on the table, took out my check, and set it before him. He picked it up, looked at it, and flipped his eyebrows up and down, laughing.

"Proud of you!" he said. He stood from his chair and gave me a big hug and kiss. The way he held me was like God was holding me in his secure arms. Then Dad said, "Sit down."

I sat, and he reached over and gave me another kiss on the cheek. He folded his arms, which was Dad's way of letting me know that he had something important to say.

"Do you know what we are going to do with this tomorrow?" he asked.

"Not a clue."

He took the check and held it up. "We are going to the bank to open a savings account for you."

"But, Dad," I said, "I wanted to get some new clothes and an Elvis record."

He nodded. "Yes, you can do that, but first there is a responsibility now about having money and using it wisely."

"But it's my money."

He placed his hand over mine and held it tight. "It is yours, but there are rules to follow." I stood up, and Dad pulled me back down. "Angelica, stop acting like your mother and listen to me."

I took an annoyed breath. "Okay."

Dad walked out of the kitchen, through the living room, and into the master bedroom. He returned with a small book in his hand. He placed the book, which read Astoria Federal Savings Bank, on the table. Then he opened it and showed me some numbers.

"This is Mom's and my bank savings account book," he said. "This is how much money Mom and I have saved in the past few years."

I nearly gasped when I saw the amount of money that was in the bank. I thought we were rich. But as I see those numbers in the caverns of my memory, I realize it was a pittance. Dad was a laborer and didn't make a lot of money. He and Mom had worked hard for their savings, and as a mother now myself, I understand his need for me to learn to earn my keep and be responsible for it. Back then, though—despite being impressed with how much he and Mom had saved—I kept thinking, *This is my money! Why is Dad trying to take it from me?*

"So what does that have to do with my paycheck?" I asked.

"Sweetheart, if you want your money to grow, you need to start saving now."

He held my paycheck in his hand. "I'm not trying to order you around, but now that you're making good money, you need to know what to do with it."

"But I wanted to buy some new clothes and a record," I repeated.

"You will, Angelica, but first you need to pay yourself."

"I don't get it."

Dad took paper and pencil and stated making columns: Rent, Clothes, Music, Bank, Misc.

"Who pays rent?" I asked, annoyed.

"Don't roll those eyes at me, young lady. You're going to learn how to save a buck if it's the last thing I teach you—understand?"

When Dad spoke to me in that demanding voice and looked me square in the eye, I could not say no. "Okay, so how do I save money?"

Dad took thirty-five dollars from his pocket, made separate piles, and wrote the amount of each pile on the paper: rent, three dollars a week; clothes, ten dollars a week; music, one dollar a week; miscellaneous, two dollars a week. The total came to sixteen dollars a week with nineteen dollars left over. That went in the bank column.

I continued to watch Dad as he multiplied nineteen dollars by fifty-two weeks a year. The total came to almost twelve hundred dollars. He tapped the paper with his pencil. "That is what you will have saved at the end of the year if you put your money in the bank."

My eyes bulged out of my head. "Dad, I'll be rich!"

Dad laughed. "Well, maybe not rich, honey, but at least you'll be off to a good start."

"But what is this rent column?" I knew what he meant, but I was not giving in right away.

"One of these days, you'll be out on your own and you'll have to pay the landlord, so I think three dollars a week is a good way to learn."

I was not happy with the idea, but I knew that when it came to money, Dad knew what he was talking about.

Just then, Mom came in and set several paper grocery bags on the table. "What's this?" she asked.

"Mommy, I got my first paycheck today." I handed the check to my mother. "Dad and I are going to the bank tomorrow to open an account."

Mom stared at my paycheck. "Congratulations. It's about time!" Her voice was cold when she added, "Are you going to buy something for me with that?"

I was still sitting next to Dad and curled my legs around the front legs of the chair, squeezing so tightly that my knees began to ache. I had worked so hard for this money and now Mom wanted me to *buy her something?* Dad kicked me under the table to keep me quiet.

"You know Carmen's son Patrick buys his mother something every week with his paycheck." Mom began to unpack the grocery bags.

Carmen and my mother had known each other all of their lives. They had done everything together, except that Carmen had married somewhat younger than Mom, so her children were older. Her son, Patrick, was a high school teacher, lived at home, and was able to treat his mom like a queen every week.

Dad tapped the pencil on the table. "Patrick is twenty-six, V, and is making a good salary. Angelica is just starting."

"I am her mother, and she should buy me things with her salary."

A knot of guilt tore into my stomach and up my back. I looked at Dad for answers.

"What does that have to do with her buying you anything?" Dad cocked his head and pursed his lips; it was obvious that he was annoyed.

"I carried her for nine months."

Dad scratched the back of his neck. "Virginia, Angelica is not buying you, me, or anyone else anything. She is putting her money away for the future."

Mom's voice rose. "Oh, so I'm not important. Is that what you are saying?"

I began to sink in the chair, with the same feeling I'd had when she punished me during my birthday party. Here it was again, a wonderful day for me, and Mom was pulling the attention to herself.

"Mom, you are important. You know that," I said.

"Apparently not enough," she replied.

"Virginia, the money goes in the bank!" Dad said.

Mom and Dad began to argue about *my* paycheck, and I felt as though nothing I did in life mattered to her. What was wrong with me?

The next day, Dad and I went to the bank and opened my account as if the argument with Mom had never happened. When the branch manager put my bank savings book in my hand, I felt as if I owned the world. Outside the bank, Dad gave me a kiss before heading home. I went to the store and, for five dollars, bought my very first pair of Wranglers. Groovy!

On my way home, I passed the Woodside Florist. An arrangement of roses beckoned to me from the window. I knew that Dad didn't want me using my money for Mom, but the knot in my stomach was still there from last night. I walked in and bought the flowers.

When I got home, Mom was in her room putting away some laundry. I stood by the doorway and held the roses behind me. Would this make everything okay?

"Hi, doll," she said, catching me in the doorframe.

I pulled the flowers from behind me and into her view. She looked down at them and continued putting my dad's clean underwear in his drawers. Finally, when she was done, she gave me a half smile and said, "Thank you."

I gave her the flowers and a kiss on the cheek, and she laid the roses on the bed.

Dad came in then to put his wallet on his dresser. He shook his head when he saw the flowers but smiled and rubbed my forearm, knowing that I was just trying to keep the peace.

Keeping Mom at bay meant, at times, purchasing her love. It wasn't easy. I was making just enough to pay for my own clothes or maybe a record, if I wanted one, and just as Dad taught me, I was putting some money away for college. My education was worth more to me than anything else. Mom and Dad were blue-collar workers, and I wanted more for myself.

Despite Dad's interventions and my attempts to appease her, one day Mom lashed out. I was working on a Saturday, and, as usual, Mom strode into the store as if she owned the place. She would breeze past the cosmetics counter, where I worked, and go right to Mr. Zarchy, talking to him as though they were long-lost friends. At times, I could tell that Mr. Zarchy was annoyed. He had to fill prescriptions, and Mom pressed conversations about nonsense. I was afraid she would eventually get me fired.

This time, she brought her items to my register, and I punched in the price and told her the sum. She gawked at me. "Don't you have a discount?"

"For my stuff, not yours," I said.

"What do you mean, *your* stuff? Isn't this your stuff, too? I am your mother."

"I have to ask Mr. Zarchy if I can give you a discount. It's his store," I said. "Not mine."

From my register, I could see Mr. Zarchy in the pharmacy, watching my mother and me talk. Trying to seem nonchalant, I cast my gaze away from him, toward the shampoo section and perfume display. Finally, I looked back at my mother, who was still staring at me expectantly.

When I did not give her the discount, Mom marched right over to Mr. Zarchy. Here we go again, I thought. I wanted to walk out the door, but I quickly stepped away from my station and stood near my mother.

Mr. Zarchy was standing behind the black and white counter. He was a plump middle-aged man with gray hair, and he was wearing his white pharmaceutical coat with a silver nametag that read, "Mr. Jerome Zarchy—Pharmacist." I took a fast, deep breath, but Mom's words flew before I could open my mouth.

"So, Jerome," she said, "Angelica tells me that you gave her a discount for working here. Does that imply that I get one, too?"

Mr. Zarchy looked at me disapprovingly. I felt my face go beet red.

My mother had no compunction about asking again, but Mr. Zarchy cut her off. "Mrs. Marquise," he said, "you can have the discount this time, but I only give discounts to my help—*not* their families." He looked at me sternly. "Go back to work, young lady."

Mom and I returned to my workstation, and I ran up the items again, giving her my discount. I packed the groceries in a bag and handed them to her. She gave me a kiss and left the store. If I could, I would have thrown the bottle of Heaven Scent perfume she had left on my station across the store, but I kept my cool.

After Mom left, Mr. Zarchy's voice came from the back of the store: "Angelica, may I see you?"

I left my work area and walked through the cosmetics aisle and up the steps to the pharmacy. Mr. Zarchy was waiting. I braced myself. *He is going to fire me right now,* I thought.

"I like you, young lady," he said. "You're a good kid and you do good work."

I beamed, my heart in my hands as he praised me.

"But if your mother ever comes in here again and demands a discount, I may very well have to let you go. Do you understand me?"

I nodded silently, then returned to my station to sort out the lipsticks for the display shelf.

From that day on, I never let my mother come in to shop. If she needed anything from the store, I made sure that I purchased the items myself. Mom's head games drove me crazy, but I was not going to lose my job because of them.

CHAPTER 5:
RELIGION
OR
HEALTH

While I was focusing on staying out of the house, my mother went into early menopause. She was hemorrhaging every month, and her doctors wanted to perform a hysterectomy. Despite the devastating effects on her health, she refused. She was so religious by now that she felt that having such a surgery was tantamount to murder.

We didn't talk about things like menstruation in our house. When I first got my period at the young age of eleven, I would not have understood what was happening if a friend of mine hadn't gotten hers first. For my mother, a woman's menstrual cycle was part of human sexuality, and that, according to the church, was an evil thing to discuss.

I always felt that Mom's practice of her faith teetered on madness. She was joining more and more prayer groups, and they were meeting at our house. My parents' bedroom was the largest room in the house, and Mom would take their bed apart and move the night tables to make space. Then she'd open the wooden folding chairs she borrowed from the funeral parlor around the corner so that she could seat as many as twenty or thirty people at a time in the bedroom. After a while, my brother and I saw more priests and nuns grace our home than real friends.

At this time, the abortion issue was on the rise, and Mom's so-called friends would raise Cain over the issue and pray long and loud, planning marches on abortion clinics, houses of ill repute, and drug rehab centers.

They even employed my brother and me to make protest signs. I hated it!

This was in the seventies, when we girls were dressing in miniskirts and bandanas and psychedelic dresses, and disco music was surging past the old rock and roll that our parents had danced to in their youth. We were the new radicals, the "Age of Aquarius."

It was my friend Gail's birthday, and my mom had another of her prayer groups at our home. I had promised Mom that I would help with the meeting and get ready to leave only when one of the priests said the final prayers. Mom agreed and when the time came, I went in my room to change. I slipped into my white fishnet panty hose and yellow sunflower minidress. I had a bandana and a purse to match, as well as the greatest white shin-high go-go boots. I felt like Susan Dey from "The Partridge Family." Before I left my room, I grabbed Gail's gift (the newest Partridge Family album) and took one last look in the mirror. I couldn't help lifting my thumb in approval.

Mom was in the kitchen, readying refreshments for her guests.

"Bye, Mom," I said, kissing her on the cheek.

"You look beautiful," she said, smiling. "Have a good time."

I thanked her and kissed her again. Then I left the kitchen and walked through the living room to leave the house. My hand was on the doorknob when the deep voice erupted from behind me.

"Daughter of Satan!"

A man I had never seen until that afternoon came before me and blocked my path.

"Daughter of Satan!" he yelled again, this time right in my face.

"Mom!" I yelled. "Mommy!"

My mother came into the hall, looking at me questioningly.

"You let her dress in the devil's clothes," the man said, pointing first at me and then at Mom.

Mom looked at the man, then at me. She raised her hand, and I thought she was going to open the front door to let me go, but a few of her prayer group friends came to see what was going on. Mom looked at them and then again at this strange man.

"The devil's dress!" he said.

I stood there with a cold feeling in my gut. Fear began swelling in me, making me uncomfortable in my own skin.

"Go change," Mom said.

"Change? I have to leave. I'm late!"

"Go change," she repeated. "Now."

I didn't know what to do. I thought about leaving, but Mom grabbed me by the shoulder.

"Mom, you *made* this dress for me."

She took a deep breath and said it again: "Go to your room and change."

I turned and headed straight for my room, slamming the door. I sat down on the floor, crying. My dog, Colonel, came and placed his head on my lap. I stroked his fur, and he nuzzled closer to me. Colonel was a golden retriever/German shepherd mix. His body was that of the shepherd, and his coat was gold with a black streak that ran down his back. He had a long, squared-off snout and deep brown eyes, with brilliant gold flecks that made me melt but that others feared. Three years earlier, when I was ten, I had picked him out of a litter of ten. He, too, had felt the arm of my mother's abuse. He was always a good and faithful dog, and that night he stuck to me as the constant bodyguard he was destined to become.

I could not understand this turn of events. Mom had made this whole outfit for me! She loved to sew and belonged to a women's sewing circle at church. She made the most beautiful clothes, not just for me, but also for herself and as gifts. Two months earlier, Mom and I had walked up to Greenpoint Avenue in to the Singer Sewing Center. We were there for hours, rummaging through patterns for the perfect dress for this party. Mom went to one side of the shelf and I to the other.

"Mom, look!" I cried. "This is it!"

I showed Mom the pattern, an A-line with a v-neck, long bell sleeves, and a hemline right above the knee. It was perfect. Mom smiled and nodded, and then it was off to find the right material.

Again, we spent time at the shelves, searching through rolls upon rolls of fabric. We pulled out purple with yellow prints, blues and greens, and hated every one. I went over to the left side aisle and Mom to the right. A few seconds later, I heard, "Ang, come here!"

Mom had a roll of fabric in her hands. The base color was yellow with pretty green leaves and stems and the most adorable sunflowers the size of half-dollars all over the dress. The fabric was soft.

"This would be easy to work with," Mom said.

"I love it, Mom. Let's get it!"

The lady behind the register helped us pick out a zipper for the back of the dress and the two gold and green buttons for the cuffs on the edges of the bell sleeves. I was in designer heaven.

After we left the store, we stopped into a coffee shop for hot chocolate. It was late March and still cold outside.

"Oh, Mom, I can't wait to wear this for the party," I said.

"I like it, too, honey." Her voice was happy as we sat at the table looking at the pattern. "Friday night I'm going to need you at the sewing circle. I need Elizabeth to help me figure out how to cut those sleeves."

"Sure," I said. "I'll make sure I get home from work right away."

Elizabeth was Mom's sewing instructor. She led a group of twenty-five ladies every week, and if I had the time, I went with Mom and learned how to sew. Sewing was Mom's passion, not mine, but I enjoyed spending time with her.

That Friday, I went with Mom and Elizabeth to the sewing circle. Some of Mom's friends loved the pattern and material as much as we did. I watched Mom fold the material and place it on the measuring board. She took the pattern and began to lay it out, and I helped her pin it to the material. When we were done, Elizabeth, a full-bodied Italian lady with short white hair and a loose dress, came to stand near me. She took her measuring tape and measured my arm length, torso, bust, and waist, and then she and Mom used those numbers to measure the pattern. After that, it was time to cut.

Mom gave me a pair of scissors, and we cut the pieces from the direction of the pattern. With every piece done, she smiled at me. Elizabeth came over to guide me, and Mom laughed straight from her belly as we worked; it was a laugh of happiness and pride for me. I felt like the luckiest girl in the world when Mom laughed like that. While I was cutting the material, Mom wrapped her arms around my shoulders and gave me a great big hug and kiss. I could feel how much she loved me, and—at that moment—I felt as if I owned a piece of heaven.

Mom had the patience of a saint when she sewed. The sewing machine, needle, and thread sang in her hands, and she taught me how to hold the needle and thread the same way. As if by magic, my dress now had a hem, but Mom's stitches were so intricate that you could not even see them. I was in love with the dress and the experience of making it with my mother.

The morning of the party, Mom had shown me how to steam out the wrinkles and block the fabric so that it would hang right on my body. When it was done, I'd put the dress on for a final fitting, and it was perfect. I'd spun around in the living room, and Mom had given me an exuberant kiss. Satan's daughter? I could not understand what had happened.

There was a knock on the door, and my brother came in. We were both confused and wanted everyone to leave. Adam sat on my bed, just as dejected as me. We both felt like prisoners in our own home.

"I wish Dad were home," he said.

So did I, but Dad had to work late that night. Though he allowed these meetings at his house, even he, at times, did not accept all the mumbo jumbo of these fanatics. As Mom stayed close to the priests, Dad hung out at the back of the room with Adam and me.

My brother slid down on the floor next to me. We listened to the voices rising and falling outside my room.

A few minutes later, Adam stood up and hovered over me. He was eleven and husky in stature. He had a medium olive complexion, jet-black hair, wide cheekbones, and big baby brown eyes. "I know how to get us both out of here," he said.

"Okay, how?" I said sarcastically.

"Put this back on." He reached over to my corner chair and handed me the ugly navy blue dress I had been wearing at the prayer meeting.

"Okay, smartie—how the heck is that going to help?"

"Just shut up and put it on." Adam placed his ear to my door. "Kitchen's empty."

"So?" I asked, shaking in my go-go boots and dropping the dress on the floor.

"You know all the times when Mom and Dad say I can't take out my toys?"

"Yeah ..."

He giggled. "I hide them under one of my coats or pants legs, and when the coast is clear I run out the door."

"Are you nuts? You want Mom to punish you?"

My brother's big brown eyes glinted mischievously. "Do you want to go to the party or not?"

"Yeah!"

"Then put the blue dress on over that one, okay, stupid?"

I picked the dress up from the floor and threw it on over my new one.

Adam peeked out my bedroom door. "Come on."

I stood there half-frozen, and my brother pulled me out the door. Mom was talking to a friend as we passed the living room doorway, and I jumped as she looked right at me. She said nothing as we slipped out the front door.

Outside, in the alley next to our house, I took off the blue dress, and my brother took it to the backyard and hid it in the shed. Then I ran to the party.

As the days passed, our home life got crazier. The more Mom was around these people, the more she involved Dad, Adam, and me. We went to all-night vigils where we stayed up in church and prayed for long hours, and then Adam and I went to school exhausted the next day. We were good kids, but being good was getting hard to maintain.

Meanwhile, Mom's cycle was getting worse by the month. There were days when Adam, Dad, and I would come home to find Mom sleeping on the couch, pints of blood soaking through the sheets. Yet she would not listen to her own body. She was dying for the sake of what—religion?

It was August 1969, and the Apollo 11 astronauts who had landed on the moon were being honored by a ticker-tape parade through Manhattan and Queens. Mom was not well all day, and Maureen came over with her daughter to take Adam and me across Queens Boulevard to see Neil Armstrong, Michael Collins, and Edwin Eugene "Buzz" Aldrin, Jr. Mom had been watching the ceremonies on the television. When Maureen came over to pick us up, Mom put her sandals on and said, "I'm going, too."

"You don't look good, Virginia," Maureen said. "You're pale. You should stay."

Mom moved away from the couch. With determination no one could argue with, she said, "Let's go."

Queens Boulevard was across the street from us. We filed up 61st Street, crossed the Boulevard, and waited in front of one of the Big Six Towers apartment complexes. A half hour later, the motorcade came down the boulevard. There, sitting in an open black Cadillac convertible, were the three now-famous astronauts. Everyone cheered and threw homemade confetti, applauding and greeting our heroes of space. We had witnessed real history on television as these brave men placed their boots on the face of the moon, and I felt special just by seeing them in my city.

After an hour, it was time to go home. Mom leaned up against the fire hydrant, her skin white as the clouds.

"Virginia, are you all right?" asked Maureen through the noise on the street.

"I'm okay." Mom cupped her hands between her legs and began to rock back and forth.

Maureen held onto Mom, helping her stand. "I knew this was a bad idea."

"Please get me home," Mom said, her voice weak.

"What's wrong with Mom?" asked my brother.

"I don't know," I said.

Maureen walked across the boulevard with my mother leaning against her. We kids followed behind. There were drops of blood on the asphalt in front of me. I looked up at my mother and saw blood trickling down her legs. I was scared.

Mom ran into the bathroom as soon as we got in the door.

"What's the matter with my mom?" I asked Maureen, crying.

Maureen held me. "Your mother is very sick and won't take care of herself. Her period is out of control!"

"Dad told her to go to the doctor this morning."

"He did, did he?" Maureen moved near the bathroom door. "Are you all right, Virginia?"

"I'm fine. I'll be out in a few minutes."

Those few minutes were a half hour. While we waited, Maureen and I cleaned up the drops of blood that ran all the way from the porch to the bathroom door.

Months went by, and it was almost the same scenario each time my mother's period came. One morning she could not get out of bed. Dad's raised voice woke me up: "V, you are going to the hospital whether you like it or not!"

"I won't go!" she yelled back, her voice booming through the house.

"You heard the doctor—you are going to die if you don't have the surgery."

"I don't care! I am not committing murder."

I sat on my bed listening. It was the same argument every month, but now the months were running into each other as Mom's issues worsened. She was not having a monthly period anymore; instead, she was bleeding the whole month, and there were days when it was horrific.

"V, let's get you in now!"

"No! I am a Catholic and cannot commit murder."

"Murder? I don't know who put that in your head, but I could care less about what the damned church has to say about this. All I care about is my *wife!*"

"No, you don't. If you did, you would worry about my mortal soul."

Dad bellowed, "Your soul! Yeah, I worry about your soul all right, because if you don't get to the hospital soon, it will be your damned soul I'll be praying for!"

"Who's going to take care of the kids while I'm in the hospital?" Mom shot back, going for practicality.

"Maureen told you she would. Enough. Let's go!"

I ran into my parents' room, with Adam close behind me. Immediately I started to cry. Mom was as pale as the walls.

"Go back to bed," Dad ordered, still in boxers and an undershirt.

"Is Mommy going to die, Daddy?" asked my brother through his tears.

"Virginia, your kids are worried about you. We are going in now!"

Dad went to lift Mom off the bed, but she pushed him away. The shove knocked Dad off balance, causing him to hit the wall with his shoulder. My brother and I helped him up, and he grabbed his arm. I could see he was hurting.

"You are acting like the devil making me commit a mortal sin!" she shouted. "Get out, all of you!"

Dad stood there for a second. Then he grabbed his pants and shoes and walked out the door.

Later that day, Dad returned to find Mom still in bed. It wasn't unusual for her to spend great amounts of time in bed, but today she wasn't waking up. Adam and I stood by the doorframe, terrified.

"V, wake up!" Dad's voice filled the room, but Mom didn't move. He pulled the covers off her. "Holy God in heaven," he shouted. "Get your brother out of here!"

My mom was lying in a pool of blood. The sheets and blankets were soaked.

Adam cried as I pulled him away. Dad pulled out a piece of paper from his wallet, then picked up the phone. "Maureen," he said, "please come down. Virginia is not getting up."

The doorbell rang minutes later, and Maureen came into the bedroom. "Dear God!" she cried. "Anthony, did you call an ambulance?"

"I was so scared I didn't think of it." Dad's hands were shaking, and I thought he was about to pass out.

She picked up the phone and dialed 911, then told me to watch for the ambulance.

I put on my coat and ran to the door. Adam followed. Minutes later, the sound of the siren blared up the block, and the ambulance came to a halt in front of our house. Neighbors opened their front doors as the paramedics removed a gurney and carried it up the steps and through my house. I had seen this on TV before, but this was so surreal.

I showed them to the bedroom and Dad explained what was going on.

One of the men lifted the blanket that Dad had draped over Mom. "This is bad."

The two began to work on my mom, and the other EMT said, "She's not responding."

Dad watched the paramedics work on Mom. His face was rigid and ashen, and he was pulling a sweat even though the house was freezing.

"Get out of here!" he yelled at me as I approached him. He pressed closer to Mom's side.

"Please, sir, let us do our job," said one of the EMTs, and Dad backed off a little. A moment later, they lifted Mom off the bed with the sheets under her and laid her on the gurney. They placed a large white blanket over her. It read Property of Astoria General Hospital.

The paramedics applied the wheels, unlocked the gurney, and began to roll my mom out the door of the bedroom, into the living room, through the hall, and out the front door. The whole block was hanging out of their doors and windows watching. Mom was placed in the ambulance, and Dad went with her.

Adam and I stayed behind with Maureen and her daughter, shaking as we went back into the house.

Maureen took us both by the hand. "Your dad and those people are going to make sure your mom is okay—do you hear me now?" ·

My dog Colonel came near us and snuggled close. Usually he barked long and loud, but this time he never whimpered. Even he knew something was wrong.

Maureen told us to pack a bag. We were going to stay the night with her, so Adam and I went to our rooms and packed up our pajamas and toothbrushes. I fed Colonel, ran him down to the yard to do his business, let him back in, and locked up the windows and the house. Following Maureen, we walked across the street to her apartment, 6B. I liked it there because I could see the Empire State Building from her sixth floor window.

Much later that night, Dad came back. Adam and I were already in our pajamas and sitting on the floor playing a game called Mouse Trap with Maureen, her husband Vinny, and their daughter. I watched as Maureen opened the door to let him in. He looked exhausted.

"Did you eat?" asked Vinny.

"No," said Dad.

"I'll make you a sandwich." Maureen took Dad's coat, hung it on the coat tree, and then walked into the kitchen. Dad came over and embraced both of us. I could feel his body shaking.

"How'd it go?" called Maureen.

Dad let go and moved to the kitchen. We followed, and Maureen placed a sandwich and a cup of coffee in front of Dad, who gobbled down the food.

"By the time we reached the emergency room, Virginia was almost in a coma from losing so much blood," he finally said.

Adam and I stood near Dad while he sipped his coffee.

"The first thing they did was take blood and give her an IV." Dad stared at the pattern on the lace tablecloth. "If her blood count had been nine and a half points lower, she would have died. I told the doctor to operate right away."

Maureen gave Dad a piece of apple pie. He took a few bites and pushed away the plate.

"So did they operate?" asked Vinny.

"Yeah—it took them five hours." Dad made the sign of the cross. "Thank God for those good doctors. My wife is going to live."

Maureen placed a hand on Dad's shoulder. "Yes, thank God. Tony, if you need anything, please know we are here."

"Thanks," said Dad.

Dad went home a while later, as he had to go to work in the morning and talk to his boss about Mom. Adam and I spent the night with Maureen and her family.

A few days later, we all went to see Mom. She had tubes and needles coming out of her arms. I asked the nurse what all that stuff was, and she told me that what hung on the IV pole was a bottle of whole blood, saline, and antibiotics to prevent infection. Mom's blood count was so low she'd needed a transfusion. I heard Dad tell my grandmother over the phone that Mom had needed sixteen bags of blood during and after the surgery to sustain her life. She had some color to her face but could manage only a tiny smile when she opened her eyes to see us standing there.

Though we were told she'd be okay, Mom scared the hell out of Adam and me. We were having a difficult time understanding how Mom had allowed herself to get that sick. She always took us to the doctor when we were sick; why not herself? She drifted off to sleep, and Adam and I stood there watching her.

"Why did she say that having surgery was committing murder?" Adam asked.

"I don't know, Adam," I said. "I'm not understanding much of this at all."

While Mom was resting and getting better, Adam got sick with the flu. Dad had to work, so I stayed home from school to care for him. That was not easy, as my brother never listened to me, but I was lucky enough that Mom's friends came over to help. I was then able to go to school and take care of the house, too. This went on for the three weeks Mom was in the hospital.

The day she came home, Adam and I had a "Welcome Home" sign made for her and hung it on the wall of our living room. When she arrived, she hugged us as hard as she could, and we reveled in her embrace.

The surgery had taken a lot out of her. Her once white hair, always clean and in place, was now a greasy yellowy color and falling into her face. Her face was gaunt and her eyes looked tired, but she managed to crack a smile for us. I was so glad that Mom was home and safe.

Later that day, Dad told us that Mom was going to need all of us to help her, as she was not allowed out for a while. For the next two months, I would be responsible for all the chores, taking care of my brother, and going to school. It was not easy, but I had no choice.

It seemed from that time on that Mom changed drastically. She was becoming more and more ill-tempered, and we were too young to understand why.

One day, Mom was on the couch with her feet up, watching television and sewing the hem of Dad's pants.

"Mom, the laundry is done and I cleaned the kitchen," I said.

"Did you take out the garbage?"

"No, Adam said he would."

37

"Where is your brother?"

"He's outside on his bike playing with Mike."

"Get him in here." Mom got up in a hurry and could not stand. Her abdomen was still sore, and she leaned forward, holding onto her suture site. "I want Adam in this house right now!" she yelled, her voice echoing off the walls.

"Mom, please lie down. You're going to fall."

Mom half-stood there, holding onto the arm of the couch. She was pulling a sweat and looked at me with a strange, glazed expression.

"Okay," I said, unnerved. "I'm going."

I went outside to look for my brother. There was a group of kids on the corner of where the second six-story building stood adjacent to our house. As I approached, I saw that he was riding his bike down the hill. I ran halfway up the block, shouting, "Adam, Mom wants you!"

"What now?" he said, out of breath.

"She wants you to take out the garbage now."

"Can't she wait?" he asked, but he jumped off his bike and began walking toward the house with me.

"I'm not telling her that."

Adam dropped his bike by our front door, and we walked inside.

"It's about time you come in—take the damned garbage out!" Mom yelled.

"Mom, I told you I'd take it out later," he said, standing by the door.

Mom picked up a throw pillow and hurled it at Adam. "I said now, damn you!"

The trim of the pillow caught Adam's eye, and he winced. He rubbed his eye as it glinted with tears.

"I'm so sorry," Mom said. She started crying like a little girl.

Adam and I looked at each other and shook our heads. Then Adam picked up the pillow. "Mom, its okay. I'm okay."

He sat on the couch next to her and went to kiss her, but she pushed him away.

"Leave me alone!" she yelled.

Adam stood up, dejected. I was livid. How could she just push him away like that?

I watched my little brother go into the kitchen. He grabbed the garbage and twisted the bag good and tight with all his anger, then lifted it and dragged it out to the front of the house, where he slammed it into the garbage can. He got back on his bike and sped up the hill past the break where the kids were waiting for him, and they all rode off together. I went past my mother and got a glass of water. I picked up a dishtowel from the table and twisted it until my hands hurt.

My beautiful loving mother was turning into a monster. And there was nothing we could do about it.

CHAPTER 6:
WHOM CAN I
TRUST?

I t seemed as though becoming an adolescent meant skipping straight to adulthood. As my mom recovered from surgery, my grandmother's diabetes worsened. Between the two of them, I became a caregiver. I was always cleaning house, doing laundry, and going food shopping. If I wasn't at school or at my job, I was working at home and doing homework late at night. I had aunts, my father's sisters, but most of them lived out on Long Island and had families of their own, so Grandma became my responsibility. Even Mom had an excuse: when she was in her twenties, she had taken care of her own mother until her death, and she was not inclined to do it again. Therefore, I was sent to do the job.

"Grandma, I put Channel 9 on the TV for you—the movie this afternoon is *Ben Hur* with Charlton Heston."

"Great, Filimea. Just bring my coffee in for me."

Filimea—I hated that nickname. It was an endearment-shortened version of my middle name, Filomena, which was Grandma's name.

I walked into the kitchen, where Grandma sat in her wheelchair. She was a broad, well-endowed lady, with short, wavy gray hair, blue eyes, and chubby cheeks. She wore a beige housedress with pretty pink flowers on the collar and pockets. She smiled as I walked in, grabbing me for a big wet kiss.

"That was a good sandwich," she said.

I smiled back.

I didn't mind taking care of Grandma. She liked to cook and so did I, and we enjoyed baking and reading the newspaper to each other. Grandma may have been in a wheelchair, but that did not stop her from cooking. I was her legs and would stand in front of the stove, stirring the sauce and helping her mix the batter for her coffee-can breads; the house always smelled delicious, and to date I am the only grandchild who knows the secret to her sauces.

Meanwhile, my Uncle Thomas had come back to live in my grandparents' house with his four-year-old son. Uncle Thomas and his ex-wife, Marsha, had lived in the basement apartment of my house for the first two years of their marriage. Their son, Paul, was born in our house. I had liked them living with us. My brother and I would go down and play with our cousin, and Aunt Marsha would treat us to snacks after school. After Paul was born, though, the apartment just got too cramped, so they moved to a small four-room flat in Maspeth. They'd divorced after five years of marriage, and I now sometimes baby-sat my cousin along with caring for Grandma. While Grandma rested in the living room, Uncle Thomas would stay in the kitchen and talk to me. It was a routine I was accustomed to by now.

That day, the back door opened and Uncle Thomas, a much heavier version of my dad, walked in. Where Dad was broad and handsome, Uncle Thomas was a sloppy-looking obese man with black hair and brown eyes. I hated being around him when he came in from work. He drove an eighteen-wheel truck delivering goods to the tri-state area of New York, New Jersey, and Pennsylvania. Sometimes the company would send him to New England and he would be away overnight; he'd return with filthy clothes, smelling like the inside of his truck, all diesel and smoke. Still, I greeted him with a smile, and he came over to me and kissed me on the cheek. Then he went to the sink to get a glass of water.

"Where's cousin Paul?" I asked.

"He's next door, playing with Bobby."

Grandma had just finished her lunch, and I picked up her dishes and placed them in the sink. Then I unlocked the wheels on her wheelchair and rolled her through the dining room and into the living room. I had always loved that room; it must have been twenty feet by twenty feet, with two large arch-shaped windows at one end. Between the porch entry and the living room were two gorgeous French doors. The light from the porch shone through the white Italian lace curtains. The room held a plush green couch on one side and, across from it, Grandpa's brown club chair. Though Grandpa was gone, his chair lived in that corner. Next to it was Uncle Thomas's smoker's tray, always dirty with his cigarette butts.

When Grandma was settled in the living room with her coffee, I walked back to the kitchen. Uncle Thomas was sitting at the table with a lit cigarette and a cup of coffee. I was heading to the sink to do the dishes when he grabbed me and sat me on his lap. I tried to get up, but he held me close for a moment, jiggling me up and down on his thigh. His hold surprised me. I was not a baby anymore, and I felt degraded by this gesture.

"How was Grandma today?" he asked.

"She's fine, Uncle Thomas." I pushed away from him and hurried to the sink. I had prepared not only lunch but also dinner that day, and there were a good amount of dishes to wash. I turned on the hot water and began to run it over the dishes.

Uncle Thomas went over to the stove to pour another cup of coffee. Then he took a piece of pie from the fridge. He ate his pie and drank his coffee as he watched me wash the dishes. I wanted to finish quickly and go home. I had homework to do and needed to catch the bus.

When he finished eating, Uncle Thomas put his plate in the sink. Then he lightly tickled my neck.

Laughing, I cocked my neck and pushed his hand away. "What was that for?"

"Just wanted to see you laugh. You look so serious!"

I continued to wash the dishes, and he touched me again, this time caressing my upper arm. I pulled away. "Uncle Thomas, c'mon, I have to get this done."

He snickered and did it again. I moved a few inches away. I felt as though Uncle Thomas were sucking the space away from me.

Uncle Thomas moved behind me and began to stroke my hair and then my shoulders. I could feel his warm breath on my neck, and a peculiar chill ran down my back. It made me shiver, and I felt strange: the tickle felt good and not so good at the same time. I didn't know what to think. I shut off the water, turned, and pushed his hand away.

"Stop!" I said as I pushed him toward the bathroom door. "Uncle Thomas, leave me alone, okay?"

His face was blank. He walked back to his chair and took a sip of his coffee, then left the room for a minute. I returned to washing the dishes, but my heart was racing and I began to sweat. I felt as though an alien had entered my body. I shook it off.

A few minutes later, I finished the dishes, wiped the table, and went back to the living room. Grandma sat watching her movie while Uncle Thomas smoked his cigarette in Grandpa's chair.

"Grandma, everything is done," I said. "I'm going home."

Grandma smiled. "Thanks, honey."

I grabbed my jacket from the porch and shrugged it on, then retrieved my purse and school bag. When I went back to kiss my grandmother and Uncle Thomas goodbye, he said, "I'll take you home."

"That's okay, Uncle Thomas," I said. "I can grab the bus."

"Come on, the car's in the driveway."

I stood there for a minute, deliberating. I really wanted to take the bus home and be by myself for a while. I knew that once I got home, I had chores to do for my mom, but if I denied my uncle, I would never stop hearing it from either him or my dad. So I walked out of the house with my uncle and got in the car.

After about five blocks, Uncle Thomas pulled over near the deli. "I'll be right back," he said, leaving the car on. He went into the deli and emerged a few minutes later with a pack of cigarettes and a newspaper. Back in the car, he just sat there.

"Aren't we going home?" I asked. It was getting dark—my watch read six thirty—and I didn't want to get in trouble for being late.

"In a minute." He turned away from the steering wheel and looked at me. "How is school going?"

I looked at my watch again. "Mom is going to be mad at me. I'm late."

"You're with me." He twisted the key in the ignition, turning the car off.

I looked out at the cars coming and going up 69th Street. "I could get on the bus."

Unexpectedly, I felt his hand stroke my hair away from my face.

"You do know that I love you," he said.

I turned to look at him. "Uncle Thomas, yeah, I know, but please take me home."

He went to touch me again and my heart started pounding. His hand went from my shoulder down and around my armpit. I pushed his hand away.

"What's the matter?" he asked.

"Nothing. I just want to go home; Mom is going to be really mad at me."

Again he touched me and again I pushed his hand away.

"I want to go home!" I shouted.

"What's the matter?"

I reached for the car door and he leaned over me with his fat sloppy body and big filthy hands, stopping me from getting out of the car. Fear swept over me.

Uncle Thomas pulled the car door shut and took my face in his hands. His scratchy beard scraped my cheeks as he kissed me on the mouth. I couldn't breathe and pushed my hands against his, trying to move away, but he shoved me against the car seat with his two hundred and seventy pounds. I was small, not even five feet tall and around one hundred pounds. He tried to force his tongue in my mouth and I slid my hand between his lips and mine. I pushed him away and held my hands up, shielding myself from him. I had the stench of saliva all over my mouth and began to cry as I wiped my lips with my sleeves. He laughed. Then he started the car.

I cried all the way home, not looking at him once.

Uncle Thomas parked the car up the block from my house, in the area where all the trees hid the light from street lamps. He touched my face and laughed again. "You know you can't tell your parents about tonight."

Why was he doing this to me? The way I was feeling, I wouldn't even know *what* to tell my mom or dad. I grabbed my purse and school bag and slid out of the car. Uncle Thomas got out as I did, and he followed me as I ran down the block and into the house.

"Where were you?" my mother yelled as I came in the door. My dog, Colonel, barked in greeting.

Uncle Thomas came into the house right behind me.

"Hey, brother!" my father shouted. He got up from his chair and shook Uncle Thomas's hand.

"Hi, Uncle Thomas!" Adam echoed. He ran up to our uncle, and Uncle Thomas lifted him and gave him a big kiss on the cheek.

I ran to the bathroom, not saying a word to anyone. I washed my face, rinsed out my mouth with hot water, and took a long pee. My stomach was hurting so badly it felt as if I were going to get my period. I was shaking. From behind the closed bathroom door, I heard my mother say to Uncle Thomas, "Stay for dinner!"

"Please say no," I begged from the inside the bathroom. He said yes.

I opened the door a few moments later, knowing that I'd better set the table quickly or my mother would be mad at me for not doing my chores. Dinner was ready, and Mom started putting the food on the table as soon as places were set. We sat down, made the sign of the cross, and said grace, thanking God for our food. Then Uncle Thomas started filling his plate. He looked at me and I could not eat.

"May I be excused?" I asked.

"Eat your dinner," Dad said.

"I'm not hungry."

"Not hungry?" Dad repeated.

Uncle Thomas shot me a look from across the table, and Dad noticed it. "What gives?" Dad asked.

I glared back at my uncle.

As if he knew I was about to say something, he said, "Ang forgot to pick up milk for Momma. That's why we were late."

You're lying! I wanted to scream. I had gone to John's Deli that afternoon and bought everything that Grandma had on the list. Why was he doing this?

"Did you get it for her?" Dad asked.

"Yes, we did," said Uncle Thomas.

"So what gives?" Dad asked me again. "Why aren't you hungry?"

"Nothing, Dad," I said. "I just want to start my homework."

I pulled up from the table and was about to go to my room when Uncle Thomas grabbed me around my waist. He held me hard enough to hurt my stomach. I pushed my hand against his arm and tried to force it away, but he had me in his grip. He laughed and kissed me on the cheek. Colonel was between my bedroom door and the kitchen, and he growled at Uncle Thomas.

"Colonel, go lay down!" Mom yelled.

"Ang takes the bus home," Uncle Thomas said. "I can drive her here after work."

"Dad, I'd rather take the bus home." I wanted to punch my uncle. Every fiber of my being hated him at that moment.

Dad smiled at his brother. "Ang, just wait for Uncle Thomas to get home from work."

Uncle Thomas had a twisted, snide look on his face. "Thanks for taking care of Grandma today," he told me.

Finally, I was able to pull away, and I rushed to my room. I grabbed my throw pillow and started punching it so hard that I ripped it open. Then I hugged it for dear life as I sat on my floor and cried. Colonel put his head on my lap and stayed there.

From that day on, as long as we were alone, Uncle Thomas touched me in places that no man should touch a child.

Once, Grandma asked if I could spend the weekend at her house. Uncle Thomas was supposed to go on a tri-state delivery that would keep him away for a few days. Knowing he would not be home, I told Grandma I'd be happy to stay over.

I was asleep one night when I heard noises from downstairs. I crawled out of bed, feeling a bit dazed. As I neared the stairwell, a strange, sweet, yet pungent odor made me nauseated. Thinking it was coming from outside, I decided to go downstairs to close the windows. What I found were my Uncle Thomas and his buddies Derrick and Bobby smoking at the table. There was a funny-looking white powder on a flat plate near my uncle.

"Hey, come here, you sexy thing you," Uncle Thomas slurred.

It was hot, and my nightgown was light. All I wanted to do was get my robe on. Embarrassed, I eased away, but Uncle Thomas rose from his chair and grabbed me.

"Make some coffee!" he demanded.

"I want to go back to sleep," I said.

"Sleep? Come on, baby, make some coffee."

Bobby got up from his chair and swung me around. Bobby was tall and skinny. He had been my father's friend since childhood, and as thin as he was, he had a grip. Finally, I yanked away and started to back out of the room.

"Uncle Thomas, make your own coffee," I said. "I'm going back to bed."

"Come on, Thomas, let her go back to sleep," said Derrick. Coming to my rescue, Derrick took off his own shirt and placed it over me.

Uncle Thomas tugged at the shirttails. "Get over here," he said. "Take it off. Show us some skin."

I glared at him and saw Bobby lean down and breathe in the white powder with what looked like a mini straw. "Is that cocaine?" I asked in shock. I only knew about that from the cop show I watched every week.

"Now look, she knows!" said Uncle Thomas.

I turned and dashed toward the stairs, but as much as my uncle was fat, he was swift on his feet and ran after me.

"You little bitch, you tell your father or my mother anything you saw here tonight and I'll kill you. Do you hear me?" Moonlight from the open window fell over his face. His eyes were crazed.

"I hear you," I said, swallowing my fear.

"Good." To make sure I heard him, he grabbed my right breast and squeezed it hard. I took his wrist, trying to pry his hand off, and he laughed and walked away.

I placed my hand on my breast and tried to rub the pain away, but I hurt from humiliation and fear.

Back in the bedroom, I pulled the sheets over me and sat at the edge of the bed, almost paralyzed.

My cousin came into the room. "Daddy's friends woke me up." He pushed under the covers with me and snuggled close. "I don't like Uncle Bobby."

"Neither do I," I said, snuggling back with him.

I had no idea how my grandmother did not wake up from all the noise, but what I did know was that it was after three in the morning, and I could not leave my cousin alone. Besides, I wasn't sure how I would get home at that hour. Seeking comfort from each other, my little cousin and I cuddled together under the sheets. He fell asleep next to me, and I sat guard all night, too afraid to close my eyes.

CHAPTER 7:
A
FURY
BOILING

Two years pass slowly when you are constantly working a job and taking care of loved ones. I socialized at times, becoming a member of the teen club at St. Sebastian's Parish Center, but most of my time was spent with family. The year I turned fourteen, Uncle Thomas married a woman who had a ten-year-old daughter. The person I now had to call "aunt" had a part-time job she was not quitting to stay at home and care for her ailing mother-in-law, so I was given the added responsibility of caring for my new step-cousin. Unlike my cousin Paul, who was a sweet kid, this one was her mother's princess and got everything she wanted, which meant I had more work to do. However, when I griped to my parents, both of them just told me to be a "good little girl" and take care of her.

Being a good little girl had its price. If I wanted to go to the teen club meeting on Friday nights or teen dances on Saturday nights, I had to do chores at home, take care of Grandma, baby-sit, and work my part-time job at the pharmacy. Meanwhile, I watched my friends hang out on the block and go shopping and to the movies; I had no time for any of it. I was grown up already.

It was June 1971, and my eighth-grade graduation was approaching. Despite all the obstacles, I was graduating with a 94.03 average, and I knew

I'd be receiving merit awards. Mom had promised we would go to the new boutique for my graduation dress, but Dad could not afford it, as his hours had been cut at work. Mom felt it was up to her and my dad to dress me for the celebration, so she blew up every time I suggested paying for my own dress. Finally, if it meant getting through May and June with some peace, I yielded to Mom's insistence that she would make the dress herself. Yielding, always yielding for the sake of peace, but there was a war raging inside me and all I wanted to do was explode.

It was a time in my life when I should have been reveling in my accomplishments. Instead of reveling, I was taking care of things for my grandmother. There were many times that she would ask me if I was all right ... I think somewhere in her heart she knew that something was wrong.

Sometimes Grandma wondered aloud why Mom did not believe that I was doing my chores for her. Grandma asked me why my mother kept asking her if I was doing what I was told. That was the funny part: Grandma never *told* me to do anything. She asked me in a kind and gentle voice, and it was my pleasure to help her. I wanted to tell her that I was taking beatings from my mother because Uncle Thomas kept lying about me. He told my parents that I stole money from my grandmother and that I did not help her—that I just sat on the couch and watched TV. He did this to cover his desires for me, breaking the trusting bonds I had with my parents. All the while, he showed his "love" by touching and groping me, threatening more lies if I told anyone about it. Meanwhile, Uncle Thomas's new wife had dubbed me "the troublemaker" because I would not give in to her daughter wanting me to buy her candies with my grandmother's money. Not only that, but they had moved into Grandma's house and taken over—every closet, cabinet, and curtain that I had taken such care of was redone to suit this woman. Grandma told me that if it weren't for her grandson, she would have asked my uncle and his new family to leave.

One day I came home from graduation practice with my cap and gown in my hands. I was so happy—this was it! The day was coming. I went into the kitchen, looking for my mother.

"Mommy, I got my cap and gown today!" I gushed.

"Did you do the laundry for Grandma and your aunt?"

"Huh? Mom, look—my cap and gown." I placed them over the chair in the kitchen.

Mom picked them up. She shook her head and cracked a smile. "You did not answer me."

I was sinking quickly, as if the floor were quicksand. Here it was, my cap and gown day, and all my mother could think of was whether I'd done something for Grandma.

"Mom, I did everything yesterday for Grandma and Aunt Carol. Everything!"

She held my gown. "Aunt Carol told me that you didn't go to the store for your new cousin."

I was livid. "I didn't, huh? Well, you can tell Aunt Carol that I am not spending Grandma's money on candy and stupid stuff for her daughter."

"That's not what Aunt Carol told me." Mom opened the box with my cap. It was white with a gold tassel.

"You know what, Mom? I hate taking care of that kid. Grandma gave me money to buy milk, bread, and the chicken cutlets she likes. Susan wanted candy and ice cream. I told her that Grandma didn't give me money for that, so I didn't get it for her."

Mom stood there a second with that I'm-trying-to-make-up-my mind look.

"Mom, please believe me this time." I stood by the table, holding onto the red and white kitchen chair. "Please."

Mom picked up my gown again and said, "I'll talk to your aunt tonight."

I stood there and took a relieved breath. For once, was Mom on my side?

"Put your gown on, honey. Let me see what it looks like."

Without even taking off my uniform, I pulled the gown over my head and put my cap on. Then I walked to my room and looked at myself in the mirror. There I was—the graduate. Was there anything better than how I felt just now, so proud?

Mom came in my room. "That needs ironing."

"I know, Mom."

She smiled at me. "You look beautiful." She hugged me and I felt as though I could touch the sky.

Dad came home from work a few hours later, and I ran into my room to put on my cap and gown again. When he walked into the kitchen, I ran out of my room. "Tah-dah!" I said, wearing my robes.

Dad put his bag down and stared at me. Tears formed in his eyes, and he began to laugh proudly. "Ah, sweetheart." He placed his hand on my cheek and kissed me.

"Okay, dinner is ready," said Mom. "Go call your brother."

Adam was across the street playing with his friends, and I ran outside with my robes on. "Hey, knucklehead, Mom wants you!"

"What's that on you?" he asked.

I swished my gown back and forth. "My graduation gown, stupid. Now get in before Mom gets mad!"

Adam crossed the street to where I was standing. He was filthy. "You look stupid," he said jokingly, stretching his dirty hands toward me.

I pushed his hands away. "Stop! You're going to ruin it!"

"Heck, can't you take a joke?" And there were those mischievous baby brown eyes of his that irritated me and made me smile at the same time.

I went to my room and hung up my gown, then set the table. At dinner, all we talked about was graduation, my party, and what Mom still had to do before the big day. For once, the house was buzzing with happiness.

I did the dishes, and my brother and I sat down to watch my favorite television show, "The Mod Squad." Then the phone rang.

"Hi, Carol!" I heard Mom say.

What does she want? I thought. I heard my name mentioned a few times, and with it, my mother's tone of voice changed.

"But Angelica told me that Susan wanted candy and she didn't have the money to get it for her."

I got up from the couch and went into the kitchen, where my mother's eyes had adopted that angry glare. "Mom," I tried to cut in, but my mother put her hand up to me.

A few seconds later, she said goodbye and hung up. "I thought you told me that you didn't have the money to get what Susan wanted."

"I didn't."

"Aunt Carol said you did."

"It was Grandma's change, and I was not getting candy if Grandma did not tell me to." I was furious. "I am so tired of that snot nose kid getting her way!"

Mom came over to me with her finger in my face. "Carol tells me that you didn't fold the clothes, either."

I crossed my arms and locked myself in that defensive stance. "She's lying!"

"You don't talk like that about your elders!" Mom yelled.

"What gives?" said Dad, coming into the kitchen.

"You do what you are told, young lady!" Mom yelled.

"What happened?" asked Dad again.

"She didn't—"

"Let Angelica tell me," said Dad, putting his hand up to Mom.

I braced myself. "Grandma gives me money to go to the store."

"Okay, what then?" said Dad.

"I go to Johnny's around the corner and pick up what she has on the list."

"And then what happens?" Dad was listening intensely.

"Every time I go lately, Susan has to come with me."

"So what gives with that?"

Mom was about to say something, but Dad put his hand up again.

"Dad, she always wants candy and ice cream. I only have so much money to spend. You know you get mad if Adam and I spend money that you give us to go to the store and we come back with things that were not on the list—that is what Susan wants me to do. She keeps wanting things that Grandma didn't say it was okay to buy." I held my own. "I'm not buying it for her. No way!"

"Is this the truth?" Dad asked.

"Yes."

Dad nodded. "Then you did the right thing."

I almost felt light-headed with relief.

"Carol said that you didn't fold the clothes," Mom said.

"Susan is old enough the fold the clothes, too, Mom. I helped you when I was her age. Why can't she do it for her mother?"

"Your aunt told *you* to do it."

"Well, Grandma doesn't *tell* me to do anything. She asks me in a nice way, and I do it for her because she is my grandmother."

"If your aunt tells you to fold the clothes, then you do it!"

"She's right, Virginia," Dad said. "Susan can help, too."

"You're on her side!" Mom yelled at Dad.

"Wow, someone believes *me* for once," I said. "Hurray!"

I did not see it coming, but all at once, I felt a hard slap come across my face.

"You never speak to us again like that!" Mom shouted. "Do you hear me?"

I ran to my room and closed the door, crying myself to sleep.

The next day, I woke up with a black and blue mark that stretched from my cheekbone to my jaw. I was so mad that I wanted to break the bathroom mirror.

Mom was having her coffee in the kitchen, and when I walked in, she looked at me with surprise and remorse. She sat tall in her chair and shook quietly but said nothing.

I took a shower and then covered my bruise with some Maybelline foundation and powder I had purchased at Zarchy's Pharmacy. It had taken quite a lot of convincing from my mother's friends and from Grandma for my mother to finally allow me to wear makeup, and I had bought it from my own cosmetics counter only two weeks before. Frantically trying to cover up yet another mess my mother had created, I kept looking at the mark while I blended foundation over it and thought, *Please be gone by graduation. Please!*

It was Flag Day, and we were off from school. I put on my play clothes, had breakfast, made my bed, did a load of laundry for Mom, and then went to Grandma's house.

Carol was on her way to work when I arrived. She was a broadly built woman, about five feet four inches tall and very well endowed. She had short curly black hair and wore black pants and a black and white blouse with hideous bold black roses all over it.

"Where's Susan?" I asked.

"She's at her friend's house," said my cousin Paul, coming from the kitchen.

Carol took her red sweater off the chair and left for work. As the door closed behind her, all I could think was, *Thank God!*

Grandma was sitting in her wheelchair by the dining room table. I went over to kiss her.

"Hi, honey," she said.

I began to unset the table of the dirty breakfast dishes. The house was quiet. For the first time in weeks, it was just Grandma, my little cousin, and me. The only noise came from the television in the background.

"Angelica, are you all right?" Grandma asked.

I was in the kitchen making some iced tea. I heard her but didn't answer right away. I was trying to avoid the inevitable.

"Angelica *vieni qui!*"

I went into the room, drying my hands with the dishtowel. "Why do you ask?" I said.

"You are too quiet today. Come here."

I moved over to her, and she took my face in her hand. "What happened here?" she asked, pointing to my left cheekbone. I thought I had covered it enough, but I should have known better—you couldn't hide anything from Grandma.

"I got in the way and Adam hit me with his bat."

Grandma looked at me skeptically. "How did that happen?"

I twisted the towel in my hands, trying to keep my anger inside. But tears began to well up in my eyes, and Grandma pulled me toward her. She held me so close that the rim of the wheel on her chair dug into my thigh.

"What really happened, Angelica?" she asked gently.

"Adam and I were playing and I got in the way of a swing." I shrugged off the lie.

Grandma took a napkin from the table and wiped off my makeup. "Now sit here and tell me who did this to you."

I could not keep lying to my grandmother. She knew me so well, and I loved her too much to keep up the charade. "Mommy hit me last night."

"I knew your mother had a temper!"

"Please, Grandma, don't say anything," I begged. "Graduation is in two weeks, and I don't want Mommy to take my party away from me."

"This is not right. She should not hit you like this." Grandma held herself up in her wheelchair. If she could, I knew, she would have stood and walked right up to a fight.

Again, I begged, "Please don't say anything."

"I am going to talk to your father."

"Grandma, Dad was there. He tried to defend me."

Shaking her head again, she kissed me on the mark. "If Dad was there, then I won't say a thing. I promise."

Pressed close to Grandma's warmth, I wanted to tell her about my uncle and all the horrible things he had done to me for the past two years. I wanted to tell her that his second wife was calling me vicious names. But by then I was so afraid of him that it was just easier to take another beating than tell anyone the truth. He'd already built a wedge between my parents and me; I couldn't have him do the same with my grandmother. At times like these, I wanted to punch someone, anyone—the rage was always there and always suppressed, and I dreaded the day it would come to a boil.

Carol came home early that day, giving me a chance to grab the bus and get home before dinner. Mom was napping on the couch when I arrived, and in my room, Colonel was lying on the rug in front of my bed. I sat down to pet him, and he jumped up and licked me. I hugged him hard. When I let go, Colonel crawled under my bed and emerged with his blue ball.

"Okay, let's go in the yard," I said. We ran through the basement and out to the yard. "Catch!" I shouted.

I threw the ball across the yard, and Colonel ran to fetch it, dropping it back at my feet. The two of us played in the hot June sun, running around in the grass, around the roses in the back and through the swing set near the neighbors' fence. There was a cool breeze that wrapped around the yard as it came from the alley, around the parking garage wall of the Winston Apartment Building, and then across the back of our neighbors' garage around the corner.

"You're home early!" Mom called from my bedroom window a few minutes later.

"Aunt Carol came home early!" I shouted back to her.

Mom looked down at me, right at the mark she'd left on my cheek, but said nothing.

An hour or so passed, and Mom started dinner as I set the table. Colonel started barking up a storm, letting us know that Dad was on his way in. The phone rang as we sat down to eat, and Mom rose to answer.

"Hi, Thomas!" she said.

Okay, what did I do now? I thought. *Go ahead and make my night another nightmare.*

My mother's face went white. "Mom's in the hospital?"

Immediately Dad took the phone. "Thomas, what is going on? Heart attack? When, how?" My father's voice cracked.

"I was just there a few hours ago," I cried, jumping up from the table. "I swear Grandma was fine!"

We didn't have a car, so my dad said to Uncle Thomas, "You are coming to get us."

"Dad, I don't understand," I said when he'd hung up. "Grandma was fine when I left the house."

Dad stroked the back of my head. "Honey, these things happen. Go get ready."

An hour later, we were at St. John's Hospital on Queens Boulevard. Uncle Thomas pulled Mom and Dad aside in the waiting room. I caught the words "massive heart attack," "ambulance," and "intensive care unit" and felt as if I were in a bad dream.

"Carol is up there with her," Uncle Thomas said.

Dad came over to Adam and me. "Stay down here. Mom and I are going up."

"Dad, can I come?" I asked.

"Let me see how Grandma is first, okay, honey?"

Dad, Uncle Thomas, and Mom got into the elevator, and I went to sit by my brother, who was playing with his handball. I looked out the window of the lounge toward Queens Boulevard. Across from the hospital stood A&S Department Store and Fairyland Amusement Park. It was getting late, and the street lamps had just turned on.

I started to cry. I had just *been* there, sitting with her, eating lunch with her. How had this happened?

Dusk turned into night and my parents came down the elevator. Dad looked so tired and worried. He, Mom, Uncle Thomas, and Aunt Carol huddled near the information desk, talking.

"Is Grandma okay?" I asked, approaching them.

Dad put his hand on my shoulder. Behind him was the statue of St. John the Baptist, the hospital's patron saint. "Grandma is very sick."

Adam was standing near Mom. We looked at each other.

"Is she going to die?" asked my brother.

"I don't know, son," said Dad, "but we have to say a lot of prayers for her."

For the next week, my parents—along with my aunt, uncle, and all of my dad's family—went back and forth to the hospital. Since we did not have a car, Uncle Thomas brought my two cousins to our house for me to baby-sit while the adults went to see Grandma.

When things were looking up and Grandma was out of the intensive care unit, Dad told me that I could finally go see her. I was scared. Mom and Dad explained what Grandma looked like, but I did not really know what I was walking into.

Mom had to stay down with Adam as he was only eleven and too young to go up. I was so nervous as Dad and I waited for the elevator. The mirrored doors opened, and we got in. Elevators had never bothered me, but this time

I felt as if I were in a box, choking.

We walked out into organized chaos. Nurses in white dresses and caps were scurrying around with their medical carts. A few patients walked the floor in hospital gowns, and I cringed at seeing them. There was an orderly mopping the floor, and there on the right was Grandma's room. I stood there, frozen, but Dad walked in ahead of me. "Hi, Mom," he said. "Look who I brought with me!"

The room smelled of cleanser and something else. I could not see her yet, as there was an ugly blue curtain around the end of the bed.

"Where's my girl?" I heard Grandma say.

Dad beckoned to me, but I was too scared to move. Dad knew, and he took me by the hand as we walked toward the bed. "It's okay, honey," he said. "It's still Grandma. Just in a different place."

Grandma was half-sitting, half-lying down, her head propped up on pillows. A mess of tubes connected her to an intravenous pole.

She reached out for me. "There's my girl!"

I just stood there.

"Go give her a kiss," said Dad.

I wanted to run, to cry, but did not want her to see me upset. I stood near the bed, leaned in, and forced myself to give Grandma a kiss on the cheek.

"I missed you," she said.

"Are you going to be okay?" I asked. The tears swelled in my chest. "I don't want you to die."

Dad took me in his arms. "Grandma is not going to die," he tried to assure me.

I wrapped my arms tightly around him. I could not turn and look at the person I loved most in the world. Those tubes! They looked like tentacles on an octopus.

"Come here," Grandma said, her voice weak.

The courage to push away from Dad came over me, and I turned and looked at my grandmother. She smiled that reassuring smile of hers.

"Are you ready for graduation?" she asked.

"Are you going to be there?"

"No, sweetheart, I won't, but can you do me a favor?"

I felt as if someone had kicked me in the stomach. "Anything, Grandma."

"After graduation, can you come see me wearing your cap and gown?"

I looked at Dad and he nodded.

"I'll come right after church," I said.

We stayed until a nurse came to tell us that visiting hours were over. I did not want to leave, but my stomach kept pressing on my throat and I ran to the first bathroom I could find. I could handle my uncle's evil, my mother's abuse, and taking care of everyone. But this I could not endure. I purged in the ladies' room and then sat on the cold tile floor, alone and scared.

The next week was hard. There was school, graduation practice, the graduation dance, and getting the house ready for my big day. But my graduation was getting lost in the shuffle with Grandma in the hospital, and I wondered if it was all right to celebrate. My emotions were wild. One minute I was ecstatic that I passed all my finals and attained honor status. The next I felt surges of guilt and grief, hearing from my parents that Grandma was not getting better or going straight to the hospital to see for myself.

June 26, 1971, arrived with the sun shining and the temperature in the high eighties. I was thrilled that it was not raining. Mom and I went to the hairdresser that morning and had our hair and nails done. I changed into the dress Mom had made me—Wedgwood blue taffeta with chiffon overlay, tiny embroidered stars, and a silver collar and hem. Mom had made her own dress, too. Hers was blue as well with a tiny, pretty white floral print. Dad wore a navy suit with a white shirt and red tie. My brother had to wear a suit whether he liked it or not, so he matched Dad, except he wore a blue tie. We took pictures in front of the house, and then we were off to St. Sebastian's School for lineup.

Dad, as usual, had his camera going like a firecracker. Dad loved his camera and always took the greatest photographs of the family. We took pictures with the nuns and priests by the main entrance of the school, which was on 58th Street and Woodside Avenue in Woodside. It was perfect, even with the 7-train chugging above us. Our parents and siblings were told to go to the church, and then only we were left: the excited graduating class of 1971, the boys dressed in blue and gold and the girls in white and gold.

Commencement began with "Pomp and Circumstance" playing, and we filed down the long aisle of St. Sebastian's. I passed my parents, my godparents, and my brother, but the excitement was dulled by my grandmother's absence. A deep sense of sadness engulfed me as my eyes lifted to the beautiful crucifix of Jesus.

After we sat, the priests entered the altar and Mass began. The liturgy was read and the homily given by our pastor, and as I listened, my gaze shifting from the altar, to the Stations of the Cross, to the statue of the Sacred Heart of Jesus, and then to the statue of the Virgin Mary. Grandma loved Mary very much.

After Mass, our teachers stood on the altar and gave out the awards. I knew I had done well and received the gold cord of honors in English and history, and a Certificate of Merit for religion. I knew my mother was going to love that one. Father Curran, our pastor, and Sister Lourdes, our principal, began handing out our diplomas. I moved up the line, and Sister gave me my diploma. Then there was a handshake from Father, and it was official: I had graduated!

When the ceremonies were over, we all sauntered up the aisle and out to our families. I gave my parents my awards and diploma, and they both hugged me. Mom held me so tightly she was shaking.

"I am so proud of you." Tears were flowing down Mom's cheeks as she said those words. She hugged me again. "I love you, doll."

My heart skipped a beat when she said that. I had not heard her call me "doll" in so long I thought she had forgotten it.

Dad embraced me. "You are something else, sweetheart."

My godparents hugged me and told me how proud they were, and then came Adam. "Congratulations," he said, and he kissed me quickly on the cheek. Short and sweet—we had to be cool in front of our friends.

My classmates and I were screaming in the streets. Our energy could warp out the Enterprise on the show "Star Trek." We took pictures with friends, teachers, the nuns, and the priests, and none of us wanted to say goodbye. But it was time to go, and everyone headed their separate ways.

With all the commotion around me, I had almost forgotten my promise to Grandma. It hit me when I heard Mom telling my teacher, "I'll bring Angelica's cap and gown in tomorrow morning."

Dad had rented a car that day to make traveling easier, and we arrived at the hospital shortly after graduation. Dad stopped by the nurses' station to get an update on Grandma. In the hall, Mom helped me back into my cap and gown.

There were only two people allowed into the room at a time. My godparents—my father's sister, Marie, and her husband, Uncle Joey—went in first. They stayed for a little while, and my poor aunt came out with tears in her eyes. Mom and Adam, who was allowed in for ten minutes because of the special occasion, went in with Dad. As much bravado as my brother had at eleven, he came out looking like a shaken leaf. Mom had to take him down to the lounge to comfort him.

Then it was just Dad and me.

There was a glass door to the side of the room, and I used my reflection to fix my cap and gown. Inside, I was surprised to see Grandma sitting up in bed. The nurses had dressed her in a pink gown with a white and pink lace bed jacket. For the first time in a while, her hair was all in place. Once silver, it had turned snow white in the past weeks.

"Grandma, you look nice," I said, walking toward her.

Grandma reached her arms out to me, and I couldn't help but notice that they were black and blue from the needles.

I pointed to the bruises. "Do those hurt?"

Grandma's eyes dropped. "A little, honey."

I leaned carefully and gently onto the bed and gave her a hug and kiss.

"Let me look at you," she said.

I moved back, and she looked at me in my robes.

"I am so proud of you!"

A few minutes later, the floor nurse came in with a tray of food. She retreated to the back of the room as Dad began to cut Grandma's chicken into small pieces. I gave her a piece of the meat, and Grandma chewed and swallowed it with a smile. When I went to give her another, she pushed my hand away. Grandma had always had a great appetite, even on her worst days, but in the past few weeks, she had not been eating. I knew instinctively what that meant. She was not fighting anymore.

She patted the bed and asked me to sit near her. Weary, she cradled her head on the pillow and took my hand. "I had a dream about Grandpa last night."

"You did?" I said, trying to sound enthusiastic.

"I did. He was wearing a white suit, and on his chest was a gold cross."

I felt myself sink into that mattress. I gripped her hand and begged inside, *Hold on, Grandma, please don't leave me.*

She caressed my forearm. "There was a beautiful angel with Grandpa. She was all lit up."

Dad's eyes were fixed on mine with a stare that didn't need words. His heart was speaking through that look, and he was trying to be brave even while his heart was breaking.

Grandma was only sixteen when she had my dad. She was a child herself, and he was not an easy boy. He quit school at thirteen and got in trouble with the law. With the help of the police and the church and all the love she had for him, she put Dad in a Catholic protectory for boys. Dad spent three years in that home and came back the responsible man she hoped he would be.

Dad had his camera bag on his shoulder. He took it off and placed it on the table, then bent low and took his mother in his arms. I watched him holding her, loving her. He propped her back up on the pillow, and she said, "Let's take a picture."

"A picture?" said the nurse from the corner of her room. "Well, why don't we?"

The nurse fixed Grandma on her pillow and brushed her hair. She took the camera as Dad and I stood near the bed. Dad held Grandma's hand.

"Say cheese!" the nurse said.

We shouted, "Cheese!" and the nurse shot the photo. Then Dad suggested, "How about one with the graduate and Mom?"

My heart skipped a beat and I smiled at Grandma. I fixed my gown, then stood next to her. She reached for me and I took her hand.

"Ladies, look at me now," Dad directed.

Grandma and I looked right at Dad. The camera flashed, and Grandma barely cracked a smile.

"I'm sorry, but it's time you both left," said the nurse.

After all the excitement of the day, I did not want to leave. I knew that everyone was waiting for me down in the hospital lounge to go to dinner, but my feet were fixed to the floor.

"Come on, sweetheart," said Dad.

I braced my heart and went over to my grandmother. She was so tired, trying to stay awake just for me. Resting on the bed, I took her hand, leaned over, and gave her a kiss on the cheek and then on her lips.

"I love you," she whispered to me.

"I love you, too, Grandma."

"See you tomorrow, Mom," said Dad as he gave Grandma a kiss and packed his camera.

The next day I woke up knowing that I was officially a high school freshman. I was growing up and excited about vacation and working at the pharmacy. Since I had graduated, Dad took a few vacation days to help Mom and me get ready for my party. It was good having Dad home.

In my room, I was proudly gazing at my diploma and my awards. Mom had just come back from school where she had taken my cap and gown back to my teacher.

As we were getting ready for lunch, the phone rang.

"Hello?" I answered.

"This is Dr. Smith," I heard. "Is Mr. Marquise there?"

"That's my dad. I'll get him."

A knot formed in my stomach as I went to my room and opened the window. Dad was in the yard playing with my brother and Colonel. "Dad, Dr. Smith is on the phone!" I called down to him.

I heard my father's steps through the basement, up the steps, and right into the kitchen.

"Yes, Doctor, I'm here," said Dad.

I watched as Dad's face went from flushed and relaxed to distressed. He gazed at the picture of Jesus on the wall and then looked at my mother. Silently, he hung up the phone.

"Mom just died," he said. "She died in her sleep."

My world fell apart at that second. On June 27, 1971, my grandmother, Angela-Filomena Marquise, passed from this life into the next.

When I think back to the moment Dad took that final picture, I see that I was standing in two worlds with my grandmother. I was with Grandma here on earth and also with her at the beginning of the road to heaven. My grandmother loved me so much that she waited for me to graduate and enjoy my celebrations before giving herself permission to leave. That was her loving gift to me—and I vowed to make her proud.

CHAPTER 8:
WHO WANTS
TO
GROW UP?

"Bye, Mom!" I called.

Adam and I were on our way to the 57th Street park that was in back of Public School 11 in Woodside.

"Be good, be careful, and behave!" Mom yelled from her bedroom. "Angelica, take care of your brother!"

I heard that line every day from the time I was old enough to walk my brother to school without Mom being with us.

"Okay, Mom, see you later!" I yelled back as my brother and I dashed over to the park.

Adam, of course, always ran ahead of me and jumped on his bike. Even though I had been on the track and field team at St. Sebastian's and won the bronze and silver medals consecutive years, my brother was a bullet racing out of the house and up the hill on his bike before I could straddle mine and reach him. He was by far the champion of bike riding.

That summer of 1971 was bittersweet for both of us. I was anticipating the beginning of high school, and Adam was not happy that he was going to be alone at St. Sebastian's. He was going into sixth grade and was hoping that Mom would let him walk to school alone. However, we were both feeling the same pain; the death of our grandmother was hard to take.

After Grandma passed away, I went over to Uncle Thomas's to baby-sit a few more times, but I could not keep going back there. It wasn't the death of my grandmother but a feeling in my bones that once Uncle Thomas had a chance to get me alone, he would molest me again. It had stopped briefly after Carol and Susan moved in, but after Grandma passed away, he started getting too close to me again.

It didn't matter if his wife and children were home; he would get close enough to brush against me as I walked through the kitchen into the dining room, pushing me against the doorframe. Once, while I cleaned off the table, he patted me on the behind while his wife watched. I was not expecting it and jumped out of my skin. I pushed his hand away, feeling like a piece of chattel. Carol laughed so loudly you would think a magician had pulled a rabbit out of a hat, and my uncle and cousins, who were playing in the room, laughed with her. He gave me that smirk that made my skin crawl.

That was it for me. This was the last time.

I finished my chores and grabbed my purse. As I walked out the door, Uncle Thomas grabbed his car keys.

"Nah, I'll go home by myself," I said.

"Your father will be mad," said Carol.

"So? Who cares?"

I walked out the front door, ran up the block, crossed 69th Street and up 53rd Avenue to 65th Place in Maspeth. I looked back and all I could think was, *Go to hell!*

Instead of going straight home, I went to the pharmacy where I worked and asked for more hours. I knew it would give me the ammunition to tell my parents that my job came first and that I could not take care of family matters anymore. At least I hoped it would go that way.

"Can I talk to you?" I asked Dad that night after dinner. He was having a cup of coffee and reading the newspaper.

"What gives, sweetheart?"

I sat down at the table and this time, it was I looking at the picture of the Sacred Heart of Jesus that hung on the wall behind Dad. I swallowed hard.

"Well?" he said.

I bit down on my finger. "I asked Mr. Zarchy for more hours today," I spat out quickly.

Dad's face was a bit perplexed. He shook his head. "How come?"

My leg was shaking under the table even though I was trying hard to control it. "Dad, you know it's the summer and I could use the extra money for new clothes for school and my future." I felt my shoulders hunch and my right cheek pull up in a knot that actually hurt my eye.

"What about baby-sitting for Uncle Thomas and Aunt Carol?" asked my mother, coming into the kitchen from the living room. "You did promise them."

I looked at my mother and my stomach lifted into my chest. Then I realized something. "Did Uncle Thomas or Aunt Carol call you?"

"No, not today," Mom said. "Why?"

"Um, nothing. Just wondered."

"Did you tell them about your job?"

I stood, held onto the chair, and braced myself. "Not yet. I wanted to make sure that Mr. Zarchy needed me first."

"I don't like this," Mom said. "You promised your aunt you would baby-sit for her during the summer while she worked."

"Yeah, I did, Mom, but she is not giving me a dime, and why should I waste my time going there if I can work and get paid?"

"They are family. You don't ask them to pay you," Mom said.

"Mom, you know if I was just baby-sitting Paul and Susan I wouldn't mind, but I am doing all the chores for Aunt Carol, just like I did for Grandma."

"So? She's your aunt," Mom shot back. "You respect her."

I looked at my father, then back at my mother. "I took care of everything because it was for Grandma, and I loved her with all my heart." Tears began to roll down my face. "Aunt Carol is not my grandmother, and Susan is not my real cousin. I won't do it for free." I looked at Dad. "It's not fair."

The phone rang. *Here we go,* I thought.

"Hi, Carol!" said Mom.

"Dad, I don't want to baby-sit—not if I can make extra money," I whispered to my dad while Mom spoke to Carol.

"How did you get home today?" Mom asked me.

I knew it was too good to be true, I thought. "I walked home."

Dad gave me that perplexed look again.

"Come on, Dad, I can walk home. I'm not a baby anymore."

Dad smiled. "No, you are not."

Mom's face went beet red. She covered the mouthpiece. "So are you going to work at the pharmacy or take care of your cousins?" she asked curtly.

"I am working," I said.

"Carol, I'll call you back." Mom hung up the phone.

"Lady Jane," she said, using a nickname whose origins I didn't know but that drove me crazy. "What am I supposed to say to your aunt about this? It will look as though I taught you to disrespect your family."

"What?" I was stewing. "Disrespect?"

"Yes, it will be a reflection on me!"

"On you? This has nothing to do with you, Mom! I am not going back there. I have a *real* job, and from now on I am working there."

"Well, you're the one who's going to have to tell your aunt you're choosing to work instead, Lady Jane." Her voice was snide and condescending.

"Don't worry, I will!" I shouted, the words vibrating in my chest wall.

My mother's hand began to fly in my direction, but Dad was quick and blocked it. "V, enough. Leave it be. Angelica is working."

Mom screamed when Dad's forearm made contact with her hand. "You hit me?"

"No, I stopped *you* from hitting Angelica!" Dad slammed a rolled up paper on the table. "Enough, V!" He looked right at me. "She has a job. That's more important."

"But what am *I* going to say to Carol?" She rubbed her wrist and gave Dad a look as if she could kill something.

Disgust drew across Dad's face. I had seen it before; he was getting tired of Mom's tirades, too. "I'll call my brother—just leave it alone."

"Neither one of you love me!" she yelled. She lifted her hand to pick up the phone.

Dad put his hand out to stop her. "I said I'll call Thomas. You leave it alone."

"You both hate me!" she screamed. "This looks as though—"

"V, I said enough!"

Mom looked at Dad and then at me as though we were steaks she could devour in one bite. She took the phone off the hook and slammed it on the table. It pulled back on the cord and hung there like a noose as Mom stalked away from us into the living room.

"I'll call Thomas tomorrow and tell him," said Dad as he kissed me on the forehead.

Dad was a stickler when it came to the responsibilities of a job and making a decent living. I was so relieved that I wanted to confide in Dad about my mother's beatings and tell him what my uncle had put me through, but I held both truths in my gut. I was afraid of both Mom and my uncle and, for reasons I didn't understand, still loved them both.

Loving my mother was hard, but I tried to remember the woman whom I'd sewed with, the one who gave my brother and me baths after we dirtied her house, laughed with us, and then gave us Ovaltine and cookies. The mother who took care of me when I was sick and the mother who made me a red velvet coat for Christmas, sewing through a fever.

As for my uncle, there was always the hate/love war inside of me. This was the man who, along with my grandmother, had saved my life when I was only a month old and turned blue in my sleep. This was the man who played Santa Claus at Christmas for us cousins, and made us laugh, the man who took my brother and me fishing on his boat. And when I thought of both him and my mother, I kept remembering what Jesus said in the Bible: "Let he who is without sin cast the first stone." I hated that line when someone hurt me, but somehow those words kept me grounded when I felt hot with hate for my uncle and my mother.

"I'm proud of you," Dad said before leaving the room that night.

I was proud, too. I had stood my ground, and Dad had stood with me. And I won: from that day on, I never went back to Grandma's house unless we were all there together. Victory was a new feeling, and one I wanted to get used to.

CHAPTER 9:
BRAND NEW
DREAMS

In September, I started William Cullen Bryant High School. I had been accepted into Christ the King Catholic High School and a few other Catholic high schools, but my parents could not afford the tuition, so I applied to Bryant and got in. After wearing a uniform for eight years, I felt like a fish out of water. Where St. Sebastian's took up one quarter of a city block, including the schoolyard, Bryant covered four whole city blocks and included a track and field court, basketball court, and football field.

Mom and I went to orientation during the last week of August. Arriving at the school, I thought I had arrived on another planet. There was an iron gate around the front entry, with small spruce trees and manicured bushes on one side. On the other side were a six-by-four foot bronze plaque dedicated to poet and journalist William Cullen Bryant, and a sign in black iron letters that read William Cullen Bryant High School. The enormity of the building intimidated me.

Mom and I walked up the main entrance on 30th Avenue in Long Island City. The entry had marble steps, brass handrails, and three brown and black metal doors with a glass window cut in the center of each door. The lobby was so huge I felt as if I were in a movie house. On both sides were glass display cases holding trophies, special projects, and sports uniforms. One was strictly dedicated to the theatre workshop. To the left was a winding green and black marble stairwell that I later learned rose up to the second floor and a mezzanine section of the theatre balcony. There was not one religious article around. It felt very strange.

We were greeted by a student and given a welcome packet, then escorted into the auditorium. I noticed a plaque dedicated to actress and singer Ethel Merman, a graduate of the school, as I walked through the door. My eyes followed a long aisle that led to a stage with red velvet curtains. Hundreds of dark brown wooden folding seats filled the orchestra area of the room. On the side near the orchestra pit was a beautiful Steinway piano and seats for the musicians. I was in awe. St. Sebastian's auditorium had been a small church in the school.

Orientation began, and the freshmen advisor, Mr. Handelman, spoke about what he expected of all of us and the rules of the school. Then Mr. Ryan, the principal, addressed us. "Remember that this isn't just *my* school," he said. "It is also *yours.* I expect you to respect your school as you respect your home and your parents." His words have always stayed with me.

After the speeches, we were given papers to see what clubs we might be interested in joining. The list was long, and my eye fell on the English Club, A Journey in Social Studies, Student Government, Modern Dance, and Arista, the honors society. I smiled and checked all of them.

Parents had been given similar papers, and I looked over Mom's shoulder to see her list. There was door duty, lunch and hall monitoring, and the Parent Teacher Association. I could see my mother's mind in motion as she read what each entailed. Sure enough, she took her pencil and checked off door duty and PTA. I wanted to yell, *No, Mom, just stay home!* But I did not want a scene in my new school before I'd even started there.

Exactly forty-five days into the school year was parent-teacher conference and report card time. Mr. Handelman was my homeroom teacher. He was a tall stately man, with green eyes, a light olive complexion, and dark hair that was balding at the top. He wore turtlenecks, a gold Star of David amulet, and jeans to school every day.

As I sat at my desk, he took attendance and, a few minutes later, began calling us in alphabetical order to give out report cards. I sat there doodling Paul McCartney's name in my notebook until I heard, "Miss Marquise!"

I shot up to the desk and Mr. Handelman smiled at me. "Good job, Angelica!"

I took the paper from his hand and looked at it. "I got B's!" I was mortified.

"Angelica, come see me after class."

The classroom filled with, "Oooohs" from other students.

Once the bell rang, I stood next to my teacher. "Am I in trouble?"

Mr. Handelman's kind green eyes smiled at me. "You, in trouble? Nah, you're one kid I enjoy having around!"

"So what gives?" I asked, shrugging.

"Did you look at your report card?"

"Yeah." I put my head down.

"What's bothering you?"

"I got two B's. I'll never get into Arista with those B's."

Mr. Handelman laughed. "Oh, dear girl, you received *nine* A's, including excellence in conduct and overall participation in class. And you worry about two tiny B's?"

My breath caught in my chest. "Don't you have to have all A's to get into Arista?"

"No. What they are looking for is the overall grade for the year. You need to get at least a ninety-two grade average for the year to attain membership in the club."

I swallowed hard. "So if I continue this, I'll be okay for a May entry in the club?"

"And I will be the first to recommend you."

"Okay. Thank you!" I looked at my watch. It was three thirty p.m. I had to run for the bus and get to work.

That night, while I was at work, my parents attended the parent-teacher conference. I arrived home at my usual nine thirty. I opened the door, and my dad shot up from his chair. He greeted me with a great big hug.

"I am so proud of you!" he said with love.

I looked at Dad. "Did you go with Mom?" I asked. Dad had never gone to a conference with Mom in all my eight years at St. Sebastian's.

"I did, sweetheart." He gave me that look that told me the whole world was okay. "Every one of your teachers had such great things to say about you!"

Mom called from the kitchen, "Bought your favorite ice cream!"

I walked into the kitchen, where Mom had the stainless steel banana split bowls that Dad had made at work sitting on the table. She opened the freezer and took out the box of Breyers chocolate chip ice cream.

"You made me so proud tonight!" Mom kissed me sweetly on the cheek.

"Go get comfortable and we'll celebrate."

A few minutes later, I was in my pajamas, and my whole family sat down at ten o'clock on a school night to enjoy homemade banana splits with lots of whipped cream and chocolate sauce. I wanted to hold onto the sweetness of that night forever.

That joy lasted up until right after the Christmas break. Mom received the call she'd been waiting for: the school needed her for door duty.

I was about to leave classroom number 119—social studies—and go upstairs to class number 213, English. I looked down the long hall with brown wooden doors and posters that art students had made, and there was my mother. She was sitting at a desk wearing her favorite white lace blouse and red pleated skirt, monitoring the goings-on in the hall. I could hear her voice: "Don't run; walk!" I wanted to throw up.

I usually used that hall and stairwell to get to my class, but I ditched that idea and used the stairs at the other end.

Class began, and Mrs. Wolff, my English teacher, was at the front of the classroom. "And so the Montagues and the Capulets were at war with one another—"

A knock on the door interrupted her.

"Mrs. Wolf, excuse me. Mr. Diggs wants to see Eileen in his office."

My heart skipped ten beats when I looked up and saw my mother handing my teacher the yellow excuse slip. She looked over to me. "Hi, Angelica!"

I slid halfway under my desk. "Hi, Mom," I mumbled.

The kids laughed under their breath.

"Thank you, Mrs. Marquise," said Mrs. Wolff, and the door closed as Mom walked Eileen out of the classroom.

That was the beginning of the next three and a half years at my school. From that day on, Mom was at school at least twice to three times a week for door duty, PTA, and anything else the school needed her for. I hated it! I did not want her there, especially on the days after we had a fight or some other family affair. I wanted to be my own person in school.

It was the end of May, and we received our report cards. My average was just over ninety-three. I was ecstatic, and attached to my report card was a letter:

Dear Miss Angelica Marquise,

Your grades and accomplishments have not gone unnoticed. We, the Arista Honors Society, wish to invite you to join this auspicious club. Please report to room 423 to Mr. John O'Connor, Moderator, if you accept this invitation.

Sincerely,

Miss Carolyn Amatto, Student Bryant Senior Arista President

I read the words over and over again. Tears began to roll down my cheeks. *I did it! I made the club!* I wanted to shout, but there was silence in my soul.

I felt Mr. Handelman's hand touch my shoulder. "I told you that you would do this."

I looked up at my teacher. He gave me a wide proud grin, and I smiled back at him.

June arrived, bringing with it the end of my first year. In the auditorium of Bryant, I was inducted with twenty-five fellow students from all grades to the Arista Club. Over four hundred students and their parents sat in the audience, and Mr. O'Connor introduced us and spoke highly of each of us. When he called my name, I rose from my chair and stood by him. Dad was standing at the bottom of the stage with camera in hand.

Carolyn, the Arista president, drew closer to me. She stood five feet four inches tall, with jet-black hair that hung to her shoulders, blue eyes, blue eye shadow, and black liner. That day she wore the black kilt of the club and a baby blue ruffled blouse. She took the gold ribbon with the Arista Bryant owl with wings spread on the emblem and draped the ribbon over my neck. I watched as she took the gold and silver pin with the same symbol from the box. She opened the pin, held the yoke of my dress, and pinned it on.

She smiled and kissed me on both cheeks. "Welcome to Arista!"

"Thank you!" I said proudly and gave her a kiss on each cheek in return. Principal Ryan joined her, shook my hand, and gave my certificate of membership to me.

I went back to my seat and listened as Principal Ryan stood at the podium and spoke about how proud he was of his students. He told our parents, friends, and classmates of our many accomplishments and why he felt that we were the leaders of tomorrow. *I did it,* I thought. *I am now an Arista!* I felt as though I had won an Oscar. It was wonderful. Again, I found my eyes on the certificate, where the date read June 27, 1972. It was one year to the day that my grandmother had passed away. I had chills, remembering how she'd told me that if I worked really hard, I could attain anything. I smiled and felt that she was with me, watching and proud.

CHAPTER 10:
STREET
FIGHT

R ight before my sophomore year of high school began in fall of 1972, I was getting to a point where the income I was making at my job was not enough. I was fifteen years old and paying all my own bills, including medical and dental, and since I was using the telephone, Dad handed the invoice to me one evening and told me that this was now my responsibility. I was miffed, to say the least; Mom used the phone as much as I did, talking with her friends and being president of so many organizations. When she was home, she could be on the phone all day and night, yet I was the fallback. My tiny paycheck only went so far, and now this bill was breaking it.

By midterm, Mom, who was a paid floating teacher's aid in other schools, was not only working her part-time job but also volunteering full-time at my school. She spent more time in school with me than at home. It was getting to me in many ways. I was gaining weight and losing sleep, and it was starting to play a game of hardball on my grades. This was not me, and I was getting angrier by the day.

In March, I was coming out of my science classroom. The principal's office was two doors down, and I could hear Mom speaking to Mrs. O'Hare, the school secretary. Mom's laugh echoed, quivery and boisterous. Trouble!

"Hi, doll!" Mom said as I approached the door to the stairwell.

"Oh, hi," I said.

"Hi, Angelica!" Mrs. O'Hare stood there dressed in her black pantsuit. She was short, with a blond pixie haircut, blue-green eyes, and a constant smile. "Your mother has some great news."

"She does?"

Mom smiled and held up a white sheet of paper: Application for Employment. "I am going to be Evelyn's new assistant secretary!"

My mouth hung wide open. *"What?* You're kidding, right?" I was ready to drop my books on the floor.

"Your mom is here so much and does so much for me that I thought I'd make it permanent and pay her for her hard work," said Mrs. O'Hare.

The loud clang of the class bell rang out in the hall. "Oh, shoot, I'm late!" I said.

I was about to open the door and leave when Mrs. O'Hare said, "Wait!" She walked into her office, took a piece of paper, and gave it to me: Late Pass. "Here, tell Mr. Nash that you were in my office."

I took the pass and walked slowly up the steps. At the landing, I sat on the bottom step. A mesh fence surrounded the landing so that no one could fall down the winding stairwell. I felt as though I were in jail.

"She's calling Mrs. O'Hare by her first name?" I said out loud, my voice resonating off the walls. This could not be happening. My right hand grasped the handrail as though I were choking someone by the neck. Then I pulled up and finished my climb. From that point on, I understood—my job would be my only solace.

It was May, and spring was in the air. It was a slow day at the pharmacy, and I was glad just to be able to take inventory of the products and stock the shelves from the "new order" boxes. The FM station Mr. Zarchy liked was playing tunes from Broadway shows. I heard the door open and looked into the mirror in the perfume display cabinet. *Joy,* I thought. It was Mom with her friend Maureen. The ladies had been at a meeting down the block for one of their organizations.

"Hi, doll!" she said

"Hi, Mom," I muttered.

Mom came to my counter and stood there with Maureen. She picked up a sample perfume bottle and spritzed her wrist.

"Mom, I need to get to work. The store closes in an hour."

"Guess what?" Mom said, ignoring me.

"What?"

"I've just been nominated for County Trustee in the Ladies Auxiliary."

Sure enough, she was wearing the white dress uniform of the Catholic War Veterans Ladies Auxiliary and the blue-gray cape and cap of her station. Adorned on the left breast of the cape were all the medals of her accomplishments, including her president's pin. *More?* I thought. Great—now my brother and I could expect to hear her scream that she needed more help in the house.

"That's nice," I said.

I was annoyed that she'd just come in to tell me this news. She could have passed the store and walked home, then told me there. But stopping in was a bad habit of hers, and Mr. Zarchy had already warned me that in addition to not getting my discount, my mother could not come in and take up my time.

I turned my back on her and went about my work. In the mirror, I could see Mom rummaging through all the items I had just inventoried and put in order.

"Maureen, why don't you and Mom go for coffee across the street?" I suggested.

Maureen winked at me, fully understanding. "Come on, Virginia," she said. "My treat."

Mom put the lipstick sample down, kissed me on the cheek, and left with her friend.

An hour or so later, everything was put in order and my register drawer tallied out. I went up to the office, punched the safe's eight-digit code, and placed the drawer inside. Then I went to my locker to pick up my jacket and purse.

"Good night, Mr. Zarchy," I said, making my way down the office steps.

"Good night, Angelica. See you tomorrow." Mr. Zarchy gave me a fatherly smile that let me know he was pleased with my day's work.

Before I opened the door that went out toward Roosevelt Avenue and 61st Street, I checked to see if Mom and Maureen were still at the Stop One Diner across the street. The diner was a Woodside artifact. It had been there since the railroad was built and had only been modernized a few years earlier, when some of the brick walls were cut through and wide-open windows set to replace them. All one had to do was peer through the glass to see who was in the diner.

Mom was not there.

Relieved that I did not have to worry about walking home with her, I strolled to the corner to cross the street. I was waiting for traffic to pause when I heard, "Bitch!"

I was struck and fell flat on my face. My chin hit the pavement, and I was shocked by the sudden pain.

"Bitch!" I heard again, and then I felt a hard kick to my right thigh.

I managed to turn around. There, looming over me, was Debby, a friend from school.

"I hate you!" she screamed at me.

"Debby!" I dragged myself up from the street. "What did I do?"

"You know!" Before I knew it, I felt my left eye stinging like a match had been set to it. Debby had smacked me hard across the face.

"What the hell did I do?" I screamed.

"You know, bitch!"

I wanted to hit her back, but I was shaking and noticed that blood had begun to drip onto my blouse. I placed my hand on my chin; my fingers came away wet with blood.

"No, I don't!" I screamed back.

"Your mother ratted on me!"

I felt dizzy, and from the corner of my good eye, I could see people watching the fight. "What do you mean?"

"You know!"

"Hey, you—girl! Stop that!" yelled a man from the top landing of the train station. The fight was drawing more people as Debby kept screaming at me.

Every bone in my body wanted to retaliate, but my hands were shaking with the rest of me. Tears began to wet my face, stinging my pavement-scratched cheek. I wiped my face and again saw blood on my hand.

"Debby, you cut me!" I said. "What the hell did my mother do to you?"

"She called my mother and told her I cut class!"

I was so dumbfounded I could barely move.

"I hate you, and I hate your mother!"

Debby and I had known each other since kindergarten. We were friends. She was at every party I had, and I went to all of hers. We went to the movies together, shopped together, and sometimes even wore the same blouse to school, just to be Bobbsey twins. Now here she was, beating the crap out of me.

"What is wrong with you two?" yelled Grace, a waitress from the diner, as she ran up to us. She pulled off her apron and started to wipe the blood from my face. "Tom, get Mr. Zarchy!" she ordered. Tom was the short order cook who had worked at the diner for years. He must have followed Grace out.

"I've known you girls since you were babies. What the hell is going on?" Grace was middle-aged and Irish all the way. She had shoulder-length blond hair and was wearing the black and white uniform of the diner.

"I walked out of the store and Debby hit me." I was shaking and wanted to sit down.

"Well, Debby?" demanded Grace.

"Her bitch mother ratted on me—again! I hate her!" Debby stepped closer to me and spit in my face. Her warm sputum washed over my cheek.

"Debby! What the hell is wrong with you?" Grace said, appalled.

"I don't know what she is talking about." I wiped my cheek.

Grace started to pick up my things. "You have some talking to do, young lady," she told Debby. "Look at Angelica!"

"I'm going to call the cops," said Tom as he and Mr. Zarchy came from the store.

"Dear God!" said Mr. Zarchy as his eyes fell on my face. "Angelica, get in the store—now!"

"Mr. Connor, don't call the cops!" Debby begged before she bolted down the block toward 37th Avenue, but Tom was swift and caught her. He brought her back, pulling her by the forearm.

"You have some explaining to do, young lady!" he said.

Debby began to cry. "I'm sorry, please, please don't call the cops!"

"Well, explain yourself!" said Tom.

"Mrs. Marquise is always getting me in trouble. She keeps calling my house and telling my mother everything I do wrong at school." Debby was sobbing right there in the street. "Please don't call the cops! Please!" she wept, falling to her knees.

I shook like a leaf. I didn't know if I should be angry at her for doing this to me or side with her. My mom and I had fought not two weeks earlier after she called another friend's parents and told them what their son, Frank, was doing in school. Frank told me in class that my mother had gotten him into a lot of trouble. When I confronted her, she and I argued about whether it was her job to tell parents if their kids were doing wrong in school.

"Let's get those wounds looked at," said Mr. Zarchy.

I went back in the store, and Tom and Grace followed, escorting Debby inside. Mr. Zarchy called my parents, and Grace—who was good friends with Debby's mother—phoned Debby's parents.

It was a good thing that I worked for a pharmacist. Mr. Zarchy sat me in the back of the store where he filled prescriptions. He took some medicines off the shelf and began to clean my wounds with peroxide and sterile gauze. I pulled away, the peroxide burning the hell out of my open cuts, and my stomach cramped as I bent backwards. I doubled over in pain.

"What's wrong?" asked Mr. Zarchy.

"Nothing," I said, but I began to feel nauseated.

"You look pale," he said.

"I'm fine ..." I held onto my stomach again, lifting the bottom of my blouse to find the source of the stinging. My flesh was scraped from my belly button up to my rib cage, and it was already turning black and blue. Mr. Zarchy pulled my hand away and looked at me with alarm.

"Angelica, when your parents get here, I am telling them to take you to the emergency room."

"No," I said. "I just want to go home."

A few seconds later, I heard my mom and dad rush into the store. Mom ran up the steps.

"My God in heaven!" she screamed when she saw me.

"I'm okay, Mom."

Dad followed behind her. "My God, what the hell is going on?"

Mom had a look of fear on her face. She knelt next to me and wanted to hug me, but I pulled away. I was hurting so badly I didn't want to be touched.

Then there was chaos when Debby's parents walked in.

Mom went in for the kill before Debby's parents could say a word. "Your daughter is a troublemaker in school, and now here—look what she did to my daughter!"

I heard Debby, who was sitting in Mr. Zarchy's office, break out in a terrific cry. I began to cry, too. Here I sat in my place of employment and now my parents and my friend's parents were arguing like animals in the jungle.

The truth was that Debby and I were victims of similar circumstances. Today she would be labeled ADD or ADHD; she always struggled in school, and her parents tried their best to deal with her learning problems. As for me, it was my mother whose issues were crossing dangerous boundaries.

"You need to control your daughter!" yelled my mother.

"Maybe you need to mind your own business!" Debby's mother shot back.

"I will not have this behavior in my establishment. I will call the police if you all don't quiet down and show each other some respect!" Mr. Zarchy's words resonated in the store.

"Please don't call the cops!" sobbed Debby. "I am so sorry!"

I slowly made it down the stairs, my head feeling about to explode.

"Mr. Zarchy, please don't call the cops," I said. "I'll go to the hospital."

"Debby, did you do this?" asked her mother, aghast.

Debby folded her arms around her torso. She was shaking, and so was I, though her tremors were with anger and mine with shock.

"Mr. Marquise, I will pay for the doctor's fees," said Debby's father. "Let us handle our daughter our way."

"Thank you," said Dad.

Since my parents did not have their own car, Mr. Zarchy drove all of us to the hospital. My mother complained about Debby's misbehavior in school the whole way. My head and stomach were killing me, and I sat quietly in Dad's embrace.

We arrived at Elmhurst General Hospital in Jackson Heights, and Mr. Zarchy helped us in the emergency door. He looked at me again with that fatherly expression, then said to my mother, "Mrs. Marquise, please call me later and let me know if they keep Angelica." He wrote his number on a piece of paper and left.

We were there all night and most of the next day. Thankfully, I was fine, just badly bruised, but the doctors wanted me to stick around for a while to make sure that it was safe for me to go home.

When I woke at home on the third day, I could hardly sit up in bed. The wounds on my stomach ached. I used my desk to pull myself to a standing position, taking a small step toward the door. When I looked in the mirror on my bureau, it appeared as though I had been in a war zone. My lip was swollen in the corner and scraped to my chin, and my cheek had three long scratches that started at the corner of my eye and ran down to my lip. My stomach felt as if it were encased in a tight girdle.

The hospital emergency room doctor did not want me in school for a few days, so I slowly made my way to the living room and onto the couch. Before

I knew it, I was asleep.

"Adam, start your homework!" Mom's words startled me from my nap. My dog Colonel was right by my side, keeping watch on me as he always did when I was sick or lonely.

"Oh, man," Adam said as he walked into the living room. "You look like hell. Is that lip ever gonna go down?"

I struggled into a sitting position and gave him a wry smile.

He sat next to me. "You scared the heck out of me."

"Sorry," I replied.

"Are you okay?" Adam's voice croaked, the way it was doing often lately, and we both laughed.

"I'm okay." Then I started to cry. "This is all Mom's fault." I could barely turn my head, but I turned my neck and saw my brother's baby browns staring at the cuts on my face.

"I know, Ang," he said.

"It's not her job to call the parents. It's the advisor's job. I don't know why she does it."

Adam shrugged. "She does it to me, too. Then when *I* get into a fight," he pointed to himself, "she punishes me."

At that point, I began to realize that my brother and I were suffering the same fate, except with him it was more with his friends on the block. Mom was always calling their parents and telling them if the kids were playing on our sidewalk, or somehow she knew which boy broke a car window or one of the windows on the apartment houses on the block. She seemed to think it was Police Mom's duty to call the boy's parents. Then my brother, oblivious, would go play with his friend, and the fights would erupt. Adam often arrived home with a gash on his knee or eyebrow, or a black eye.

Meanwhile, I was losing lifelong friends and hating Mom for it. Debby was not the first of my friends to fall under her scrutiny, and I sensed that I would spend my high school years losing one friend after another. I wished that I could sign myself out of Bryant and into another school. The only other alternative—the only way to escape my mother—was to quit school and work full time, but I didn't want that. I wanted my own identity, yes, but I also wanted an education. That was one thing I was not willing to sacrifice.

Chapter 11:
The
UGLY
Duckling
of Bryant
High School

That summer all I did was work, and thank God, Mr. Zarchy did not fire me. It was a hard summer, though. I was blossoming as a young woman, but all I felt like was the ugly ducking from the Hans Christian Andersen story. My body had grown ... all over the place. I was fat and hated every piece of clothing I wore. I couldn't even fit into Wrangler jeans; they were cut too small in the hips, and mine felt as if I could crush a baby under them. Finding a boyfriend seemed impossible. Who wanted an elephant for a girlfriend? I wouldn't.

If being self-conscious wasn't enough reason to hide in school, by September all the kids who lived in Woodside knew about how Debby had beaten the crap out of me. I said hi to friends passing in the hall but, one by one, they shunned me. I would have done the same if it had been the other way around. After all, who wanted to risk befriending a snitch's daughter?

One friend who didn't drop me was a girl named Angela. She was my height, about five feet, and had brown eyes and dark curly hair that hung to her shoulders. She wore the greatest fashionable clothes of the day: Wrangler jeans, peasant blouses, platform shoes, and a bandana tied around her thigh. I wanted to be her, but how? I wore ugly navy blue stretch pants with an oversized brown pullover, black low-heeled pumps, and Indian "love beads" that hung low on my neck. I was eating anything I could get my hands on just to calm my nerves.

In the cafeteria, where it was always chaos during lunch, we joined the food line and Angela picked up her tuna sandwich and diet Tab. I took turkey on a roll and a piece of chocolate cake.

We sat in our usual seats on the left side, near the door that led to the second floor, where our next class was.

Angela was sipping her soda. "You know the place I work?"

"The supermarket?"

"Shop Wise in Jackson Heights."

"Yeah. What about it?" I asked.

"We need checkers for the express line, and Mr. Shapiro asked me if any of my friends were interested."

I kept chewing on my sandwich and swallowed hard. I looked up by the black and white tile wall at my mother, doing her usual strut of the school, looking for kids who were cutting. I kept eating and watched her stroll the black tiled floor of the cafeteria, right toward Angela and me.

"Hi, Mrs. Marquise," said Angela.

"Oh, hi, Mom," I said.

Mom handed me an envelope. "On your way home, please drop this off at Woodside Bakery."

I opened the envelope. It was a list of pastries that Mom had ordered for her Ladies Auxiliary party and a check for fifty dollars. "Mom, I have work after school, remember?"

"I know, but I need this in today, and I have a staff meeting after school."

"But I need to get to work on time. It's order day, and I have inventory and shelving to do."

"I already called Claire and told her you would have the list and money to her today."

I wanted to throw the milk container at her. "Mom, I cannot be late. Not today."

"Just get that to Claire!" she shouted. I felt the eyes of my fellow students staring at me.

"Okay," I hissed and placed the envelope in my purse. My stomach was so tight after that, but I shoved my chocolate cake down my throat.

The bell rang, and Angela and I put our trays on the cart. I passed Mom in the hall, where she was yelling at a student for smoking in the girls' bathroom. The girl looked at me as if she would punch me out. I kept walking to class.

"Sorry I'm late, Mr. Zarchy!" I said while hurriedly placing my jacket, books, and purse in my locker.

I went to the vault to take my money drawer from the shelf. I was about to close the vault door when Mr. Zarchy approached. He stood before me in his white pharmaceutical jacket, blue shirt, and dark blue tie, and he was not happy at all.

"You are almost a half hour late, Miss." His voice was annoyed.

"Mr. Zarchy, I had to do something for my mother. I'm sorry."

It was written on his face, that expression you get when you know all your excuses are done. I held onto my money drawer for dear life, hoping he was not about to fire me. He placed the brown manila order envelope on top of my drawer. Relieved, I smiled and went to my counter to start my day.

It was four p.m., and I placed the drawer in the register, counted the money, and closed the drawer. I had five hours to get my work done and decide whether I wanted to take Angela up on her offer to work with her.

It was five thirty, and I was taking care of a client at my cosmetic counter. The phone rang in the office, and I heard Mr. Zarchy mention my name. A few minutes later, I heard the phone again. My client paid for her goods and left the store.

"Angelica, phone call," Mr. Zarchy said.

I locked my drawer and went in the office to pick up the phone.

"Finally!" It was my mother with that condescending inflection of hers. "Why didn't you answer the phone before?"

"Mom, I was busy with a customer."

"Did you give Claire the list? It's important to me."

If I could, I would have thrown the phone across the store floor, but I contained myself. "I did and I was late for work. Mr. Zarchy was mad at me."

"Thanks. During your break, please pick up a loaf of Italian bread."

"Fine."

I hung up and went back to my station. *She didn't even care that I was late for work,* I thought, and started to cry at my counter. I decided to call Angela and see if the job was still available.

That Friday, I met Angela on the 30th Avenue side of school and accompanied her to work. If I took the job, this was going to take getting used to. I no longer would just take the Triboro bus home to 61st Street and Roosevelt Avenue. I was looking at a forty-minute commute each way. I was not happy with this, but at least the distance would keep my mother away from me—I hoped!

As I walked up 37th Avenue, Angela pointed out the many clothes boutiques she liked. "Here is Gurdies. That's where I get all my jeans and tops," she said.

There were banks and restaurants, coffee shops and bakeries. It was more upscale than Woodside. Where we had the usual mom-and-pop stores, these were higher-end and corporate.

"Here we are!" Angela pointed to the supermarket.

I looked up at Shop Wise and felt like hurling. I really liked working for Mr. Zarchy, but I had to move on; I just could not have my mother in the store anymore. Angela and I walked in, and again my stomach wrenched. The store was enormous—aisles and aisles of food and produce, and on the side were a bakery and deli. Not one supermarket in Woodside had a bakery or deli counter. Could I get used to working in such a huge place?

Angela went to the office and brought down an application. I filled it out, protesting silently all the way. I was so angry that my mom was pushing me out of a job I enjoyed, but I needed to break away from her. She was at home, school, and—all too often—my job. I had to find someplace that was mine and mine alone.

Angela took the written application to the office, and Mr. Gibner, the owner of the store, called me in. I felt my legs give way. I was so far out of my element. Mr. Gibner, a tall lean bald man in a white shirt and black pants, rose from his seat.

"Angela tells me you go to school with her," he said.

"I do, sir."

"Do you enjoy school?"

"Yes, sir. I want to go to college, too."

He read my application while I stood there. "So you have experience at the register, I see."

"Yes, I've been working for Mr. Zarchy for two years now."

"Why are you leaving him?"

I had to think quickly. "To be honest, sir, I like working for Mr. Zarchy, but since I am paying all my own bills, I need a job that pays more. I am making two-fifty an hour, and Angela said the starting pay here is three-fifty."

"Can you work Monday to Friday, five to nine o'clock at night, and Saturday from seven in the morning to seven at night?"

Mr. Gibner stood tall over me, and I felt intimidated by him. "I can work those hours, yes," I stammered.

"Can you start next week?"

"No, Mr. Gibner, not next week. I need to tell Mr. Zarchy first. It wouldn't be fair if I didn't."

Mr. Gibner extended his right hand. "That is the answer I was hoping for—honesty. Welcome to Shop Wise."

The next day, Saturday, it was work as usual. My alarm went off at six a.m., and I was at my counter at the pharmacy by eight thirty. As always, my register was ready to go and the day began. My first customer was a lady named Mary. She was a regular, and I knew what color lipstick, eye shadow and what perfumes she liked. I filled her order and out she went. As I wiped down the glass, my heart began to pound. I had to tell Mr. Zarchy that I was quitting. How could I? The man had always been patient and kind with me.

The day went so fast; funny how that happens when you don't want it to. I tallied out my register, locked up the display cabinet, and made sure that all was in order for Monday morning.

As I turned the last number on the vault, in one breath of courage I said, "Mr. Zarchy, may I talk with you?"

"What's up, young lady?" he said with a smile.

"I-I-I have to tell you something."

"Is everything okay, Angelica?"

"Not really, Mr. Zarchy. I have to quit." I felt myself choke on the words.

"I am not surprised. Please sit down." He gestured to the chair.

"I don't understand," I said.

Mr. Zarchy opened the refrigerator and poured some apple juice for both of us. As he handed me a cup he said, "I know you have been unhappy for a while. I wasn't sure if it was the job or other issues."

"I have never been unhappy here," I said, "but I can't stay. I found a new job out of Woodside where my mother won't be able to walk in any time she wants."

Mr. Zarchy raised his eyebrows, then took off his glasses and rubbed his eyelids. "Angelica, if you weren't such a good kid, I would have thrown you and your mom out a long time ago, but I was not going to punish you because of your mother."

Tears began to well up and drip down my cheeks, wetting my lips. "I'm sorry, Mr. Zarchy. I never meant any disrespect to you."

He handed me a tissue. "When is your last day?"

"Next Saturday." The tears kept coming down, and my heart was pounding.

"I'll ask my wife to fill in for you until I find someone else, but I don't know how I'll be able to find an honest kid like you."

I gave him a half smile, wiped the tears from my face, and stood up. Mr. Zarchy gave me a warm hug. "You do what is best for you, you hear me?" He lifted my chin.

"I will."

"Now go home before you're late and your mother calls."

A week later, as I finished up my last day, Mr. Zarchy beckoned me into his office. As I sat across from him, he opened his desk drawer and pulled out two business envelopes.

"Here," he said.

I took both envelopes. One was my pay, and he instructed me to open the other. To my surprise, there was a check made out to me for two hundred dollars and a note that read, *College fund money.*

"Thank you," I said, choking on the words.

"You earned every penny, young lady." With his fatherly expression he added, "Angelica, if you don't like it over there, you can have this job back any day."

I needed to hear that. "Thank you, Mr. Zarchy."

I shook his hand, retrieved my belongings, and walked out.

With the job change, it inevitably got harder to get up for school, run to work, and have time to do homework and keep up my grades. As if that wasn't enough, my mother took the bus with me to school some days. The neighborhood kids would see us get on the bus and hide behind their book bags, baseball caps, or anything they could hold up just so we would not sit near them. The alienation I felt was exacerbating some new health symptoms: every day in school, I was coming down with stomach cramps.

There were days when the cramps would start as early as mid-morning and last all day. I was tired, hungry all the time, fat, and in pain.

It was the end of my sophomore year, and we received our report cards. For the first time in my life, I failed a class by getting a sixty in gym. It was no surprise to me. I couldn't keep up with my classmates. I couldn't even keep up with myself.

My only solace was my literature class. Every day, I couldn't wait to enter Mrs. Wolff's room.

"'Once upon a midnight dreary / as I pondered, weak and weary ...' Who wrote these lines?" Mrs. Wolff asked.

I raised my hand, but Mrs. Wolff pointed to another girl.

"Edgar Allen Poe," Vanessa said.

My head was down, reading the words of the poem. I heard my teacher asking questions, but I could not lift my eye from the page. I was immersed in Poe's words and could not tear away.

"Angelica, what do you think Mr. Poe meant to say?" I vaguely heard Mrs. Wolff ask. "Miss Marquise, are you with us today?"

The sound of my classmates laughing snapped my daze. "What was the question, Mrs. Wolff?"

She came and stood over me. "What do you think Poe wanted to say in this poem?"

I began to read the poem again. Then I looked up at my teacher. "I think Poe was longing for a lost love, but somewhere there was guilt within the relationship."

"Go on," she said.

I read the words again. "The raven became a symbol of the darkness in his soul. It was a place that no one could enter."

"Go on."

"A secret that felt so evil only a bird as black as a raven could penetrate it without becoming ravaged."

Every eye in the room was on me, and I felt like sliding down under my desk.

Mrs. Wolff stared down at me. "Your answer is profound, Angelica."

My heart stirred in a way I had never felt before.

Riding the bus and train to work was the only time I had to read. I did my homework assignments, and I began a quest for books from the authors I was learning about in school. Edgar Allen Poe, Shakespeare, L. Frank Baum, Hans Christian Andersen, and Margaret Mitchell were my new best friends. I wandered into their tales and allowed myself to become part of the story-lines. What would it be like to be Juliet to my own Romeo? Would someone live and die for me like that? How would it feel to have a lithe waist like Scarlett O'Hara and wear the gowns and corsets she wore in *Gone With The Wind?* I imagined myself so beautiful that no man could resist my whims. But it was only the dream of a schoolgirl.

In reality, I was no Scarlett O'Hara. There were boys everywhere I turned at school, but not one ever saw me. My friend Angela had met a boy at a dance in her neighborhood, and they were now dating. Some of my friends from Woodside had boyfriends, but not me. I nicknamed myself the Ugly Duckling of Bryant High School.

On the bus going to work one day, I had these words running in my head:

What's wrong with me?
Am I so hideous no one will look at me
I am horrendous
Why am I slighted, pushed aside
Cast away like a rag
I am horrendous
Who will look at me
Will someone see me for who I am
I am horrendous

That was my first poem—the day I became a writer. I was sixteen years old.

As time passed, I wrote more and more poems and feared my mother reading them. I could not stand anyone reading my poetry. This was the only way I could say what I wanted without my mother slapping me in the face for expressing my opinions. The older I got, the more she beat me, and the more I retaliated, the worse the abuse. My body was wearing down. I felt old already, and—someplace in my horrendous world—I needed a place for solace.

My poems were on loose-leaf paper, and one day in the school supply section of the supermarket, I noticed a red spiral notebook. I purchased it. I took the time during my breaks to copy my words on the pages of this notebook. Some poems were dark and others about my dreams of boys and young love.

Behind every word I wrote was fear; to my mother, all boys were evil, and I was evil to have the feelings of a young girl who was growing into a woman. I decided that if some of the famous poets had pen names, I could find one for myself. I renamed myself Octavia Greer.

The poems I wrote as Octavia Greer were too personal to share with anyone, so I hid the red notebook behind our basement steps. I did not want anyone to read my words, the good or the bad ones. They were words of anger and rage, and some were spiritual, asking God why no one loved me and whether He loved me. Writing was the only outlet I had, my secret argument with the universe around me. The words became a secret panacea, a way for me to yell at the world and my mother for hurting me without getting beaten by anyone in return.

CHAPTER 12:
THE PRICE
OF BEING
GOOD

Gym—every unfit girl's nemesis, especially the locker room, where everyone could see the flaws and sins of everyone else's bodies. My stomach was killing me one day, the elastic waist of my gym shorts digging into the lower left quadrant of my abdomen, near my groin. We were playing basketball, and the more I jumped, the more it hurt. As I ran guard past a girl on the court, the pain got so bad it ran down my thigh. It cut so hard I doubled over and dropped to my knees.

"Angelica! What's the matter?" Mrs. Yanodious, the gym teacher, ran over to me, and the rest of the class followed.

I was on fire. My stomach was so hot I could not get up.

"Kathy, go get Mrs. Marquise," said Mrs. Yanodious.

That was all I needed: my mother coming to my rescue. "No, I don't want my mother."

I had been suffering secretly with these pains for months and had so far managed to fight through them. I pushed my teacher aside and fought my way onto all fours, bracing myself on the gym floor with both hands. I breathed deeply through the pain and lifted myself to one knee. With another hard breath, I pushed up to a near standing position and allowed my teacher to help me to a chair.

I held my side and pushed in against the pain. It was the only way I could control it. I was sweating as the pain seared down my leg and into my back.

"Are you pregnant?" asked my teacher.

"Pregnant? My mother would kill me! No, I am not pregnant!" I laughed through the pain, but soon tears were wetting my face. "Why would you ask me that, Mrs. Yanodious?" I was hot with embarrassment.

"Some of the kids said that lately you look like you are pregnant."

"Does my mother know this?"

"I don't think so. Do you have your period, then?" asked Mrs. Yanodious.

"No. I can't remember when I last had a period. It just disappeared."

"Angelica?" My mother's voice cut through the chaos in the gym. "Where's my daughter?"

And there she was before me, concerned and pale as her eyes looked into mine. "What's wrong?" she asked.

I was afraid to tell her that I had stopped getting my period almost a year earlier. There were some teenage girls who had gotten pregnant, given birth, and come back to school. At home, Mom had only one word for them: *"Putana."* Whore. She would look me straight in the face and add, "If you ever come home like that, I'll break your legs and kill you."

I knew that even though I was a "good girl," my mother's questions would come if I told her about my period. And no matter how much I told the truth, her mind would hear otherwise and a beating would ensue. So I had kept my pain and female issues to myself—but now I was sick.

The school nurse came into the gym and quickly took my blood pressure, my pulse, and my temperature. Mrs. Green had been the school nurse for years. She was a tall lady who wore blue pants, white lace ruffled blouses, and a white blazer. She had short gray hair, blue eyes, and a kind smile.

"Did you eat today?" she asked.

"I ate lunch." I gripped my side as hard as I could.

"You go to the bathroom?"

"Yeah, so what about it?" My skin crawled with embarrassment as my whole class stood in the background and watched. I started rocking back and forth to calm the pain.

"What do you think it is, Yolanda?" asked my mother.

"Virginia, give me a minute with your daughter," Mrs. Green said. "Do you have your period?" she asked me.

I looked at her and then my mother. I wanted to hide, but I couldn't, and I did not know how to answer her.

"See? I told you she was preggers," came the voice of a fellow student.

"Pregnant? I'll kill her!" yelled my mother.

"No, Mrs. Green, I am not pregnant. Please believe me, Mom!"

"Do you have your period?" asked Mrs. Green again.

"Can we go to your office?"

I strained to rise from the chair. My legs felt like lead pipes, yet I managed to walk out of the gym and down the short hall to Mrs. Green's office, with Mom striding after us. Mrs. Green opened the door and I followed her to the desk, where I quickly took the seat beside it. My back was trembling from the pain.

"Look at me now, young lady, and tell me you are not pregnant!" Mom screamed in my face.

"I'm not pregnant, Mom—but I don't have my period, either!"

"Get up on the table," Mrs. Green said.

I struggled to take the few short steps to her examining table. Mrs. Green helped me up.

"Lay down," she said gently.

As I lay down, I felt my whole body give way. I was so tired. All I'd wanted to do for the last few days was stay in bed.

"Show me where it hurts," Mrs. Green said.

I had my hand on my left side. She put her fingers there, and I moved my hand away. When she pressed down, I screamed.

"This is too tender. You need to go to the hospital," she said.

"No, please. I want to go home."

"When was the last time you had a period?" Mrs. Green asked.

I closed my eyes, opened them, and looked right into the florescent lights above me. "I don't know …" I shrugged. "About a year ago, maybe."

"What do you mean a year ago?" my mother demanded. "Why didn't you tell me?"

I focused on Mrs. Green while answering. "Because you would have thought I was pregnant."

"Yes, I would have."

"Mrs. Marquise, I am surprised. Your daughter is a good girl; why would you think such a thing?"

"Well, look at two of her friends," Mom sniped. "They are both pregnant."

"Mom, what does that have to do with me?"

"Show me who your friends are, and I'll tell you what you are," she chanted. It was a saying she used often, implying that my friends' actions directly reflected my character.

"Yeah, I know. A *putana*, right?" I said sarcastically.

"Don't talk to me that way, you hear me?"

"Virginia, look at her," Mrs. Green said. "She is a beautiful girl who is a very good kid at school."

But between the lies my uncle told to keep himself clean, and my mother's own undiagnosed mental illness, she was unable to trust me or the friends I had. Every word I said was suspect to her.

"If you won't go to the hospital," Mrs. Green said, "you should at least see a gynecologist. It isn't right that you haven't had your period for so long."

Mom's face was hard when she nodded. "I'll take her."

A few days later, I sat in the office of Mom's gynecologist among a sea of women in the waiting room, some reading magazines and others with what looked like watermelons under their blouses. *What am I doing here?* I wondered. Mom filled out the papers while I sat beside her, afraid.

The nurse, a short Italian lady named Alice, called me in, and Mom followed me into the examining room. The nurse launched into a series of questions, such as when I had my last period, how old I was, and whether I was sexually active.

"No, I'm a virgin," I said, but damn, what a question to ask in front of my mom.

"Take everything off from your bottom down," Alice said. "Put on the gown and get on the table."

I looked at the strange table. "What are those?" I asked.

"Don't worry about that. Just do what Alice said," Mom said brusquely.

"Virginia, this is her first time," Alice said. "Those are stirrups for you to put your feet in so that the doctor can examine your vagina."

I felt my stomach jump into my chest. "I can't do this!"

"If I can do it, so can you, Lady Jane. Let's go!" Mom said.

Alice shot my mother a disapproving look. "I promise Dr. Brucata will be gentle with you," she said. "He just needs to find out where the pain is coming from."

I was holding back tears and clutching the gown in front of me like a shield. "Let me help you," Alice said.

After a few moments, I allowed Alice to help me disrobe. She placed the gown on me and tied it in the front. I felt so naked. She then helped me on the table, covered me with a sheet, and called in the doctor.

"Hello, Virginia, how are you?" Dr. Brucata was a short, broad man in a brown suit and blue tie. He wore a long white coat over his clothes, and his short brown hair was graying at the temples. "So what is going on with this young lady?"

"I don't know," Mom said. "Angelica has not had a period in a year."

He placed his hand on my forearm, and I jumped. "Don't be afraid," he said. "I won't hurt you."

"Is everyone going to watch?" I asked.

"If you were eighteen, your mother would not have to be in the room, but you're still a minor," said Alice.

I was shaking. "Okay."

Alice helped position me. I turned away, mortified.

After the examination, Alice helped me sit up and placed a large white sheet over me. I was so glad to cover up.

"Young lady, I believe you have a small cyst on your ovary," said Dr. Brucata.

"What is that?"

"It's like a small sack of water. And it is causing pressure and pain."

"So what can we do about it?" asked Mom.

"First, Angelica is a pretty girl, but she is overweight and that is part of the problem," said the doctor. "Her weight is, I believe, part of the reason her period is being held back. Once she loses weight and resumes her menses, I hope the cyst will dissipate."

"And if not? What then?" asked Mom.

"Then we may have to operate."

Dr. Brucata placed his hand on my shoulder and smiled. "We're going to make you well again. Now get dressed and we'll talk in my office."

"Virginia, let's give this young lady her privacy," Alice said, walking my mom out of the room.

I sat there a minute and looked around. On the wall was a picture of a baby in its mother's womb. I stared for a few moments before dressing and meeting Dr. Brucata in his office.

The office was paneled in dark wood, and the walls displayed certificates with Dr. Brucata's medical degrees and fellowships. I could see that he was a respected man.

"Ang, this is the man who saved my life a few years ago," said Mom.

"Gee, Mom, now you tell me," I said. "I didn't know that."

"Your mother was on her deathbed when she came to me," Dr. Brucata said. "I'm just glad I had time to change that." He smiled at my mother.

"So am I, Doctor," I said, and Mom smiled at me.

Dr. Brucata opened his drawer and took out some sheets of paper. He handed them to me, and I read, *1600-calorie high-protein diet.*

"I want you to begin this diet today." Then he pulled out a prescription pad, scrawled quickly, and tore off three pages.

"What is Dexamine?" I asked as he handed me the prescriptions one at a time.

"That is a diet pill. It will help you lose weight by curbing your appetite."

"That sounds okay, I guess."

"I am also starting you on Provera. Take one a day starting today. It may take about ten days, but it will kick-start your hormones and bring on your period. The last," he said, passing me a final prescription, "is Norlestrin 21. These are birth control pills—"

"Birth control!" my mother interrupted.

"Yes, exactly. It will regulate her cycle."

"*No!* I won't allow it!" Mom's voice was raising.

"What do you mean, Mom? They'll help," I said defensively.

"Oh, no, Angelica." Mom pointed her finger of justice at me. "Taking those pills is murder. I *won't* have my child commit murder."

"I don't understand, Virginia," said Dr. Brucata.

Mom flailed her hand in front of her face. "I am a Catholic, and so is she. In my faith, taking those pills is murder; she is preventing a baby from being conceived!"

I stood, and my purse and the prescriptions dropped to the floor. "Mom, I am not having sex, so a baby can't be conceived anyway. I want the medicine to help me."

Dr. Brucata reached out to touch Mom's arm, but Mom pulled away. "Virginia," he said, "it was this same scenario four years ago that almost killed you. Please don't do this to your own daughter."

"I'm taking the prescription to Mr. Zarchy. He'll fill it for me."

"He can't, Angelica," Dr. Brucata said quietly. "You are underage." He had a look of pity on his face.

"You've got to be kidding me," I said. "I'll ask Dad, then. He'll listen to me."

Mom was stewing, and I could tell by the way she was clenching her fist that she wanted to hit me but was holding back. Her voice was loud and clear when she said, "This is one thing that your father and I agree on."

"Not all the time! Dad gets mad sometimes when your holier-than-thou friends take over the house."

Dr. Brucata lifted an eyebrow. "Maybe we should speak to your dad about this."

"No, Doctor, you will mind your own business with my family." Mom pointed her finger at the man who had saved her life.

Dr. Brucata stood tall on his own turf. "I cannot, Virginia, not when it comes to the health and wellbeing of your daughter."

Mom bent down, picked up the prescription, and tore it up. She let the pieces fall back to the floor.

"Virginia, I advise you to change your mind," Dr. Brucata said. "Your daughter needs to heal."

"Our religion comes first."

"Can she at least take the Provera?" he asked cautiously.

"That I will allow," said Mom. "And the diet pills, but that is as far as I will go."

I held back tears as Dr. Brucata picked up the torn prescription and threw it away.

Then Mom and I left the office and walked to the bus. I said nothing all the way to Zarchy's.

"Hello, young lady!" said Mr. Zarchy with a smile. "Been a while."

Mom handed him the prescriptions.

"Angelica, have you been sick?" he asked.

"Yeah. So what?" Embarrassed, angry, and dejected, I walked around the store. I remembered when I worked for him there were doctors who called in prescriptions for their patients. I knew this because I sometimes answered the phone if Mr. Zarchy was busy. I wanted to ask if this was a possibility for me, but if I said anything in front of my mother, it would be hell to pay. I took a magazine off the rack and placed it on the counter.

Mr. Zarchy prepared both prescriptions while we waited. He handed me the bag and I paid for my meds and the magazine. I laughed inside, and thought, *I'm old enough to pay for my pills, but I am too young to take the pills—go figure!*

CHAPTER 13:
UPPERS
AND
DOWNERS

I waited a week to broach the subject of the birth control pills to my father. Mom had gone to one of her meetings, and I had saved dinner for Dad. While he washed up, I placed the chicken cutlets, mashed potatoes, and peas and carrots on a plate. Dad came out of the bathroom and I set the plate before him. He made the sign of the cross and quietly said grace before cutting his chicken and taking a bite.

"You made dinner tonight!" he said.

"How do you know?" I asked, smiling from ear to ear.

"I know my mother's recipe when I taste it." He smiled with pride and filled his mouth with food. Dad had a hearty appetite.

I sat next to him and braced myself. "Dad, can I ask you something?"

"What, sweetheart?"

I knew I could cut to the chase him. "What are your ideas about birth control?"

"Is this about what happened at the doctor's?" Dad asked, still chewing.

"Yeah. I don't get it. Dr. Brucata is giving me the pills to help me. That's it."

Dad got up, poured himself a glass of cold water, and took a long sip. "Honey, the church states that birth control goes against its teachings."

"But I wouldn't be using it to go against the church. I would be using it to help my cycle. My health is in jeopardy. Dr. Brucata agrees," I said.

Dad fixed his eyes to mine. "Ah, sweetheart, you don't understand. If you take those pills, your *soul* will be in jeopardy, and the devil can find his way in."

I closed my eyes and breathed deeply. I picked up a spoon and from the table and tapped it before me. I tried one more time. "Dad, I won't be doing anything wrong by taking the pills."

Dad held my hand down from tapping the spoon. "The answer is no." He glared hard at me, and I knew to get up, finish the dishes, and never mention it again.

In the next few weeks, I took the medication that my parents agreed on and kept to the diet Dr. Brucata put me on. By the end of the first month, I had lost fifteen pounds. I watched my body change as the pounds and inches melted away. Shortly after that, my period returned and I began to feel like me again.

Losing weight was a great self-esteem boost. For the first time, I was able to wear the clothes that my friend Angela wore. After work at Shop Wise, we stopped into Gurdies, her favorite boutique. I had always wanted one of those peasant blouses, and Angela handed me one right away. It was blue with tiny white flowers all over. I went into the fitting room, afraid the blouse would not fit. I undressed and looked at the top on the hanger. My hands began to sweat.

"Hey, did it fit?" asked Angela from outside the door.

"In a minute," I replied.

I slipped the blouse from its hanger and undid the three buttons on the bodice. Then I slid it over my head, feeling the fabric float dreamily over my skin. I looked at myself in the mirror. *I look like Angela,* I thought. I took a breath and opened the door.

"Radical, man!" Angela said. She ran to get a set of turquoise love beads and wrapped them around my neck. "You look like Peggy Lipton on 'The Mod Squad!'"

I swallowed hard. For a minute, I did not see the new me in the full-length mirror, but the old fat me. Then the music in the store grew louder and as the song "The Age of Aquarius" played, I began to dance. "Yeah, I do feel like Peggy Lipton!" I laughed.

Angela and I spent many fun hours shopping there. We bought jeans and belts and jewelry. It was the first time since I'd started working at Shop Wise that I actually spent money on me and not the bills or medicine. It was groovy!

Just as the pills were lessening my appetite, they also minimized my need to sleep. Dexamine was an amphetamine, a kind of speed that not only took away the hunger but also boosted my metabolism in a way that made my energy levels soar. I could stay up until all hours, do my homework, and attain honor status again. Best of all, I was writing poetry in the middle of the night. I'd sneak down to the basement while everyone slept and write in my red notebook. I found peace in those wee hours of the morning.

Six months later, I had lost sixty pounds. I had gone from a size sixteen to a girly size six and felt like the attractive young woman I wanted to be. Mom was proud of me, too, and I have to admit that I enjoyed her approval. At that point, Dr. Brucata took me off Dexamine. But weaning was more difficult than I expected: without realizing it, I had become addicted. Without the pills, I had such low energy that I was back to eating again and gained five pounds in the first two weeks.

I asked my mother to ask Dr. Brucata to renew the prescription, but he said I did not need them. I was scared out of my mind that I would gain the weight back and all the health complications that came with it. I didn't realize I was already sick.

It was well known in school that some of the seniors sold drugs, and I asked a friend to hook me up with one of them.

"Are you Candy?" I asked as I approached a tall, lanky girl in bell-bottom jeans and a fringed sheepskin blouse.

She examined me from head to foot. "You're kidding, right?"

"What's that supposed to mean?"

"You ain't no drug taker—you a virgin, girl!" she said scornfully. Then her face suddenly paled. "Hey, you're not a cop, are you?"

"Just give me the damned pills," I said, flashing a twenty at her.

She stared hard at me a moment, then placed three pills in my hand.

"That's it for twenty bucks?"

"You gettin' grade-A stuff there." She laughed as she walked away.

Just like that, I began using my hard-earned money to buy tiny black pills called "black beauties." The pills gave me the energy I was lacking, but the side affects were worse than the prescriptions—I couldn't sleep at all and, in the end, found another pill called "street reds" to help me calm down.

I hated what I was becoming. I looked great on the outside, but I was beginning to feel like some of the rock stars I heard about on the television and read about in teen magazines. Strung out and desperate. Twice a week, I'd stand on the corner near school in the hot sun with some red-haired kid dressed in hippie clothes. I didn't even know his name, but I handed over a fifty for five black beauties. He placed a small brown envelope in my shaky hands.

"Thanks," I said.

He said nothing, and the silence freaked me out. I turned my back on him and hurried away to get to work. It was one in the afternoon and I was exhausted already, feeling the rebound effects of the pill I had taken earlier that morning. On the train, I took a black beauty and swallowed it with some bottled soda I had in my purse from lunch. Black beauties were fast acting. Within minutes, my energy levels were boosted. I was ready to take on the rest of the day, which would see me home by ten and doing homework until one in the morning. It was a strange kind of "balance," and it continued for months. Meanwhile, I was losing more weight. On my home scale, I was down to one hundred and five pounds from the one hundred fifteen that my doctor felt was healthy. I didn't care. "Healthy" be damned.

"Hey, Angelica, what's shakin'?" asked Roger, a friend of mine from English literature class, one afternoon.

Roger was a tall well-built African American boy. He had chiseled features and light brown eyes. He wore tie-dyed denim bell-bottoms and a psychedelic blue shirt with a white bandana around his short Afro.

"I'm rad, Rog, how are you?" I asked.

"Groovy, man—I got into modern dance class today!"

"How did you hear?" I squealed. I had wanted to join that club since I started at Bryant but had always been too fat. Now that I was thin, I had auditioned right along with Roger.

"Come on, girl—do I have to drag your pretty ass down the hall to see?" Roger grabbed me by the wrist and pulled me down the hall to the dance room. He pointed to the list on the side announcement wall.

My jaw dropped—there it was: my name! "I'm in!" I shouted, dancing in the hall.

Roger picked me up and spun me around. "Hey, girl, you lose more weight? You feel like skin and bone!" He dropped me gently back on the ground. "What you doin', girl?"

I shrugged. "Nothing."

"Nothing? Nah, girl, you better start eating that pizza pie again. You ain't supposed to be this skinny." He felt my shoulder bones. "I like some meat on my girls, you know?"

I looked at Roger's face. We had known each other since freshman year. Hearing him say that things weren't right made me nervous, but I was not about to confess. I knew he had a point, though. Half my new clothes were hanging on me.

A few days later, modern dance commenced. I was ready to go, feeling great in my black Danskin leotard and tights. I slipped on the periwinkle blue Qiana skirt I had just bought two weeks earlier. After buttoning and zipping it up, I realized it was two inches too big in the waist. I rummaged through my purse and found a safety pin, which I used to pin the loose material closed. Roger's words resonated in my head: "I like some meat on my girls."

I was ready and joined the rest of the girls in my class. We ran down the hall from the locker room and into the dance studio. There, reflected in the larger-than-life mirror, was the truth: I looked like a skeleton. It was obvious that I was in trouble.

Trouble or not, the fear of gaining weight scared the living crap out of me, and the pattern of my addiction continued. Daily, I lived on two black beauties, one with my coffee at five in the morning and one in the afternoon around two, before the rebound effect kicked in and I could eat a house. I lived on coffee, a hard-boiled egg, and a slice of cheese before work; at the supermarket, I ate two slices of turkey from the deli and a yogurt cup. That was it all day except water.

Every Friday afternoon, the gang from modern dance class ate lunch in a classroom down the hall from the gym that we branded our own "clubhouse." We listened to music and picked out the tunes that our coach, Ms. Bariento, would choreograph for us. I had finished my one measly hard-boiled egg and cup of milk. It was bearing down on two p.m., and I felt as though I could lie on the floor and sleep. I opened my purse and removed the small brown pouch I kept the black beauties in. I undid the strings and fumbled for a pill, but it slipped from my hand to the floor. Before I could retrieve it, Roger leaned over.

"What's this for?" he asked, picking it up.

I stuck out my hand, and Roger was about to return the pill when he pulled back, looking at it intensely. His face jolted with recognition.

"What the fuck are you doing, girlfriend?" he exclaimed.

The sweating had begun, letting me know I needed that pill. "Give it back, Rog," I said quietly, trying not to draw attention.

Roger closed his fingers around it. "No way. This shit is going to kill you."

"Rog, give me my pill." I was shaking. "Now, damn it!"

Ms. Bariento strolled into the clubhouse, and Roger reluctantly pushed the pill into my hand. I shoved it down my throat, and within a few minutes, my body began to balance itself.

The awful clang of the next period bell rang through the halls. Roger had one more class, and I had to leave for work. I hurried toward the steps to leave. As I opened the hall door, I felt a strong hand tug hard on my arm.

"Where you think you're going?" Roger said.

"Where I go every day. You know, work?" I said.

"You ain't headed for work. You headed for a 'grave man,' like Tybalt in that *Romeo and Juliet* play," Roger said, shaking his head.

"I'll be fine. I know what I'm doing."

"Really, girl, you don't. You gonna die you keep taking that shit."

I knew he was right, but I didn't care.

"I'll get off them, I promise." Roger still had a grip on my arm. "I'm going to be late for work," I said sharply.

Roger let me go. "You better keep that promise, girl."

I didn't keep my promise. I just found more ways of getting my pills. If it wasn't from connections at school, it was from the kids who hung out in Pops Pizza or friends in my neighborhood in Woodside who had their own connections. I could pick up five or ten pills from seemingly anywhere, and I did.

I was lucky, though. My friends would not let me down. Roger told Angela what I was doing, and they intervened and took me to the school social worker, a man named Ira Zaiff. He had a group in Bryant called The Family. It was aligned with a program in Manhattan called The Door, which helped addicted teens without requiring permission from their parents. The group's motto was, "What is said and done here stays here!"

Mr. Zaiff was a tall man, balding with long gray hair and a beard. He and Mrs. Green, the school nurse, helped wean me off the pills. One pill, one fix, at a time, they brought me down. It took all I had to get through the stomach pain and sweats and chills the rebounds would bring.

One day at dance, our teacher put a record on the turntable. It was an Israeli ballad, and as the drums started, we all took each other by the waist. In a circle, we went left, then right, remaining bound to one another. The lights were flickering, and in the mirror, my face looked pale and clammy. The room was hot from all of us dancing, but I was ice cold. I let go of Angela and fell to the floor, shaking.

"Go find Mrs. Marquise!" said Mrs. Bariento.

"No, Mrs. B," said Roger, "she's coming down. Mr. Zaiff and Ms. Green will take care of this."

A few minutes later, Mr. Zaiff walked in with a warm blanket. I wrapped myself in it, and he took me down the hall to his office. Mr. Zaiff stayed with me, holding my hands and wiping my tears as my body came down from the drugs.

"You are such a wonderful kid, Ang," he said. "We are going to make you well again."

I held on to this kind man with blue eyes and gray hair, shaking under the blanket. "I want to get better."

"You will!" He poured me a cup of coffee, and I curved my hands around its warmth. Mr. Zaiff held my hand to steady the cup as I took a few sips. "You know, you are one of the lucky ones," he said.

I wiped my tears, black mascara streaking on my fingertips. "How am I lucky?"

"You have people who love you."

And I did. If it weren't for Roger and Angela, maybe I would have headed for the "grave man," but Mr. Zaiff helped me wean, and Mrs. Green taught me how to respect my food and eat healthy. I kept the weight off just by eating right, and staying off the pills was saving me a lot of money. I decided to reward myself. I had found out that Elvis Presley was playing at Madison Square Garden and was ecstatic at the thought of seeing my favorite artist in person.

I went into the city to pick up tickets to see the show and, while I was there, bought a great pair of Vidal Sasson jeans that I would wear to the concert. For the first time in my life, I felt as though I had some control. I hummed to myself as I walked home from the bus stop, Elvis tickets securely in hand.

PART II

WELCOME TO

ADULT HOOD,

POPULATION: 1

CHAPTER 14:
WHAT PRICE
ADULT HOOD

Life at home was never the same after Mom came at me with the knife that day, and I was grateful that I had a job that kept me away for so many hours.

By the time junior year was almost over, I was out of the house from seven in the morning until ten at night. I did all my homework at my job. I'd walk in the door each night, change, wash my face, and then go to my room to study. On days off from work, I did all my chores and was always on guard, keeping ten paces ahead in housekeeping, shopping, and everything else just to keep some semblance of peace. My biggest priority was to keep as far away as I could from my mother.

There were times, of course, when that was impossible. The summer before my junior year began, Dad rented a car and took the whole family to Jones Beach Theatre. Yul Brynner, one of my favorite actors, and Constance Towers were starring in *The King and I*, and Dad had bought tickets.

Sitting in the outdoor palladium under the stars was just the medicine my soul craved. The music, the magic of the stage set in China after the Civil War, the costumes—all of it stirred something in me. There was a scene where Anna and the king were discussing how well the dinner with the English had gone. Her gold lamé gown flowed on the stage, and the king's red Asian suit dazzled me. When he placed his hand on Anna's waist and the crescendo of the music brought up the lights and the dance began, I wanted nothing more than to be Constance Towers.

After the play ended, we went to Guy Lombardo's club, which was attached to the theatre and where Mom and Dad had booked a table for dinner. The musicians had not yet come down from the theatre, and the first thing we saw was the band shell loaded with musical instruments. I gazed with awe at the tables, covered by white lace cloths and sparkling with gold utensils. Black velvet dining chairs completed the picture. I felt as if I had walked into a dream.

The hostess, draped in a low-backed red sequined gown, guided us to our table. I could hardly believe it was just for us. I felt beautiful in my pink and white mini wrap dress that Mom had made for me after I'd lost all the weight, and my brother wore his brown suit. Mom looked gorgeous in her blue satin dress and white patent leather shoes, and Dad wore a crisp navy suit. They looked like a bride and groom. *We* looked like the typical successful American family. But there was a monster hiding within.

The host of the evening came on stage to welcome us. Waiters wearing black suits and white gloves took our orders. Mom and Dad ordered champagne and our dinner, and I felt as if time were standing still. The host introduced Guy Lombardo and his band, and everyone stood to applaud. The first song they played was "One Enchanted Evening." Dad took Mom's hand, and they glided onto the dance floor with other couples.

My beautiful mom flowed on the dance floor with my handsome dad. I sat there and watched them. They mesmerized me. Mom and Dad knew how to dance, and as the music played, all I could think was how my mother looked so wonderful and graceful. Dad had her floating on the dance floor. The folds of her dress swayed like angels' wings. She was Ginger Rogers to his Fred Astaire, but as I watched and listened to the music, I felt the same knot in my stomach that was always there, the one that made sure I stayed on guard against the other side of Mom, the side that—just two months ago—had tried to take her own life and mine.

The band played all night while we ate a scrumptious meal. Our waiter poured champagne into pretty crystal glasses, and Mom handed one each to my brother and me. The bubbles tickled my nose as I raised the glass to my lips, and I couldn't help smiling at the sweetness of the moment.

A few minutes later, Guy Lombardo introduced Constance Towers. She was dressed in a gold and white turn-of-the-century gown, her dark blond hair up in a Victorian chignon. She took the microphone and began to sing "Getting to Know You." I couldn't believe that I was just ten feet away from her. I wanted to be her—standing there, singing, and wearing beautiful dresses.

The audience stood and gave Miss Towers a standing ovation. She bowed and exited the stage, walking right past our table to join her own family two tables away. I could not keep my eyes off her. A few minutes later, people lined up near her table with the play programs in hand, and Miss Towers graciously autographed each one. I wanted to go up to her, but I was anchored to my seat. She was so beautiful. Would she sign my program? Was I even worthy enough to ask?

"Angelica, stop sitting on the edge of your seat and just go!" Dad laughed. He pulled my chair away from the table to get me moving.

I stood took a deep breath and walked over, standing with the crowd. It felt like an eternity, but there she was, not six inches away from me. She smelled like rose oil, and she was more beautiful up close than I had imagined.

I spit out the words, "Can you sign my program?"

She smiled. "Of course I can. And what is your name?"

"Angelica," I said, swallowing hard. "Miss Towers, I want to be an actress just like you."

She looked up from the program. Her blue eyes could light the sky. "You do? Have you taken any acting lessons?"

"Not yet—but there is a theatre workshop in my high school."

Again, that smile. "I advise you join it. That's the way to get started."

She handed me the program and I read the inscription: *To Angelica, a fellow actress. Break a leg, Constance Towers.* My heart skipped a beat.

After practically running back to my table, I showed my parents and brother what she had written. "An actress?" my mother said, her relaxed expression twisting into one of condescension. "You want to be an *actress?* You're not the material for that."

My high at that moment dropped to one of the lows I'd felt getting off drugs.

"Well, maybe someday," I said, trying to hold on to some dignity.

The applause of the audience changed the mood forming at our table, and I was thankful. The waiter brought our desserts, but I couldn't eat. I glared at my mother. *I will prove you wrong,* I thought. *Just watch me, Mom!*

S eptember came around, and the first place I headed on campus was the theatre department. I signed up for auditions that first week of school, even though calls for the troupe weren't until October. In class, my teacher gave me my schedule, and I noticed that I had regular English instead of honors English literature. Immediately after all my classes, I ran up to the English department to see if I could change my class. Mrs. Wolff, the English department director, greeted me.

"What can I do for you?" she inquired.

"I think Mr. Lopresti made a mistake," I said. "He didn't give me Honors English Literature."

Mrs. Wolff picked up the program mantle and ran her fingers through it to see if there was an opening in the class. Taking a program change paper, she wrote in my name for the honors class and gave it to me. I nearly gasped: Mrs. Klausman, the theatre workshop director, was the teacher. I took the sheet and placed it in my purse.

"Thank you, Mrs. Wolff."

"Remember, you have to sign out of English first and then sign in with Mrs. Klausman," she advised.

After signing out of English, I could not wait to sign in with my new class. Mrs. Klausman's class was room 273, one of the center hall classrooms. Next door were the costume and makeup rooms, which were located right off the auditorium mezzanine. All I hoped as I set my eyes on Mrs. Klausman was that she would not only be my honors English lit teacher but my theatre workshop director as well.

Mrs. Klausman was a middle-aged woman of medium frame and height, with jet-black shoulder length hair, brown eyes, and high cheekbones in a light olive complexion. The day we met, she wore a black flare skirt with a white lace ruffled blouse, black short-sleeve sweater, and a pretty red, white, and black scarf tied around her neck. I would later discover that scarves and shawls were her signature accessories.

"Welcome to my English literature class," she said.

"Thanks, Mrs. Klausman."

There was an empty seat in the back of the class, and as I sat down, I noticed that walls in her classroom were decorated with playbills and book and movie posters. There were pictures of L. Frank Baum's book cover of the original *Wizard of Oz* beside the corresponding movie poster, and Margaret

Mitchell's *Gone With The Wind* jacket was next to its respective poster. I felt as if I were in a storybook Elysium—my mythical heaven.

Mrs. Klausman interrupted my thoughts as she approached my desk and set down a copy of *Gone With The Wind*. Along with the class manifest for the term, there was also a paper to sign; it stated that we had received the book and promised to return the copy or pay a fine. I signed it and handed it in.

I found it difficult to concentrate that day. The class had opened their books, but I was not listening. My mother and I had argued the night before— again—over my chores. I could not stand it anymore. I was up at five thirty every day, at school at seven thirty, and at work at four. I left work at nine in the evening and arrived home by ten. I would then get into my pajamas, wash my face, and tackle my homework.

As much as I was glad to be in Mrs. Klausman's class, I was exhausted and distracted. Instead of taking notes, I penned a poem on my loose leaf:

Life, is it worth living
I don't know any longer
I look at it behind closed doors
I see it through those prison walls in my mind
Haven't any friends, but enemies who wish to harm
My mortal body
Can I find peace if I were an immortal soul?
I do not know, I cannot dream it possible
Everywhere I roam, my pathways flooded with blood
Every friend I seek presents me with a gift of pain
Can I find peace in death
Or will death bring me hell
Will it bring me hell
My God, my God
Take me in your arms
Caress me, stroke my brow
Place your kiss upon my lips
And never release me
Hold me close
Cradle me, cradle me
Cradle me, Lord
Cradle me

"Angelica, what do you think about the portrayal of slavery in *Gone With The Wind?*" Mrs. Klausman was standing over me. She must have been there a while, and I was so consumed in my poem I had not realized. "Come see me after class," she said.

Great, Ang! I thought. *Now you will never get into theatre workshop.*

After class, I stood by Mrs. Klausman's desk. "Hand me that paper, please," she said curtly.

"It's personal!" I said. "Respectfully."

"I understand that, but I'm pulling rank here. Give me the paper, please."

I rummaged through my binder and handed my teacher the paper. I watched her read my very personal words. When she finished, she stood and placed her hand on my shoulder. "Can you be as profound an actor as you are a writer?"

"I don't understand," I replied.

"If you can bring that kind of emotion to the stage, I would love to have you in my theatre workshop troupe."

"Would I have to audition first?" I asked.

"Yes, you would. Everyone who wants to be in *my* theatre workshop auditions!" she said with a smile.

I was shaking inside and felt a smile of vindication form on my face. "Yes, I can."

"Come to our meeting tomorrow after school."

My mood instantly deflated. "I work after school, Mrs. Klausman."

"If you want to act, then find a way." She paused, then held up my poem. "And by the way, where did these words come from? Is everything all right at home?"

I shrugged. "I like Edgar Allen Poe. I try to write like him."

Mrs. Klausman pursed her lips. "I don't buy it. Only real pain writes like that."

"Well, as I said, it's personal. I'll see you after school tomorrow."

She handed me my poem, and I walked out the door.

CHAPTER 15:
SO WHO
AM I?

B y the end of my junior year, I was enjoying theatre workshop and history. I also became an intern at The Roundabout Theatre Company, which needed volunteer ushers and costume runners. Mrs. Klausman had written me a letter of recommendation, and I was hired quickly after my interview. Meanwhile, I was still working in the supermarket. I made four dollars an hour and paid my own bills, including all my medical bills, and was saving for college. Between all my activities, time flew.

In the beginning of senior year, I discovered a new love: Arthurian lore. I was entranced by stories of the mythical King Arthur, Merlin, and The Lady of the Lake. Within my books, I found a place to run away from my woes at home. The king and his men of the Round Table became my brothers, and the wizard Merlin, my magical friend, could take away pain with a brush of his hand. The Lady of the Lake was my surrogate mother. I began to read every Arthurian tale I could get my hands on, from T.H. White to Thomas Malory. I could not get enough.

If that fire wasn't igniting me enough, another was about to be set.

"Hi, doll!" I heard as I emerged from history class.

"Oh, hi, Mom," I said. *Why are you here?* I thought.

Standing next to her was a cute—no, *hot*—guy. He stood around five feet, eight inches, had dark brown hair cut like Patrick Swayze's, and blue eyes that melted me. His tight jeans hugged every muscle from his waist down. Who *was* this?

As if reading my mind, Mom said, "This is Joseph Sergio, Angelica. He does service work for me in the office."

"Oh, hi," I said, kind of coyly.

"Joey wanted to meet you," Mom said.

Instantly it clicked: his last name was Sergio; he had to be Italian, a "good Catholic boy." Mom's dream boy for me. Sure enough, she smiled and went back to her office. I was shocked. My mother never left me alone with a boy, never mind a hunk like Joey.

We both stood there, and I could tell Joey was as uncomfortable as I was by the way he held his books and looked down the hall as the kids passed.

"Do you like pizza?" he asked.

"Hey, I'm Italian," I laughed. "Of course I like pizza."

He gave me a half smile. "Would you like to go get some this weekend with me?"

"I guess." I held my binder up to my face, half hiding behind it.

"Here's my number," he said, writing it on a sheet of loose-leaf paper. I wrote mine on his binder, and we waved as we parted for our classes.

That weekend, my heart skipped a beat when the doorbell rang. *Oh my God!* I thought. *He's here.*

"Angelica!" I heard my mom yell from the living room.

I had on a floral peasant blouse and my designer jeans. I felt like a fox. I met Joey in the living room, where he was standing with my mom. He wore those hot jeans and a short-sleeved button-down shirt with a white fleur-de-lis print. He looked so handsome.

Joey had no qualms telling me right off what he thought. "You look great, Angelica, but I have to say that the makeup artist in me is telling me that if you did your makeup a different way, you'd look amazing."

"Huh?" I was confused.

"Oh, I forgot to tell you Ang," Mom said. "Joey is studying to be a makeup artist for the theatre."

"Really? So can you show me how to do my makeup the right way?"

"Sure, I can," he said, "with your mom's permission."

Mom was grinning from ear to ear as Dad came home from work. "Hon, I'd like to introduce you to Joey Sergio," she said.

"Nice to meet you, sir," said Joey.

Dad looked Joey over like he was a bomb ready to go off. He even made *my* neck hairs stand up.

"Joey is a makeup artist intern for the theatre, and we go to Bryant together," I said.

"A makeup artist?" Dad repeated, raising an eyebrow.

"Yes, Mr. Marquise," Joey said. "I want to do makeup for the theatre and film one day."

"I see," Dad said, but there was something in his tone that was making me uncomfortable.

Joey did not have a car, so we hopped the Q60 bus on Queens Boulevard. There was an Italian restaurant on Queens Boulevard called Daisy's. It was rather pricey, but that didn't seem to matter to Joey. Here I thought we were going to pizza, and I walked into a restaurant with Roman columns, white lace tablecloths, and white and gold china and utensils. This was my first real dinner date, and I felt like a princess.

"So what do you like to do?" asked Joey.

"I love theatre and history. One day I want to be a famous actress."

"Me, too, but I'm more a behind-the-scenes guy," he said, biting down on a meatball.

"You mean sets and stuff like that?" I took a sip of soda.

"Nah, I love doing makeup and hair. You know, designing styles for the shows."

"Yeah I know what you mean," I said. "Especially in those period movies. The hair and makeup is amazing."

"So artistic," he said, putting his fork down.

Joey and I talked about everything from school to religion to having strict Italian parents. It was great to have an intellectual conversation with him.

Toward the end of the meal, Joey asked an unexpected question. "Do you know what it means to be homosexual?"

"Of course," I said.

"And?" Joey pressed.

"It's when people of the same sex go out with each other." I felt my face redden. "Aren't they also called 'gay?'"

"Yes ..." There was a long pause. "We are."

"C'mon, Joey!" I exclaimed. "You're a hot guy—no way are you gay."

Joey reached over the table and held my hand. "But I am gay, Angelica."

I stared at him in shock. Here I was, all decked out in my fashionable clothes for my "date," and Joey was gay. Why had he even asked me out? I sat at the table for a minute and then went to the ladies' room. I stood in front of the mirror, trying to digest what Joey had just told me. No matter how I tried to fight it, I broke down right there and cried.

"You look upset," Joey said when I rejoined him at the table a few minutes later.

I shrugged. "I am. I guess I was hoping I'd found a boyfriend. Finally."

"Well, I'm a boy and a friend—one you can feel safe with."

"Safe, now that's a concept," I muttered.

"What's that supposed to mean?"

"Joey, if you're gay, then why did you even ask me out? Why did I get all dressed up for you?"

"Your mom kept talking about her nice Italian daughter," Joey said, "and when I saw you, I thought we could be friends."

"Friends?" I felt tears wet my eyes. "I was hoping for more."

He placed his hand over mine. I was about to pull away, but his touch was calming, his smile gentle. I let him hold my hand and dared to hope he was telling the truth—that I could feel safe with him.

That "date" was the beginning of a relationship that was to span an all-too-short single year. During that year, Joey taught me all the makeup and hair tricks he had learned in a beauty school he went to in Manhattan. What he showed me began to empower me with the confidence I lacked. I began to look and show the world (or at least my friends) that I indeed had a sense of style. I even had my own signature scent, which was Givenchy Ladies, the other side of Gentleman by Givenchy that Joey wore. We grew to be thick as thieves, going not only to straight bars but to gay clubs as well. For the first time in years, I began to feel as though I fit in. I had proudly become Joey's "fag hag," a term of endearment for a straight girl who hangs tight with a gay man.

In addition to being a makeup artist intern, Joey was a female impersonator at the gay clubs we frequented.

"So how do I look?" he asked backstage at The Alley, a gay nightclub in Jackson Heights.

"You look just like her," I said.

118

He was standing in the wings waiting to go on. Even though Joey was an amazingly handsome man, his looks lent to him being a gorgeous woman. The lead music rang through the theatre and off he went.

"Gypsies, tramps, and thieves!" Joey's voice rang out. Everyone in the audience was in awe of him. He moved, sang, and acted just like Cher. He was in a black gown that clung to his body. His hair was Cher's signature long black locks, and his voice resonated like hers. I moved closer to the stage entrance and hid behind the curtain. I was close enough to keep an eye on him but far enough that no one in the audience knew.

The clubs where Joey performed were my weekend reprieve from my mother. I couldn't tell her where I was; after all, I knew the Catholic Church's stance on homosexuality. In its eyes (and my mother's), I was sinning just being with him. So Joey would pick me up and take me home, and we'd tell my parents that we'd seen a movie or that we had gone out to eat and for a long walk. My mother bought it, especially because she liked Joey and had met his parents. He was, in fact, Italian and Catholic and, from time to time, went to church with us. He was perfect for me, and I know Mom hoped he'd marry me one day.

On nights like these, while Joey waited in the wings to go on, I'd sit at the bar and sip a tequila sunrise while Joey's friends sang. The Alley was always standing room only on nights the impersonators sang. One night, there was a young woman at the bar. She had been there before and we had briefly said hi to each other, but this night was different.

"My name is Allison!" she yelled over an impersonation of Marilyn Monroe.

"Hi, I'm Angelica." I yelled back.

"What are you drinking?" she asked above the crowd's ovations.

I told her and a few seconds later had a fresh drink in front of me. "Thanks!" I said.

"You're welcome," she said, placing a hand on my shoulder. She gave me a hint of a smile that made me feel as if time were standing still. She stood with a medium frame about two inches taller than me, wore an Yves Saint Laurent denim pantsuit, a red ruffled blouse, and black heels. I felt her caress the back of my hair.

"I'm straight!" I declared as I pulled away.

"No, I don't think so," she said.

"What do you mean? I *am* straight."

"We'll see."

My confusion was interrupted when Joey's music came on and he stepped on the stage. I cheered and took a sip of my drink. Then it hit me. *She'd just made a pass at me.*

For the remainder of the night, I felt uncomfortable around her. I left my drink on the bar and excused myself, going backstage to hang with Joey and his friends.

The next week, Allison was there again. It was the club's impersonation contest, where the best female impersonator would win the grand prize of five thousand dollars. Joey was best by far when he was Cher. His rendition of "Gypsies, Tramps, and Thieves" drew standing ovations every time. This night was big business for the club, as not only the performers but also the audience was dressed to the nines and ready to have a good time. Joey loaned me a black sequined low-back gown that followed every womanly curve of my body. He had taken the gown in for me and helped me dress backstage. Then he did my long hair in curls that hung down my back, and my makeup was simple yet impeccable, finished with ruby red lips. I looked like I belonged on the red carpet for the Oscars.

I tried to pretend that Allison wasn't there, but when I went to the bar to get a drink, she came over quickly.

"How are you?" she said over the crowd.

"Good and you?" I said.

"Great." She leaned over and gave me a kiss on the cheek. "You look amazing."

I did not know what to say at first. "Thanks," I managed. "I need to get backstage." As I lifted my drink off the bar, I felt her hand caress my right forearm. It felt both comfortable and strange.

Backstage, all the impersonators were lined up on the benches waiting to go on. "You look like you've seen a ghost," said Joey, all decked out. He wore a red sequined gown similar to mine, except his had a slit all the way up his left leg. He had on black fishnet pantyhose and black sandals, and, at the last minute, I was helping him gather up his chest muscles under the prosthetic bra and corset to make him look as though he had breasts. Then I zipped up his dress and—careful not to ruin his makeup—gave him a soft kiss on the cheek.

"I love you," I said, ignoring his comment. "Now break a leg and knock 'em dead!"

He kissed me back, waving his hand in front of me and showing off his pretty red nail polish. "Sis, this drag queen is going to win tonight!"

I nodded. "Yes, you will. I can feel it."

"So who's the babe at the bar?" he asked.

"You don't miss a trick, do you?"

"You know my eyes are everywhere." He smiled with those baby blues that always made me feel safe and wanted.

Joey and I moved toward the back end of the stage near the dressing rooms.

"Her name is Allison, and she made a pass at me for the second week in a row."

"She's cute," Joey remarked.

"Yeah, but Joey—I'm straight, remember?"

"I know, but you were pale and had a hint of red on those cheeks of yours," he said. "She's getting to you."

"I don't know ... I mean—me, gay? I never saw myself with a girl before."

"Hey, baby, if love is finding you, then go for it. We only live once."

I sighed deeply. "Yeah, I know, but I'm not so sure if I can."

I stood and listened to the music. I had been hit on twice before there by girls I wouldn't take home even if I were gay. They were girls who sat by the bar and drank all night until they puked outside—yuck! I hated drunks. But Joey was right. Allison was getting to me. She would be on my mind at times at work or in school, and I shuddered thinking about her. I was supposed to be with a man, not a woman. How the hell could I have kids with a girl? The parts were all wrong.

One of the bouncers came over, interrupting my thoughts. "Joey, ten minutes."

"Break a leg, baby," I said. "Win!"

Joey kissed me and went to the left wing to wait for his cue music. I left the stage area to join some friends and Joey's brother and parents at our table. Where my parents were staunch Italian Catholics, Joey's parents were becoming part of the more liberal sect. They believed in birth control and, in some instances, abortion. At their home, I could talk about these issues, freely expressing my feelings without worrying that God was going to strike me down with his lightning bolt. Joey's parents were against him being gay in the beginning, but Joey told me they came to realize that he had been given to them by God, so only God should judge him. That showed them the way to embrace him. Where my mother was pushing me away, Joey's parents kept him close. I couldn't help feeling jealous.

I sat down, and Jordan, a young man who worked the club, brought over my drink. I took a cigarette out of Joey's pack and saw, from the corner of my eye, someone stretch a lighter toward me. It was Allison. She lit my cigarette, and my whole body shook.

Joey's cue music filled the club, and everyone applauded as Joey strolled onto on the stage. He sang "Gypsies, Tramps, and Thieves," and if he weren't a medium-sized man in height, you would think the real Cher was singing. He belted the last of his song, and the audience went wild.

He was the last performance for the first act, and during the intermission, the DJ played some disco hits. Everyone went crazy when the Bee Gees rang out. As the mirror ball lowered and cast its reflective lights on the dance floor, Allison grabbed me and dragged me onto the wooden floor. The music pulsed and we began to dance, the rest of the crowd gathering around us. I always enjoyed dancing, and my adrenaline was running wild with the festivities. Before I knew it, Allison grabbed me around the waist and pulled me toward her. Right there she kissed me, then started to make out with me. My heart was racing.

I had kissed guys before. When I was fourteen, a classmate named Jimmy kissed me under a tree, and though I'd been wanting to be kissed so badly, when he took me and held me around the waist, I felt trapped, almost as if my uncle were touching me again. In high school, I met Steven. He was cute and tall, and we had a lot in common, but the night he kissed me in his car scared the hell out of me. It was as if someone had sucked the air out of the vehicle and I was suffocating. Those feelings frightened me so much that I ran from the relationship, whatever it was or could be. But Allison wasn't frightening me. I felt comfortable with her. We were dancing and kissing and I was high, high on the music, high on the moment.

Then Joey took the microphone and declared over the music, "Ladies and gentlemen, I believe a couple has been born this night!"

Everyone clapped and the music got louder and for the first time in my life, except for my friendships with Joey, Roger, and Angela, I felt safe. I was dancing and singing and wrapped in Allison's arms when Joey ran to me. Holding up his gown, he grabbed me from Allison, kissed me on the cheek, and lifted me off the floor. "I am so happy for you!" he said, spinning me around.

But I wasn't sure even then. My gut told me I was doing something wrong, going against my very nature. While I wasn't scared of Allison, I was scared of being gay and what that might mean for my life.

"Hey, what are you doing tomorrow?" asked Allison.

Under Joey's watchful eye, I answered, "I work."

"Why don't I pick you up and we go out somewhere alone?" she suggested.

"I can't. My godparents are coming over tomorrow night."

Joey shot me a disapproving look, but I didn't care. I wasn't ready for this.

Allison called me almost every day for a week asking me to go out. I gave her every excuse in the book: school, homework, Roundabout Theatre. Anything real and tangible that I could reach for, I used to get out of a date.

The following Saturday night, Allison was waiting outside Shop Wise when I got off work.

"What are you doing here?" I asked.

She leaned in to kiss me on the cheek, and I pulled away.

"We need to talk," she said.

We walked up the block toward the train. The faster I walked, the more determinedly she kept up with me.

"Talk about what?" I asked.

"Why you've been lying to me."

"Lying? I'm not lying. I have to get home." I was rushing up the steps to the 7-train when she grabbed me before the turnstile and, right there in public, planted a hard kiss on my lips. Two women at the station looked at us in disgust as Allison pulled me close and then pushed me away.

"Tell me that didn't mean anything to you," she said.

The problem was that it did mean something. I was falling for Allison, and it scared the blood out of me. I kept thinking it was wrong, but why did it feel right?

Before long, Allison won me over, and we began double-dating with Joey and his boyfriend. We were regulars at the Alley. Every weekend, my life resembled the movie *La Cage aux Folles*. Allison drove and would pick me up at work or home. While I became Joey's makeup artist and costume runner, Allison waited at the table for me between acts. She filled a void in my life, giving me a love that was unconditional. I did not have to prove anything to her, nor she to me. We laughed and had a great time with the guys. Allison and I made love, and when I was with her, I was on a natural high. Nothing and nobody could drag me down.

My parents met Allison and thought she was a nice, good Irish Catholic girl. If they had known that we "knew" each other in the biblical sense, Mom would have killed us both. Though she remained oblivious to the true nature of our relationship, Mom asked more and more questions about Ally. Did she go to church? What kind of work did she do? Where did we go when we went out? I shouldn't have been surprised. With every person I had in my life, there was an interrogation at the door. Friends were invited into my house at all hours, even at three o'clock in the morning, for coffee and cake, just so my mother could see what I was up to. It enraged me every damned time, but I put up with it; I didn't need the neighborhood hearing my mom and me argue.

Eventually, rumors began circulating in school about Allison, Joey, and me. One day, I walked into the fourth floor bathroom to see that someone had written Angelica is a Lesbian on the stall door. I freaked out. How did they find out? And who was the culprit?

Around the same time, Mom's friend Maureen had gone to the movies with her family near the Alley and noticed me outside having a cigarette with Joey. To Irish Catholic Maureen, the Alley was the house of the devil, and she wasted no time telling Mom about her sighting of me.

"Are you a boy or a girl?" Mom shouted as she came into the kitchen that night. She slapped me hard and, in a mad rush, went for the wooden spoon. "You are an abomination to our faith!"

I looked up at her, shocked, as she beat me with the spoon. I shot my hands over my head to shield myself, pushed the spoon from her hands, and scrambled out of my chair. "I don't understand, Mom!"

"Are you a boy or a girl?" she yelled even louder.

"Oh, I'm a girl." I smirked.

Mom's hand flew at me again, but I dodged her strike and she hit her hand on the refrigerator. "You did this!" she yelled, holding her hand.

"Me?" I could not hold back a laugh, and Mom ran to me and grabbed my hair, yanking hard. Every nerve ending in the back of my head and neck was on fire. I pried her fingers away from my hair. "What the hell was that for?" I screamed.

"You know exactly what I mean. You're one of those gays, aren't you?"

"What do you mean, gay?" I held the back of my head where it was pounding.

"Maureen told me that Joey is a homo!"

"No, he's not," I said, trying to lie my way out of it.

"Oh, from what she tells me he sure is—and so are you." Mom pointed that knowing finger in my face. "She saw you and Joey outside that bar in Jackson Heights."

I began to sweat. *Holy shit,* I thought. That *had* been Maureen's car across the street from the club. I had seen but dismissed the old black Ford Impala with the red rosary beads hanging from the rearview window.

"She saw you and Joey smoking outside that club for Satan's army."

My jaw dropped. "What the heck is Satan's army?"

"Gay people! They are an abomination to God and life!" Mom yelled.

I looked out the kitchen window, which faced the apartment complex next door. There was a brick wall staring at me through the window, and—to stay calm—I began to count the bars around the window that could see right into my house.

"Abomination?" I said, trying to keep my voice low. "Joey is my friend. He is not an abomination, not to me."

"He is to God, Angelica!" said my father, who was just coming in from work. His curt inflection cut like a knife in my gut.

"You agree with this, Dad?" I asked, feeling betrayed.

"The Bible tells us this, sweetheart," he said.

"So if Joey is an abomination, am I, too?"

Mom went to slap me again, but Dad stopped her. "V, leave it alone, will you?"

"You're on her side again!" Mom screamed at Dad.

"Virginia, I am trying to teach her a lesson here—so let me," Dad said, protecting me in his way.

"Oh, and by the way, is that Allison girl a queer, too?" Mom asked.

"No, Mom. She is just a good friend, and you know Joey's not gay—okay?"

"He is, Angelica. I had a feeling from the first day he came here," said Dad.

"What do you mean?" I asked, surprised.

"He reminded me of the *he/she's* we saw in France during the war."

"And how would you know?" I shot back, trying to be smart.

"You don't disrespect your father!" Again came Mom's hand from across the table and again Dad stopped her. "V, enough!" To me, he said, "I'm a man and I know these things." He looked at me with both kindness and disgust.

"Honey, if you are gay or associate with homos, then in God's eyes you *are* an abomination."

"Am I an abomination to you?" I asked, fighting tears.

"Tell me who your friends are, and I'll show you who *you* are," Mom said snidely.

"Please tell me you are not one of them." Dad's hazel eyes begged me for the right answer. I wanted to spit out the truth, but I couldn't.

"I am not," I said.

"Oh, thank God," Mom said, as Dad's eyes closed in relief.

"Mom, Dad." I tried to hold onto some dignity, without shouting. "Joey and Allison are not evil. They are good people. Please, I beg you, don't call them 'Satan's army.'"

Dad's eyes slid back to me. "In order to redeem yourself in the eyes of God, you must leave these friendships."

I stood there, feeling as though I was bleeding out on the kitchen floor, but there wasn't a cut. I knew by my father's tone that there would be no changing their minds. To the church, all homosexuals, including their daughter, were the unholy of the unholies.

I was not allowed out anywhere but school, work, and church for a while. One night after work, I met Allison at the coffee shop by the train.

"What is going on?" asked Allison, waiting for her coffee by the counter. "You're as pale as these walls."

I sipped my coffee and wished it were arsenic. I was about to break it off with Allison, a person whose only sin was loving me.

She grabbed her coffee and came over to me. "Are you sick or something?" she asked, giving me a loving kiss on the cheek.

Right away, the tears welled in my eyes.

"Ang, what is going on? It's me, baby." She placed her hand over mine and held it. "You can tell me anything."

I wiped my tears away. "My parents found out about Joey."

"I don't understand," she said.

"My mom's friend told her she saw Joey and me by the club, and now Mom is calling us abominations."

"What?" She let go of my hand.

"You heard me. All homos, as they call us, are Satan's army."

"Hey, I'm not one of those Satanic worshipers," Allison said defensively. "I go to church."

"I know, but their religion tells them otherwise."

Allison took my hand again, discreetly so that no one would think of us as anything but "girlfriends."

"Allison, she beat me." I pulled my hair back and showed her the mottled mark Mom had left under my left ear.

"What the fuck? She hurt you?" Allison tried to touch me, but I pulled away.

"Please. I can't see you anymore," I said before I lost the courage.

Allison's expression went from angry to baffled. "Did I do something wrong? I don't understand."

"Allison, if she did this to me and I'm her *daughter*, what could she do to you?"

Allison grabbed my hand and held it. "We won't let her win, that's all."

"She's calling all of my friends abominations. I cannot have her hurt you."

"I can handle it—"

I pulled my hand out from under hers and walked out of the coffee shop onto Roosevelt Avenue. It was dark, and the first cool winds of fall were blowing. Allison followed me, and I shook my head.

"No, Allison, stay away from me. I am trouble to you now."

I kissed her on the cheek and ran up the steps. When I looked back, Allison stood by the bottom step in the cool breeze, as alone as I was. I tried to hold myself up on the pole waiting for the train, but my knees buckled and I slid down to the cold ground. I shook and sobbed, feeling drained of every breath. There was no air that night, only pain.

CHAPTER 16:
GRADUATION
AND
GRIEF

Giving up Joey and Allison was a great loss to my soul, and it seemed as though King Arthur and Merlin were the only ones able to fill the void. I spent any free time in the Woodside Library reading everything and anything on the bardic king. My history teacher, Mr. Chahallis, challenged me to read senior college-level books on medieval history and had me do extra credit term papers just to see how much knowledge I was developing about the time period. In April 1975, I handed in a twenty-five page report that rivaled a college thesis.

After Mr. Chahallis read the work, he said, "One day you will write a book on this subject."

"Me?" I said, laughing. "Write a book? You must be kidding!"

It got to a point where I always carried a book about King Arthur. It was as though he were protecting me from all the evils in my life. When Mr. Chahallis asked me why I was so obsessed, I could not explain. All I knew was that I felt a deep connection to Arthur and his manic-minded son Mordred.

By the end of my senior year, I was so overwhelmed with work, keeping my mother's rage at bay, and making sure I graduated with full honors that I hardly had time to worry about anything personal. At eighteen, my life was about my future.

I was interning for the Roundabout Theatre and the TV show "Dark Shadows." I had managed to score some bit parts, but I was closed-lipped at home about my adventures in the theatre. My parents and my brother never saw me on television or in my one Off-Broadway performance. It hurt me deeply, but it wasn't surprising. Neither of my parents was keen on me becoming an actress. Dad wanted me to take a trade, saying, "College isn't for girls. After all, you are going to get married some day and your husband will take care of you and provide for you." According to my mother, I should become a secretary, as she was, or give up the nonsense of the theatre and become a beautician with the knowledge of hair and makeup Joey had given me. She even joked that it would be great to have me as her very own "private hair dresser."

It got to a point where going to work in Manhattan without confrontation was like trying to see the Pope—impossible—and my mother's abuse worsened as time went on.

"What do you need with being an actress? All of them are a bunch of tramps." Mom looked me over from head to foot. I was wearing a pair of jeans and my Bryant Owl t-shirt.

"Do I look like a tramp to you?" I asked.

"Well, show me—"

"Yeah, yeah, Mom—show me who your friends are, and I'll tell you who you are."

Mom rammed her hand right across my face. "No daughter of mine is going to sleep her way to stardom."

I held my hand to my face and stared at her. "I am still a virgin!" I yelled through the pain in my jaw.

"And that is why I won't let you go tonight!"

The playhouse was showing the Arthur Miller play *All My Sons*, starring Jane Connell and Hugh Marlowe. It was my turn to be costume runner backstage, and I was not going to miss it.

"I'm sorry but I'm leaving," I said. As I walked out into the hall, I felt a hand pull at my shirt.

"You hate me!"

I turned, and there it was again—that wide-eyed madness that always frightened me. I tried to be calm. "Mom, I don't hate you, but this is what I want."

"If you go tonight, you do hate me!"

Mom shoved me against the wall. The molding slammed between my shoulder blades, and a weird tingle ran down my legs from the hard push. Dad had done some work in the hall during the week and left some wood slabs on the side. Mom whisked one up and arced it toward my head. I ducked down and dodged her attempt. She went after me again and grazed the back of my left ear and neck as I managed to open the hall door and run.

She followed me halfway up the block, yelling, "Go ahead! Be a tramp!"

The elevator to the train wasn't working, so I ran up the stairs to the 7-train. Once aboard, I tried to quiet myself, but my heart was racing like a gazelle running from a predator. Catching my reflection in the window of the train, I wanted to scream. There was blood flowing down my neck and onto my senior t-shirt. I raised my hand to touch the area; Mom must have cut me with the wood, but I couldn't tell where. My adrenaline was still rushing, and all I wanted to do was get to the theatre.

I arrived a half hour late. I showed my ID to the door manager, and he let me in.

Lucy, the backstage manager, caught me entering. "You're late," she said. "Get changed fast and put the first-act costumes in place."

"I will, Lucy!" I shouted as I ran in the stage crew's locker room.

Each of us had our own small cabinet with a lock on it. On the side wall was a vanity and makeup mirror. I stripped and began to change into my black pants and shirt. But I couldn't. Suddenly I felt as though I was going to pass out. I sat down quickly on the chair across from my locker.

"Angelica, c'mon, girl," Lucy said, coming into the room. She pointed to her watch. "Showtime!"

She rushed across the room in her black clothing, but I just stared at myself in the mirror. I had a dark purple streak running down my face, and on the other side, blood had dried on my neck. I was a mess.

"What the hell is that?" she asked.

On the train, I had tried to clean up the fragments of my day, but it was obvious that something major had happened to me. "I fell down the steps on the train station near home," I lied. "Didn't know what it all looked like until I got here."

Lucy stood tall over me. She was about thirty, and her dark hair was pulled back in a ponytail. She took a clean towel from the cabinet, wet it, and came over to help me clean up. "Who did this to you?" she asked.

"Nobody."

"Angelica, don't kid me. I've seen this on actresses who have drunk and addicted boyfriends. Things get out of hand, and *whack!*"

I took the wet cloth from her hands and finished cleaning the blood off my neck. "I fell, okay?"

She looked up at the clock. "You good to work tonight?"

"Yeah."

"Then let's go—showtime!"

I was glad that the stage would be blackened during the show so nobody would be able see me. Before the intermission warning light went on, I grabbed the costumes and props and set them in place as Act One ended. During intermission, I ran back to the locker room, where Lucy always hid a box of stage makeup so that if one of the actors needed, the supply would be there. Using the skills Joey had taught me, I began to cover up the mark on my face. As I leaned over the vanity, my back hurt so badly I could hardly stand up straight again. I felt as though I had been through a war zone. In the mirror, I noticed the crew couch against the opposite wall. I gave in that night and broke down on the couch, scared to go home.

The rest of that year was a blur. I missed Joey and Allison so much and wanted to be with them, yet I was afraid of coming home to more arguments and abuse. I needed to survive, and if that meant spending my time alone, working, then I would. At least I did not have to explain every moment of my day to Mom.

My last theatre workshop show was *You Can't Take It With You.* The title grabbed me, as I already felt that I could never take with me the things or people I loved. I played the sultry actress Gay Wellington, and I loved putting her life on like a costume for a two-night performance. I played her so well that my teachers asked Mom if she'd "given me a drink" before I went onstage. Mom made jokes of it, but the reality was that she and my dad wholly disapproved of my portrayal of an alcoholic muse.

June came, bringing with it finals and graduation. I sat onstage that day at Queens College Caldor Auditorium and received my awards in front of the graduating class of 1975. I had achieved my aim: a graduation with full honors. I was awarded honor status in English literature, history, and theatre; gold cords recognizing Excellence in Conduct and History as a Major; and a silver medal in English literature. As for Arista Honors Club, I was given the white cord of honors in Student Excellence and Conduct of High Virtue of Honor.

Sitting up on that stage, I held onto the cord as if it were my lifeline. If I could succeed in school through all my tribulations so far, I could continue to do it. I could attain my dreams and become an actress.

"Sweetheart, I am so proud of you," said Dad in the back of the auditorium.

Mom took me in her arms and kissed me. "Congratulations."

"Proud day, huh, Virginia?" said Evelyn, the assistant principal.

Mom smiled, though there was something in her embrace that made me wonder how proud she really was.

"Let's take a family picture," Dad said.

Evelyn took the camera and we stood in front of the auditorium doors. Dad placed his hand on my shoulder and bore down. It was a weight I took comfort in.

CHAPTER 17:
WHO'S
HOT
AND WHO'S
NOT

That September, I entered Hunter College. College wasn't much different from high school, at least not for me. The biggest change was that I headed for Manhattan in the morning instead of the evening. That proved easier for me, as I could go from class right to the theatre or the set of "Dark Shadows" to work my internship hours, which now were accredited to my college years. On days I did not have the theatre, I went straight to work in the supermarket.

Things were changing in our house again, but this time it had nothing to do with Mom. By the end of my freshman year, Dad was beginning to suffer with headaches severe enough to keep him home from work. Dad *never* missed work. He also always enjoyed doing things around the house, but he started to employ my brother and me to help with painting or yard work or anything else the headaches kept him from doing. Though we were worried, we also enjoyed helping and learning from Dad. I tried to focus on that side of things.

Around this same time, between my first and second years of college, I met two men who would change my life forever. One was a singer named Greg; the other a man named John.

In the summer of 1976, I began to hang out in our neighborhood watering hole, Finnegan's Irish Pub. Many of my friends from Bryant hung there, along with some of my longtime friends from Woodside. One of them was my good friend Brenda Thys, a young Haitian American woman. Brenda and I knew each other since childhood. It was a friendship that should not have been, as she was black and I white. My parents forbade me to play with her because of her race, but Brenda and I defied the rules of race wars back then. She remains, to date, one of my dearest friends.

That summer, amateur bands were invited to play at the bar. Music scouts often prowled the tavern, hunting for new talent. One hot night, a young man named Greg and his band were set to play. I was there with many of the kids from St. Sebastian's and Bryant. Together, we would either hail the new singers or bring them down—we were a tough crowd.

Bands had ten minutes to set up; if they took longer, a bell rang and they were kicked off before they played a single musical note. I did not know his name, but I could tell by the way he was dressed—in tight jeans and black satin shirt with buttons opened down to his navel—that this hot guy had to be the lead singer. He stroked his guitar and began to sing, and the crowd was screaming within one minute. For the next fifteen minutes, this long-haired fox sang his way into every girl's heart.

"Hey, let's give a shout for Greg and his Wildcats!" yelled Tommy Finnegan, the owner of the bar. We whistled, pounded on the bar, and screamed for more. Greg took it to the max with another round of hits from the late 60s and early 70s.

When Greg was done, Tommy took him over to the side bar and spoke to him briefly. The next thing I knew, Greg was standing a few feet away from me with some of his guys ordering drinks. His chiseled chest was glistening with perspiration. A long silver link chain was draped around his neck, and a sterling silver and gold cross hung from the end of it. I couldn't help noticing that he had brilliant baby blues, just like Frank Sinatra, and sculptured features like Aerosmith singer Steven Tyler. He was hot, and I wanted to meet him.

"He's so tall!" my friend Angela yelled over the other band's music.

"Over six feet, easy!" I yelled back.

Bobby, the bartender, placed a glass of red wine in front of me.

"I didn't order that," I said.

"No, but he …" Bobby pointed to Greg, "… did!"

My heartbeat went into overdrive. "You're kidding me, right?"

I looked at the wine glass. "How the hell does he know what I'm drinking?"

Bobby shrugged. "He asked me."

I was not sure what to do. Should I pick up the glass, look right at him, accept the drink, and take a sip? My chest was throbbing as I tried to be reserved and keep my gaze averted. I couldn't figure out why I was so uncomfortable. Just minutes ago, I'd been dying to meet this man.

The truth was this was all new to me—hanging out at Finnegan's, with a very different crowd than I was used to with Joey and Allison. There was no doubt that I was attracted to Greg, but relationships with boys still scared the crap out of me. Every time a boy touched me, my body remembered what my uncle did to me and shut down. I again looked at Greg. He was a tall lean fox, but my mind went to my heart, where Allison still lived. I never stopped loving her or feeling guilty for running up those train steps. She didn't deserve to be left that way. I looked at the glass of wine on the bar; the surface was rippling from the vibrations of music and people moving and dancing. I felt as though it were imitating the shiver of my own heart, pining over my Allison and wondering if I could, in fact, start a straight relationship.

"Hey, I'm Greg. What's your name?" His voice startled me as I caught his reflection in the bar mirror.

"Angelica," I choked.

"So how long you been coming here?"

"Since the beginning of the summer."

My friends were on the dance floor, and all I wanted to do was run. Here was this tall, stately guy who towered at least two heads and half a torso over my five foot one inch, one hundred and ten pound frame.

He grabbed the wine from the bar and handed it to me. "This is for you."

As he gave me the wine, I couldn't help noticing the size of his hands. Mine looked almost childlike near his.

"Do you live near here?" he asked.

"A few blocks away, actually."

I held the wine, still unsure about accepting it. I knew there were drugs out there that guys laced drinks with to get their way with girls. But watching Bobby serve drinks to the others, I realized that he was the one who had given me the glass, not Greg. I sipped the wine, took out another cigarette, and lit it. "Be right back," I said, slipping off the stool. "Ladies' room."

"Well, look at the lucky bitch tonight!" said Angela, following me into the bathroom.

I inhaled on my cigarette. "Not sure about this, Ang."

"Please, if you don't want him, I'll take him," she said, eying me in the mirror.

I fixed my makeup and then snuffed out my smoke. There was a knot in my stomach. I wasn't sure if it meant that I liked him or should stay away from him.

The following week brought the usual hustle of work and school. Then Friday night came, my weekly reprieve.

Friday night was always a late work night. I got out of the supermarket at nine, so I brought a change of clothes and changed in the locker room. I wore a scarlet peasant blouse with a white fleur-de-lis pattern brocaded on the bodice and sleeves. Wrapped around my waist was a black leather belt with turquoise and white love beads sewn into the leather sinews. Coming from the train, I met Brenda, Angela, and Roger at the Stop Inn Restaurant across the street from Finnegan's for a quick burger and fries. Through the windows, we could see Greg and his guys hauling in their band equipment. Angela nudged me, grinning.

After dinner, while my friends went into the bar, I lit a cigarette and wrapped my red and black shawl around my shoulders outside. It was a warm night, but the anxiety of seeing Greg again gave me chills. Did I want to go in or go home? Before I could make up my mind, Angela came out.

"Hey, what's going on?" she asked.

"Nothing. Been a long day is all."

"Come on," she said. "Bobby's got a tequila sunrise ready for ya!"

Reluctantly, I followed her in and sat at my usual bar stool right up near the stage. I picked up the tequila sunrise and took a long sip, washing the day away.

"Angelica!"

I turned and there he was—tall, long, and foxy Greg wearing those tight blue jeans and a red and black satin shirt with the gold and silver cross I took for his signature piece.

"Hey!" I said, nearly choking on my drink.

"You ready for a good time tonight?"

I sucked in the smoke-filled air and felt a hot sweat come over me. "Yeah, I guess."

Bands went on at ten, and at the stroke of the first guitar string, happy hour began and drinks were half price. Bobby refilled my drink and soon Brenda, Angela, and I were on the floor dancing. Greg and his Wildcats played some Elvis Presley, Ritchie Valens, Buddy Holly, and the Big Bopper. The show was rocking, and Greg was hot. His red satin shirt was sticking to his abs and rib cage, and his hips gyrated like Elvis's. Every girl in the bar drooled over him, including me. But even as I admired him, I was disturbed at how strange my body felt around him. It reminded me of hitting puberty, and I could not understand the signals.

Back at the bar, Bobby hit me with another drink. The combination of tequila, the heat, and the rock music was a fix for a great high, and I reveled in it. I grabbed a cigarette and returned to the dance floor, where I raised my arms high over my head and let the music take me over. I felt as though I were in a cloud, and the smoke in the air danced with Greg's guitar strings.

The set ended and I made a beeline to the bathroom. When I emerged, Greg was standing there.

"Hi," he said, looking like he'd taken a shower in his clothes.

"Hi." My mouth was dry, my heart pounding. Suddenly and without warning, I wanted to be kissed.

"How are you?" he asked, moving toward me.

I found myself backed up against the wood-paneled wall. Greg stood mere inches in front of me, lifted his arm, and held himself up on the wall. He towered over me.

"You look amazing tonight," he whispered, and my body shook. I felt weak in the knees, and before I knew it, Greg leaned in and I felt his warm breath over my cheek. He pressed in closer and kissed me sweetly on the lips. I reached for his shoulder and felt myself kiss him back. Every vein in my body accepted his kiss. It was the first time in my life that my body did not shut down at a man's touch.

Cameron gave the roll of the drum, and it was back to business. Greg gave me a peck on the cheek and climbed onto the stage. As I watched him perform, still feeling his lips on mine, I had the irrefutable sense that my life was about to change.

Greg and I dated for the rest of the summer and into fall. Since we were both artists, our energy for both theatre and music ignited our interest in each other. I joined a community theatre group, and we put on a performance of *Fiddler on the Roof*. I played a young Jewish mother in Tevye's village, and Greg played guitar for the orchestra.

For some reason, my parents liked Greg and would ask often if he and I were enjoying each other's company. Greg took away the fear that their daughter was a lesbian, and their relief, I can see now, lent to them trusting Greg. I was surprised to find them sleeping instead of waiting up when I came home from dates at one in the morning.

Greg and I became an item at Finnegan's, but he wanted me there earlier to help set up; since I worked late, I could not comply. It aggravated him at times, but I had no choice. Dad's headaches had intensified, and he was having problems breathing and walking straight, which meant more time out of work and more time in hospitals and doctors' offices. Dad worked in a factory, polishing stainless steel pots and pans for high-end restaurants in Manhattan. In those days, workers did not wear protective masks to keep from breathing in the dust from the metal. Doctors finally discovered that the metal dust had ended up in Dad's nasal pathways and middle ears. He needed to have his passages irrigated to clear out the tiny shards of metal and dust that were congesting him. In order for him to regain his equilibrium, he had to spend time in bed when he got home. That meant he was out of work for six months and could only return part-time for the next six, or until the doctor gave him the go-ahead. To help pay the bills, I transitioned my part-time job to full-time. I gave up my dream of college despite all the work I'd done to get there, and I felt the loss every day.

To keep the roof over our heads, I worked long, hard hours at the supermarket, and the pay was shitty. Not only did I work from nine until six every day, I worked on Fridays from eight in the morning until nine at night. I hung out with my friends at Finnegan's until one a.m., then dragged myself up on Saturday at six to be at work by eight, only to work another eleven hours. There had to be a better way!

I decided that I could no longer keep working as a supermarket checker. I wanted a career doing something, *anything*, that did not involve handling raw meat and perishable produce. Inevitably, I entered the Flexer Beauty School in Flushing. If Dad wanted me to take a trade, then at least it should be something I enjoyed doing. Joey had given me a great gift, and if nothing else, I should build on it.

At that time, budget cuts had meant a layoff for my mom. No longer working at Bryant, she was now working as a school aid at Thomas Edison High.

"Hi, Mom!" I said one afternoon, walking in the main entrance of the school.

Mom was taking visitors' names, and she greeted me with a kiss on the cheek. "Hi, doll!" she said. "Give me ten more minutes and I'll introduce you to some of my co-workers."

"Okay," I said.

I sat at the table next to her. The school was a bit smaller than Bryant, and modern all the way. It had blue tiled walls, black and white flooring, and mosaic windows that climbed up to the second floor, flooding the school with light.

"Hi, Sheila!" said Mom to her friend. "This is my daughter, Angelica."

"Nice to meet you!" I said to the buxom lady whose build and stature reminded me of my grandmother.

Sheila took Mom's place, and we walked down the hall. I was amazed at how different the school was from Bryant; Edison's halls were divided according to numbers and bridged with an overpass to get to the other side of the school. It felt as if I had walked onto the bridge of the show "Star Trek." I preferred Bryant's old-fashioned feel.

When we reached the teachers' lounge, Mom grabbed a cup of coffee and made me one as well. There was a gentleman sitting at the far corner grading papers, and she introduced me with a smile.

The stocky man stood up and shook my hand. He had brown eyes, white hair, and a beard to match. "You are just as pretty as your mother said you were."

I felt myself blush. "Thank you, sir." I looked over at the table where he'd been sitting, and next to his open valise was a book. "I see you're reading T.H. White's *The Once and Future King.*"

"I'm reviewing the book for my class at the end of this term."

"I particularly enjoyed that book in high school," I said.

"How so?"

"White gives us King Arthur from the early part of the sixth century," I said. "It's a more ancient perspective than the tales of Malory, who brings Arthur to us in the later part of the century through a more modern lens."

"Are you studying medieval literature in college?"

"Oh, Angelica goes to beauty school now," my mother interrupted with a laugh. "She just wasn't college material."

Mom's condescension came like a thief over my pride in my knowledge of Arthurian folklore. Suddenly I had nothing else to say.

It would be that way all through beauty school. Mom always had her hair done on Saturdays in her neighborhood salon, but once I knew how to do the wash and sets, I became her personal hair stylist. Once I started beauty school, instead of working on Saturdays, I was in school from nine a.m. until five p.m. She called me there relentlessly to make sure I would wash and set her hair that evening before going out. If I didn't, I would come home from either a date or outing with my friends to a slap in the face and the usual tirades that I did not love her.

That year, at least I took pride in lending my new hair and makeup to the local community shows. I became the hairdresser for the St. Mary's Players and an intern for Queens Theatre in the Park. In some ways, it felt as though I was back working Off-Broadway, and I found some solace in that.

Winter arrived, and between my work hours—I still cashiered at the supermarket—and beauty school, I was getting lost in the shuffle. I hardly had time to see Greg, whom I had been dating now for almost six months, or meet friends for a drink at Finnegan's. I must have put in seventy hours Christmas week alone.

"Hey, sweetheart, Merry Christmas!" Dad was sitting at the table having his usual cup of coffee.

I leaned in and gave Dad a kiss.

"Hi, doll," Mom said. "Saved you a plate for dinner."

I looked at the bowl of pasta and shrimp marinara. It was already ten thirty at night, and all I wanted was a peanut butter and jelly sandwich, a cup of hot tea, and bed.

"I'm not that hungry," I said. "I want to go to bed soon."

"Bed? We are all going to midnight Mass!"

I leaned on the washing machine. "Do I have to go tonight? Can't I go to-morrow morning?" I had worked all day on my feet, from seven in the morning until nine thirty that night. The last thing I wanted to do was go to church.

"Hey, if she can go tomorrow, so can I!" yelled my brother from his bedroom.

"Nobody is going tomorrow. We are all going to church tonight!" Mom shouted back in that tone no one could challenge.

In silent protest, I ran my sore body through a shower, hot rolled my hair, and applied some light makeup to mask my tired face. I dressed in black velvet pants, black satin turtleneck, and a sky blue sweater, with a silver chain belt around my waist and my peace symbol necklace. After I choked down a bowl of cereal, my parents, brother, and I slid on our coats and walked out into the cold night up the hill and four blocks to St. Sebastian's Church.

"That is what you wear to Christmas Mass?" Mom commented as I removed my coat.

"Mom, you and Dad are lucky I am here," I replied.

To my surprise, she said nothing.

A few seconds later, I heard my name called and I looked over. It was my friend Daniel from my school days.

"Angelica, do you remember the songs we sang at Christmas folk mass?" he asked.

I nodded. "Why?"

"Karen and Terrence are not here, and we need a good alto to carry some of the songs."

"I haven't rehearsed, Danny," I objected.

He shot me a sly glance that said, *Yeah, but you want to, don't you?* The actress in me pulled herself together and went to the back of the altar to join the folk group.

Patricia Gallagher, our folk mistress, exclaimed, "There is a God!" She handed me a cup of hot tea with honey to prepare my throat, and in exactly fifteen minutes summarized the two-hour ceremonies and gave me a quick vocal exercise of the scales.

My stomach was in knots, as I had not performed in a while, but once we all stood on the altar and the organist began to play the overture for the opening hymn, I felt as though Jesus had truly given me a Christmas gift. Pat lifted her baton and we began:

"Oh come, oh come, Emmanuel, oh ransom captive Israel …"

I was singing again and felt as though an angel were at my side. I shifted my eyes to the congregation; our church was filled with at least three thousand people. My dad, an avid photographer who always had his camera in hand, snapped photo after photo of me on the altar.

When Mass was over, I did not want to leave. These were the first peaceful moments I'd had in such a long time. I wanted to stay there and savor them for a short while.

I met my parents in the back of the church. Standing with them was another couple. I knew the woman, Maeve, from the Catholic War Veterans Auxiliary, the women's club I had reluctantly joined a few months back to please my mom. Her husband's name was Fred.

"Sweetheart, you sang beautifully!" said Dad with pride. He gave me a kiss on the cheek.

"Ang, guess what?" Adam griped. "We're going to Mom's friends' house for cake and coffee."

I pulled my brother aside. "What the fu—" I covered my mouth, ashamed to be cursing in church so soon after singing for God.

Adam nodded, putting his finger on his tongue as though he were going to vomit.

"*Oh,* no, I'm not," I said. "I am going home."

"No, you are not, Lady Jane," Mom said. "It's Christmas and you are coming with us."

We arrived at Maeve and Fred's house and were introduced to their sons. Maeve had already set the table, and I knew this was preplanned. I'd had no say in the matter, as usual. As I sat there, a nerdy young man and his younger brother came in the room with Doris and John LoCascio. I already knew Doris from one of my mother's clubs.

"Hi, Angelica," Doris greeted me as she took off her coat.

"Hi, Doris," I replied.

"Hi." The nerd emerged from behind his mom, waving hello. I felt my eyes roll to the back of my head. He was tall and medium-framed with curly, shoulder-length sandy brown hair, hazel-green eyes, and a mustache that severely needed trimming. Acne wove through his five o'clock shadow, and he was wearing a red Nehru jacket, maroon pants, and a green turtleneck. Immediately he sat next to me.

"I'm John," he said, grinning.

"Hi," I said back. *Oh, why couldn't Greg be here?* I thought, knowing he was in Pennsylvania with his family.

"What's your name?" John asked me.

I looked at him, then followed my dad's lead and rose to serve myself treats from the nearby table. Soon the men were caught up in talking about the poker game fundraiser the Catholic War Veterans Post had the other day, and the ladies chatted about the auxiliary, which we were all members of. John's brother and my brother talked about sports. I tried to stay invisible. I was tired and wanted to crawl in the sack; I had been awake and working for almost twenty-four hours straight.

I was startled when I heard John's high-pitched voice in my ear. "Hi," he said again. "You didn't tell me your name."

I sighed. "Angelica."

Gross me out, man, I thought. *Who dresses like this? Did your mommy pick that out for you?* My brain was tired and playing evil games when it came to John, but I couldn't make myself care.

From that day on, every time I attended an auxiliary meeting with Mom, John was there to pick up his mother at the Post. It got to a point where I bolted out of the meeting hall as soon as I could just to get away from his waves and attempts at conversation.

May came, and the Post had its usual Memorial Day community parade and picnic. I marched with the women's league and proudly carried the flag. I shouldn't have been surprised when John followed the parade route right next to me, wearing some zany red, white, and blue pants, a Mets t-shirt, and black and white high-top Converse sneakers. *Stay away—stay far, far away,* I silently begged. Yeah, okay, so the guy was funny, but I was accustomed to my trendy friends who wore the radical clothes of the day. John looked as though he just rolled out of bed and put on clothes his mommy picked out—not my style.

Later that day, in the Post yard for the annual picnic, the table was covered with the best-cooked burgers, hot dogs, and grilled corn on the cob in all of Woodside. I took a plate, sat next to my brother—who was already stuffing his face—and began to eat. That came to a halt when John came over and sat his nerdy butt next to me.

"Hi, Angelica!" he said with that high-pitched voice. I continued eating my lunch.

Everyone was having a ball, eating, cooking, and filling up their glasses with cold beer or soda. When lightning filled the sky and it began to rain, everyone grabbed the picnic supplies and took the party into the Post meeting hall. That did not dampen anyone's sprits. This day was for friendship and camaraderie, and we were reveling in it.

John and I, along with both our brothers, were playing pinball in the back of the meeting hall with some of the other young adults. We were all having a blast, and I finally got a chance to see another side of John; even though he dressed weird, he was fun to be with and was good at pinball.

"Ang!" I heard Mom call.

"Yeah, Mom?" I knew something was up her sleeve.

"Could you go home and pick up that container of apple juice in the fridge?"

"Can't I go to the A&P and pick one up there?"

"No, I need *that* one," she said.

"Mom, it's pouring out! I'll go to the store."

"No, Ang, I need that one because my stomach medicine is in there."

"Why can't Adam go?" It never failed: my brother played and I got the chores.

"John has a car!" I heard Doris volunteer from her seat near my mom.

At least while John and I were playing pinball, we'd had something of a good time, I mused. Maybe he would drive me.

"Hey, John," I ventured, "could you drive me home?"

"I could," he said, walking away from the pinball machine. "But you have to do me a favor."

"Yeah, what is that?"

He smirked. "Give me your phone number."

He'd asked me for my number at least five times since Christmas, and I'd weaseled out of it each time. I looked outside at the sheets of rain before saying, "Okay, okay." I grabbed a napkin, jotted the number, and handed it to him.

Down the block from the meeting hall was his dark gray 1969 Ford Impala. *Surely not Greg's 1965 Chevy,* I thought, but I got in and from that day on, we became friends. Even though I was still seeing Greg, John and I began hanging out regularly. He was still in college and could barely afford dinner—he'd pay for pizza or a burger and I'd pay for the movie, or we'd just go to the movies and share the bill. He also asked me to cut his hair and help him buy new clothes. I was glad to help.

That summer our friendship blossomed, and while Greg began to accept more and more gigs out of state, I had a good friend to spend time with at home. John filled a void in my heart. He was making me laugh again, just like Joey had, and it felt great.

CHAPTER 18:
THINK ON
YOUR
FEET

For the next year, I continued beauty school, hung out with John, and saw Greg every other weekend. Greg had a recurring engagement at a club in Pennsylvania and stayed with his grandparents when he wasn't home in Astoria.

"Greg!" I ran to meet him in front of Finnegan's.

Greg lifted me off the ground and swung me around. We stood outside the bar, kissing madly.

Whistling sounds came from up the block. "Get a room!"

I shot a look at my friend Brenda, who laughed at me. Tommy Finnegan—thirty years old with curly auburn hair, a beer belly, and a brown "Go Army!" t-shirt—opened the door to the bar. We walked in to a crowd already going wild. Greg and his Wildcats were playing that night, and we couldn't wait to rev it up.

Greg's band was on stage setting up the instruments. They were a motley foursome: Billie, with cream white skin, green eyes, and blond wavy hair, short with baggy jeans and black Led Zeppelin t-shirt; Emerson, skinny as a rail with dark olive skin, Wrangler fitted jeans, black Jimi Hendrix t-shirt; Mikey, tall with broad shoulders, red hair, and green eyes; and Cameron, skinny like his brother Emerson, shy until he picked up his sticks but let his drums roar like a lion on the loose.

Greg and the guys played, and—as usual—the club was hyped to the max. Couples, girls, and groupies were on the dance floor having a great time. I was stage-side, dancing with Brenda, my arms over my head, when I felt a tug at my hand. Cameron, bent over with a tambourine, grabbed me and pulled me onto the stage.

I stood next to him, and while he played his guitar, I jingled that tambourine and sang with the guys. I was jumping and dancing with the lights in my eyes and letting off steam. We sang songs from the queen herself, Janis Joplin, and I screamed the words over the music and the crowd.

"Hey, baby!" Greg said over the song. He pointed at me. "Come here to your man!"

I strolled over to him, and he grabbed me around the waist, planting a long hot kiss on my lips right there on the stage. I felt like a rock star, standing up there next to Greg, his voice resonating over the microphone with me playing the tambourine. It was heaven.

Then I saw Adam, sixteen at the time, walk into the bar.

He stood outside the dance floor, and I could read his lips forming my name above the music. I did not respond right away. Then he started moving toward the stage. I put the tambourine down, jumped off, and went to him, pulling him away from the crowd.

"What are you doing here?" I yelled over the music.

"Mom is outside. She told me to come in and get you."

"What? Why?"

He shrugged and headed toward the exit.

I turned and looked at Greg, letting him know with my hand that I'd be back.

"Well, it's about time!" Mom yelled as I walked out the door.

"What do you mean?" I asked, miffed by her even being there.

"You should have been home an hour ago!"

Adam stood beside me on the sidewalk, as pale and embarrassed as I was. I looked at my watch. "It's only midnight. I don't have to be home until one, remember?"

The door opened, and Tommy emerged from the bar. Tommy was the oldest of the Finnegan kids. We had all gone to St. Sebastian's together, and his parents owned the bar and ran it respectfully. He looked at me questioningly. "Hello, Mrs. Marquise," he said.

"Don't 'Mrs. Marquise' me, young man. Why do you have my daughter dancing around on that stage like some call girl?"

"Were you spying on me?" I cried.

"Yes, I was, Lady Jane. I saw you through the window!" She pointed to the large window to the right of the entrance. Anyone who passed by could see the bands playing on the large stage in the back.

"Mom, what the hell is your problem?" I asked. "I am singing with a band. *Greg's* band, for that matter!"

"Mrs. Marquise, this has been a family-oriented establishment for years," Tommy said. "My parents do not run a brothel."

"Well, it sure looks like one!"

"Angelica, what is going on?" There he was—my man, Greg, to the rescue. His shirt was soaked with sweat, and you could see every ripple of his ribs pushing through the fabric.

"You stop turning my daughter into some *putana* on the stage," Mom said. "Angelica, you are coming home with me."

"Oh, no, I'm not." I turned and walked back into the bar with Greg, then stood behind the doors, listening.

"Mrs. Marquise, you can't come in and make a scene in my bar," Tommy said.

"I can do what I want, Tommy."

"No disrespect, Mrs. Marquise, but you can't. This is my bar."

"I'll call your mother about this," Mom threatened.

"She will tell you the same thing," Tommy replied calmly.

When Tommy walked in alone a few moments later, I knew she was gone.

I got back on the stage with Greg, but I could see he was not happy. There was a cold wall between us.

That night, Greg did not take me home, and I was glad. Mom had embarrassed me enough. I did not need her yelling at me in front of my boyfriend. Sure enough, I hadn't even walked in the door before she was on me, pulling me by the hair into the house.

"You are a *putana*. I hate you!" she yelled, shoving me down onto the couch. She came at me with her fist, and I took the square throw pillow and shielded myself as she struck it several times. *"Putana! Putana!"* she yelled over and over again.

"What gives?" yelled my father, coming from the bedroom. I knew she had woken him.

"My daughter is a tramp!" she yelled, trying to yank the pillow away from me. It was a tug of war for a few seconds, until Dad pulled Mom away.

"V, what the hell is wrong with you? It is one in the morning. Let it be, for cryin' out loud!"

"You always take her side!" she yelled, again trying to pull the pillow from my hands. I held that pillow tightly, so tightly its trim was cutting into the palms of my hands.

"I hate her, she is a *putana!*" Mom yelled so loudly the neighbor next door turned on the light in her kitchen and looked at us from across the driveway. I wanted to bury my head in the floor.

I scrambled up from the couch, the top of my head throbbing.

"Go to your room, Angelica," Dad said. "I'll take care of your mother."

I gladly left the room.

"You hate me, you all hate me!" I heard my mother sobbing. *Oh, please stop being a child,* I thought.

She and Dad argued a bit more, and then somehow things quieted down. My head and neck hurt badly. I lay down in my clothes, and when the house went silent, I finally fell asleep.

A few weeks later, Cameron wanted me to sing again, but I chose to sit with my friends. Greg and I were not seeing eye-to-eye that week. He complained that he could not stand my mother and that I "seriously needed to put her in her place." I couldn't help laughing. Trying to put Mom in her place, I said, was like trying to tame a lion out of a cage. The argument had made things between Greg and me stiff and strange, so staying with my friends seemed safer than trying to put on a show.

Afterward, Greg and I were around the corner from Finnegan's, near Joe's Diner. It was dark and there was a summer chill in the air. Tired and aggravated, I walked slightly ahead of him.

"Where are you going, bitch?" he yelled.

I turned, shocked. *"Bitch?* Who are you calling *bitch?"*

"You!" He pointed to me. "Your mother is getting on my nerves!"

"Yeah, well, you're not the only one, bucco!" I yelled back.

Greg shoved me against his green '65 Chevy. The door handle jabbed me in the butt. Then Greg pushed himself against me, forcefully making out with me.

I pushed him away. "What the hell was that for?"

"If your mother thinks I'm turning you into some tramp, then maybe I should. Might take the chill out of you."

My jaw dropped. Since my mother had embarrassed me in front of Finnegan's, I had given Greg the cold shoulder. He wanted me to have sex with him, but I was not ready. I had decided no sex with him—with anyone—until the right man came along. Four of my friends had gotten pregnant in high school, and I was not going to make my mess of a life any worse by getting knocked up before I was married. No way.

Greg squeezed my forearm with a grip I could not shake. My arm jerked with pain as he pulled me close to him and kissed me hard again, then groped me through my clothes.

"Leave me alone!" I wriggled out from under him and managed to shove him away. Taking my purse from the sidewalk, I ran across Roosevelt Avenue, across Woodside Avenue, down 61st Street and all the way home.

That night, my skills as a makeup artist came in handy again. Greg had left black and blue finger marks on my left forearm, and I had to cover them for a week so my family would not see them.

During the next few weeks, I kept to myself, seeing Greg only when he played at the club and singing with him only when Cameron asked me. Greg wanted to see me, but I always found an excuse, whether it was "girls' night out," school, or working late. We were swiftly becoming estranged. Meanwhile, John called me from time to time and we'd grab dinner or see a movie, always going Dutch, as neither of us had much money.

The holidays came and went, and in April, I turned twenty years old. I was so glad to get out of my teens. It meant that if I could save enough money, maybe I could move out of my parents' house and into my own apartment. John's parents and mine were becoming more and more inseparable at their club meetings. It was beginning to scare the hell out of me. I knew my parents' minds all too well—fraternize with the parents of their dream groom and maybe he really would become my husband.

I knew what their plan was, but I couldn't see John as a potential boyfriend or husband. Sure, I had changed him from a nerd who went to Chicago concerts wearing red checked pants and a white shirt into a guy who wore decent jeans and Polo knit shirts, but he still wasn't my type. He was more like my best friend once removed.

Memorial Day had come around again, with the usual parade and picnic, and Greg called wanting to see me. He kept telling me how much he missed me and wanted to get back together. I decided that I would try the relationship again, but I did not want to miss the Memorial Day picnic and invited him to meet me there.

We were by the bar at the back of the Catholic War Veterans Post. It was John, his younger brother, Adam, and me. Some of the Post members sat around us watching the ball game while we pounded out points at the pinball machines.

"Hi, Angelica."

Greg had arrived, ever so stylish and hot in his tight jeans, satin shirt, and belt with a sterling silver guitar for a buckle. I looked over at John, grateful that he'd shown up wearing khaki Bermuda shorts and a red Mets t-shirt.

I kissed Greg on the cheek. "Hi," I said. "How are the guys?"

"They're okay. Cameron says hi and told me to behave." He was blushing.

"*You,* behave? Now that is a concept," I snickered.

Music was playing on the jukebox, and Greg grabbed me to dance on the Post meeting room floor. Surrounded by pictures of World Wars I and II, the Korean War and Vietnam, I was among the best soldiers of modern times. Across from us, the U.S. flag stood proudly. Greg twirled me around and around, and it felt good to be back in his arms dancing. He turned me one more time, dipped me, and then kissed me on the lips, just as he had before our big fight on the street. I felt as though the months had never passed.

The song ended, and we strolled over to the bar. Greg got a beer and I ordered a glass of wine. My brother was laughing by the pinball machine, and when I turned to look, I could not help noticing John looking at us. His expression was forlorn and jealous. So he *did* like me that way, I thought. And though it wasn't exactly a *surprise,* it made me feel incredibly special.

CHAPTER 19:
LIFE CHANGES
ON A
DIME

That summer, my mother finally convinced my father to go to Florida. They'd fought about it for most of the winter. Dad was not keen on air travel. He would rather rent a car and go to the beach or visit some museum in Manhattan than get on a plane, but one warm day they came home with their plane tickets.

"Your sister is in charge of the house when we are gone," said Dad.

"That's not fair," Adam whined.

"That is fair. She's the oldest and more responsible. She is in charge," Dad repeated.

"Fine." Adam walked into his room in protest.

I could not wait for them to leave. One whole week without my mother overseeing everything I did, a whole week of work, beauty school (I only had a few months left), and enjoying the house and television to myself.

On July 3, a yellow taxi waited in front of the house as Mom hugged us and said her famous line: "Be good, be careful, pay attention, and Angelica, take care of the house and your brother."

I sighed. "Yes, Mom."

Dad kissed me on the cheek. "Ah, sweetheart, I love you!" He picked up the luggage and walked out the door. I watched them slide into the cab and the driver turn on the ignition. In moments, they had disappeared from sight.

"Thank God!" I said, laughing.

Freedom was wonderful. I went to school at night, worked during the day, and came home to a peaceful house. No Mom yelling or crying. No wishing I had somewhere else—anywhere else—to go.

"Angelica, I'm going out with the guys tonight," said Adam, coming through the door.

I looked at the clock. "Adam, you know Mom and Dad told you to be in by ten and me by eleven. It's ten now. You are not going anywhere."

"You're not my mother," he said.

"No, I'm not, but I'm also not in the mood for either of us to get in trouble."

"Who's going to know?"

"I will, and I am not going to lie. Not for you."

"Too bad. I'm going anyway!" he yelled, storming out the door.

I heard his friends outside and followed him to the front yard. He stood by one of his friend's cars, and I folded my arms, glaring silently. He glared back. I went back inside and turned on the television. It was Saturday night, and I was tired from my usual seventy hour work and school week. I put on my nightgown, got a cup of ice cream from the freezer, and watched T.V. The next thing I knew, I was startled from sleep by the phone ringing.

"Angelica, it's Mr. Henry."

I yawned and tried to open my eyes that were gritty from sleep. "Yeah, okay, Adam stop playing games!" My brother was always good at his pranks.

"No, Angelica, it really is me," he said, and this time I recognized our neighbor's voice. "Your brother needs you on the corner!"

My stomach jumped, and I looked at the clock: it was four in the morning. "What do you mean he needs me on the corner?" I asked. A chill ran down my legs even though it was warm, and I ran to the bathroom with the phone held between my shoulder and ear.

"Angelica, hang up and meet me by the door," said Mr. Henry.

I changed quickly and put on my sandals. Mr. Henry was at the steps when I opened the door. He was a heavyset Irish man who worked as a postman, and I had known him since my family moved to Woodside. I passed him to see at least thirty people huddled on the corner of 44th Avenue and 60th Street.

An alarm went off in my head. "Where's Adam?"

"He's okay, just hurt real badly," he said.

I ran down the block, toward the ambulance in front of Pete's Bar. There were two gurneys in the street, and one had my brother strapped in. Adam's face was bleeding. An EMT was standing next to him, wrapping the cuts on his face.

"What the hell happened?" I screamed.

My brother began to cry. "I'm sorry, I'm so sorry!"

"What is going on?" I asked, fighting panic. His shirt was soaked with blood.

Adam held the bandage on his head. One eye was black and blue already and he was shaking. "We were hanging out on the corner minding our own business and some kids came over."

I looked across the way; one of them, I assumed, was on the gurney next to my brother. "Go on."

"The guys and me were drinking beers, and so were they, but somehow—" He grabbed his head. "I feel like I'm going to puke."

He rolled over a bit and heaved right there in the street.

"Are you responsible for him?" asked a police officer standing next to him.

"I'm his older sister."

"How old are you?" the policeman asked.

"Twenty."

"Where are your parents?"

"They are in Florida visiting my mother's family," I replied, holding back tears.

"I can vouch for her, Officer," said Mr. Henry. "I know the family well. They are good and respectable kids."

The streetlight glinted over some broken glass on the road. There were broken beer bottles and blood all over the place.

"What the hell were you doing out here?" I asked Adam.

He started to cry again. "I am so sorry, Angelica. These kids came and started calling us names like scumbag and wasp and before you knew it …" He paused. "I threw the first punch, and the other guys started breaking bottles over our heads."

"We need you at the hospital to sign some papers, Miss," said the policeman.

"I need to lock up my house. Where are you taking him?" I asked.

"Elmhurst Hospital," said the EMT.

"I don't drive. I'll have to take the bus down."

"I'll take you," said Mr. Henry.

Adam and the other kid were lifted into the ambulance. The siren blared and they were whisked off to the hospital. I ran to the house, and Colonel barked and jumped around me; he always knew when things were bad.

I grabbed my purse, my keys, and a jacket, and Mr. Henry met me outside in the car. As I slid into the passenger seat, the sun was announcing the beginning of another day.

Riding down Queens Boulevard toward Jackson Heights, I began to shake. How was I going to explain this to my parents?

The next day my mother called from Florida; I had given the triage nurse my aunt's phone number, and they called my parents.

"Hi, Mom," I answered, half wanting to cry, half wanting to scream.

"Why didn't you take care of things for me?" she yelled so loudly I had to pull the phone from my ear.

"It wasn't my fault, Mom. Adam—"

"I don't want to know what Adam did! I left *you* in charge. It is your fault!"

My hand was clenched so hard around the phone my knuckles ached.

"Give me the phone," I heard my father say. "Sweetheart, what happened?"

I took a hard breath.

"Dad, I still don't know the whole truth about everything. All I know is that Adam went out without my permission, I fell asleep, and at four in the morning, Mr. Henry woke me up to tell me that Adam was in trouble."

"You weren't watching him!" My mother was on the extension yelling at me.

"V, I am handling this," Dad said. "Damn it, let me!"

"We are coming home tomorrow!" Mom slammed the phone in my ear. "I hate my daughter!" I heard her say over the phone. "She brought shame to my house!"

Twenty-four hours later, Adam was on the couch resting. His face was a black and blue mess. He had ten stitches over his eye and five on his shoulder. He was swollen and in a lot of pain, but he shot up like an arrow when Mom stormed into the house.

"You do this to me!" she yelled at him.

I stood by the kitchen doorway that led into the living room.

She whirled to face me. "And you! How dare you not listen to me?"

I knew that nothing my brother or I said would change anything. My father followed in with the luggage. He took one look at my brother and said, "For cryin' out loud, look at you."

Adam got up from the couch and Dad held him in his arms. My brother started sobbing in my father's embrace, and suddenly I felt the sting of my mother's wrath on my cheek.

"You know how this reflects on me?" Her eyes looked as if the devil himself possessed her, and it would continue this way for the next two weeks.

She whipped me when I came home from work, leaving welt marks on my back that hurt so badly I could not lay down in bed and sleep. She called my job repeatedly to ask me how I could allow this to happen and to say that this whole incident made her look like a bad mother. It got to a point where my boss threatened to fire me if she did not stop upsetting me during work hours. She was even calling me at beauty school.

Fed up with the whole thing, I did not want to go home at all. One day I decided to call John from work to see if we could hang out for a while. His mother told me that he was at Shea Stadium, where he worked as a vendor during the summer. I thanked her and hung up, then returned to the register.

I began to shake as I checked out customers' groceries. I was afraid to go home. On my next coffee break, I called Greg. To my immense relief, he was free that night, and he picked me up at work right on time.

"So where do you want to go?" Greg asked, looking great behind the wheel.

I was exhausted and broke down in sobs. Greg took me in his arms and held me close to his chest. He cradled me between his arms and the steering wheel while I wept like a baby, feeling his heartbeat on my cheek.

"Cameron heard what happened from Tommy at the bar," he said. "I called your house to see if you were okay, and your mother just hung up the phone in my ear."

I looked up at him, and he wiped the tears from my face. He kissed me sweetly and held my face in his warm hands. For the first time in weeks, I felt as if I was safe.

"Can we go to your apartment?" I asked.

"Come on. We'll get a pie and a bottle and relax—groovy?" He smiled that smile that made me go weak in the knees.

"Groovy," I said through tears.

We picked up the food and wine and then drove to his apartment in Astoria. I had never been to his third floor walk-up before, and when he opened the door and turned on the lights, I was hit with posters of the best musicians of our time: Elvis Presley, The Beatles, The Rolling Stones, Jimi Hendrix,

Janis Joplin, and many others. I was in awe of his guitar collection, from Grass Roots to modern electric, all displayed meticulously on the right side of his living room. I felt as though I had walked into music heaven.

As I studied the posters, Greg retreated to the kitchen and returned with two plates and two glasses. The pizza smelled good, and I realized I was starving. Greg gave me a slice and poured the wine. The warm red felt great going down my throat, and the pizza was exactly what I needed.

We sat and watched "The Mod Squad." All I wanted to do was sleep, but I looked at Greg and we began to kiss. After a few minutes, Greg started fondling my breasts. I was sweating and my body began to quiver with excitement, but something made me stop. Visions of my pregnant unmarried girlfriends flooded my head.

"I can't do this, Greg," I said breathlessly, pulling away.

"What do you mean, baby? Come on, we both want it." His long curly hair was wet with perspiration, and he was breathing just as heavily as I was.

I shot up from the couch. "No, I can't do this. I have enough problems at home. I am not going to give myself more."

"Okay, just come over and sit near me. I won't pressure you." His face was calm and reassuring.

I sat on the cushion next to him and tried to calm myself. Yes, I wanted to make love. I wanted it so badly, but, more than being scared of getting pregnant like my friends, I was terrified of my mother and what she would do if she found out. Greg got up and went to the kitchen, returning with the rest of the wine. He poured me another glass.

"Here, calm down. Everything is going to be okay," he said soothingly.

I picked up the glass and took a sip, then another. The warm wine began to mellow me.

Greg scooted closer to me on the couch and began touching me again. I felt as if I were in a time warp and my uncle's hands were on me again. Every nerve ending told me to get out of there. I pulled away, stood up, and backed up to the hall. Greg followed and would not stop running his hands over my body.

"Come on, baby, you know you want me," he said.

This was not happening. "Get off me!" I screamed.

He grabbed me around my waist and pulled me to the floor. My back hit the floorboards, and I felt a strange tingling sensation run down my legs.

Greg held me down with his whole body. I pushed up against his chest, and he shoved my head back down on the floor. I started to feel dizzy and was losing grip on my surroundings. My head spun, and a weird taste filled my mouth. Then everything went black.

Startled by the sound of feet and keys, I woke up not knowing where I was. My eyes were blurry, and my head felt as though a hammer had split it open. I tried to get up, and pain ran down the small of my back into my pelvis. I rolled over into a fetal position and held onto my stomach, only to feel the nakedness of my body. Where were my clothes? Where *was* I?

I straightened out, my spine feeling as tight as a tangled elastic band. Through blurred thoughts running in my head, I reached down and felt my jeans at my knees. I pulled my panties up and zipped my pants. I knew something bad happened. My whole being felt violated—but how? Why?

The static sound on the TV gave me enough insight to know that it was way after two in the morning, and all shows were off the air. Trying to grab at any clear thoughts I could find, I moved to the couch, where I saw Greg was sound asleep. Adrenaline rushed through my veins, and my heart raced just as it had when Uncle Thomas molested me in the car. I knew by the feeling in my groin that Greg had raped me. I wanted to kill him right then and there but pulled myself together. I quietly grabbed my sandals, purse, and jacket off the chair and slowly walked to the door. Then I ran down the steps for dear life.

Outside, the cool summer air hit my face, and my head began to clear. I stood there on 36th Street in the dark. I wanted to call someone, anyone, but who? My legs shook and I wanted to pee so badly my stomach hurt. I walked over to Crescent Street, and stood for what felt like an eternity until a yellow cab drove by. I hailed it, got in, and went home.

As I paid the driver, I noticed the kitchen light on and knew that my mother was up. I was about to walk into another hell.

"Where the hell were you?" she screamed.

I wanted to tell her that her tirades had sent me to hell, but I said nothing. I walked past her. What in the world could hurt me now? She was about to hit me, but I felt my stomach about to hurl and ran to the bathroom. For the next two hours, all I did was vomit and pee. My body could not stop expelling whatever was inside me.

"I'm getting a cab and taking you to the hospital," said Mom. "Something is not right here."

I was sitting on the kitchen chair doubled over with pain. I kept rocking back and forth, as that was the only way I had to control the pain in my gut and my groin.

"Mom, please, it must be something bad I ate," I managed. "I'm going to see if I can get some sleep."

"Ang, what is going on? I know you're hiding something from me," she said, calmly this time.

"It must be something I ate. Just let me rest, okay?"

Mom didn't buy that story, but she left me alone, as it was evident that I was not well. She made me a cup of tea, which stayed down. I cleaned up and crawled into bed. Just being in my own room felt safe, for the most part.

When I woke up, I nearly jumped out of my skin. I could still see Greg on top of me, but there was a time span that I could not remember—why?

I sat up in bed and looked out my window into a clear afternoon sky. My back and the insides of my thighs ached badly, like a sore that wouldn't go away. I got up to go to the bathroom, my head pounding as if I had a horrible hangover. I pulled down my panties and noticed that I was bleeding. I wanted to cry but was afraid that my mother would question it. Instead, I ran a shower and tried to rinse every thought, word, and deed of Greg from my body. But even the water hurt me.

Afterward, as I wrapped a big bath towel around me, all I could think was, *Why did this happen to me?*

It was Thursday morning, and I called in sick. I had never done that before and hated how I felt bad lying to my boss, but my stomach still felt as though I could heave at any moment. My face in the mirror was monstrously exhausted. All I could think was that if my uncle, my mother, and now my own boyfriend could wish me harm, maybe my life was not worth living.

CHAPTER 20:
WHY
LIVE?

If raping me wasn't enough, Greg stalked me for the next few weeks. He knew my work and school schedule and followed me in his Chevy as I walked to the train. One evening, from the school's second floor window, I saw his car idling outside. I shivered, wondering how the hell I was going to get out of there. The school had a door that led to the Parson's Boulevard exit, where the teachers and students parked their cars, and I let myself out that way. I took the long way home on the bus. From that night on, he stopped looking for me.

In the next few months, I changed drastically. I was withdrawn to the point where my friends called me, concerned, but I always made up excuses of work, homework, or other chores to avoid being with them.

John and I had a few friendly dates, going to the movies or grabbing a slice at Peppino's Pizzeria, talking about our parents or school. John had just graduated from Baruch College with a Bachelors of Business Arts in Accounting but was having trouble finding work in his field.

I struggled to get out of bed in the mornings. My body was so tired, and I could not fathom why. For two weeks, I suffered with severe abdominal cramps. At first I thought it was my spastic colon acting up, but one day the escalator to the 7-train was out, and I had to walk up eight flights of stairs to the station. Usually I could easily make the climb, but I almost doubled over in pain that day. I stood there halfway up, took a breath, finished my climb, and went to work. There, I was in and out of the bathroom, feeling as though I had the flu but fearing it was something more. I decided to make an appointment with my dad's union doctor in Manhattan.

A week later, Miriam, a buxom African American nurse, greeted me at the desk. She wore her hair in a short Afro and had kind hazel eyes that made me feel comfortable the minute she looked at me.

"Take a seat," she said gently. "The doctor will see you in a few minutes."

From the waiting room, I could see straight out to 34th Street in Manhattan. I gazed at the tall buildings and flashing yellow signal light that reflected on the 15th floor window across from the office.

"Come in, Angelica," Miriam called.

"How's Dad doing these days?" asked Dr. Steiner. He was the man who had saved my dad's life a few year back. He was middle-aged and balding, thin, with brown eyes and a Jewish accent.

"He's fine. Back to work full time and getting on my case about everything."

"Guess he's back to normal then." He smiled and placed his hand on my shoulder. "So what is going on with you, young lady?"

I shrugged. "Don't know, Doc, but for some reason my stomach keeps cramping up, and I feel sick at times but I'm not."

"Okay, sweetie, put this on and we'll see what is going on," said Miriam, handing me a gown as Dr. Steiner left to give me privacy.

A few minutes later, Dr. Steiner came in. I was lying back, and he put pressure on my stomach. "When was your last period?"

I shrugged again. "I can't remember. I never know when it's coming. Been that way all my life so far."

He applied gentle pressure to different areas of my abdomen, paying special attention to my uterine area. I pulled up when he hit my pelvic area.

"You're a bit swollen," he said thoughtfully. "I'd like to take some blood and run a few tests."

I nodded, and the next thing I knew he was tying a tourniquet around my upper arm and slipping a needle into my vein.

His face carried so many questions. "Are you seeing somebody these days?"

"Not really. I mean, he's a friend from my area, but we are just friends. Why?"

"Are you having sex with this friend?"

Shocked by the question, I exclaimed, "No, not at all! Why are you asking me these questions, Dr. Steiner?"

"You say you don't remember when you had a period last?"

Signals were blasting off in my head. I swallowed hard. "No, I don't, actually."

"Get dressed. Then we'll talk." He left the room.

A few minutes later, I was dressed, and Miriam came in and told me that the doctor was waiting for me in his office. I walked down the hall and sat before him.

Dr. Steiner looked at me with caring eyes. "I know you, Angelica. You are a smart girl … but I'm afraid you might be pregnant."

Three days can feel like three years when you are waiting for blood test results.

"Angelica, phone call."

I turned from my register. My boss, Mr. Gibner, held up the phone, and I went to the office to take the call.

"Angelica, this is Miriam. Dr. Steiner told me to call you."

"Did the blood tests come back?" I looked out onto 37th Avenue, gripping the phone.

"Honey," Miriam said softly, "you are six weeks pregnant."

I dropped the phone, the room spinning around me.

"Are you okay?" I heard Miriam's voice, tinny and echoing, from the dangling receiver.

I lifted the phone back to my ear. "What am I supposed to do now?" I tried to hold back tears, but they were flowing down my cheeks.

"Dr. Steiner wants you to go to the Hillcrest Women's Clinic in Flushing. He wants you to see a lady named Rebecca there. Do you have paper?"

I took a napkin and began to write the address Miriam dictated.

"If you need me, honey," she added, "please call me."

Placing the paper in my pocket, I went back to work. I counted the aisles, the boxes of cereal on the sale shelf, the lights above me on the ceiling. The tears kept flowing. My worst nightmare had come true. What was I going to do now?

That week, one of my mother's good friends from Woodside found out that her daughter was pregnant by her fiancé, and they were moving up the wedding day. Mom came home that day calling Margaret every foul name in the book. To her, this girl she'd watched grow up was "a shame to her family and a disgrace to the area."

I braced myself and asked, "Mom, hypothetically, what would you do if I were pregnant with my boyfriend's child?"

With shock on her face, she said, "You would be a disgrace to me and to this house." She paused from drying her hands. "You would be a *putana,* and I would not want you living under my roof."

The next day, I stepped into the waiting room of the Hillcrest Women's Clinic. I had given most of my savings to my parents to keep the roof over our heads, so I'd had to ask John to borrow the four hundred dollars it was going to take to get me out of danger. Four hundred dollars—blood money.

I waited three hours among a sea of pregnant women and young girls before seeing a gynecologist named Dr. Harding. She had a small frame, long blond hair, and green eyes, and her examination confirmed Dr. Steiner's findings: I was two months pregnant.

Her face filled with compassion, she asked, "What have you decided, Angelica?"

I touched the gold cross on my neck, and guilt flooded my heart. Tears began to well up and uncontrollably stream down my face. Dr. Harding took me in her arms and held me. It was more kindness than I had felt in a long time.

"I can't go home and tell my mother," I blubbered. "She'll kill me!"

"Do you want her to come here and maybe I can talk with her?" Dr. Harding asked.

I was shaking to a point where I peed right there on the examining table. Every part of me was in horrific fear of what my mother would do to me. And then there was my father, who had said of Margaret, "You know how the church feels about these matters—she and her boyfriend have sinned greatly in the eyes of God."

All I could think was, *Where were God's eyes when my uncle molested me, or when Mom beat me so hard I couldn't lay on my back? Where was he when Greg raped me?* What had I done so wrong in his eyes?

Dr. Harding helped me clean up, gave me privacy to get dressed, and brought me into her consultation office.

"Are you here with anyone?" she asked.

"No, I'm alone."

"Do you want me to call someone for you?"

"No, I just want you to tell me what I need to do to have this abortion."

"We need to do this before you finish your first trimester. Will you have someone with you that day?"

"No. Let's just get this over with."

I told my parents that since my beauty school graduation was approaching, my teacher, Anna, had invited us to an overnight stay at her house. I thought my mother would question the heck out of me, but because she knew my teacher, she bought the story and let me go.

I checked into the clinic that Friday morning, alone and frightened. The triage nurse helped me fill out the paperwork, and then Maria, Dr. Harding's nurse, greeted me. She approached in her white nurse's uniform, smiled, and took my hand.

"Everything is going to be okay," she assured me. "I promise."

In an exam room, Maria helped me disrobe and put on the gown. I lifted myself onto the table, and she gently placed the intravenous line in my arm and told me to count backwards. The next thing I recall was opening my eyes in the recovery room. Maria was there with a loving smile, stroking my forehead and my hair.

"It's over, honey," she said. "Everything went well."

I turned my head, letting my tears wet the pillow.

I stayed overnight, and the next day, Dr. Harding signed me out and called a cab. The first thing I saw when I got home was the statue of the Virgin Mary sitting ever so gently in the main window of my house. My mother was devoted to her. I thought I would be relieved to arrive home, but I suddenly understood that my burden of grief and shame would never go away.

Chapter 21:
I Pray
the Lord
My Soul
to Take

"Angelica!" I heard Betty, my parents' tenant, call from the stairs. The house my parents owned was a two-family house, and Betty and her family rented the six-room apartment that was upstairs from ours. She and I had become friendly.

"Hi, what's up?" I asked.

"You! That is, you have *not* come up to see me since Amy was born!"

Betty was kind and loving, a woman as beautiful inside as she was outside, and she'd had a baby the week before.

"I have—" I started to make up an excuse for not going upstairs to see her baby.

"Oh, no, you don't," she cut me off. "Get up here and talk to me."

I walked up to the living room and there was Amy in her bassinet. She looked like her mother: blonde, light-skinned and pink-lipped, sleeping in her pink pajamas with little teddy bears on them. She whimpered, and Betty picked her up.

"Would you like to hold her?"

I ached for my own child at that moment. "Nah," I said. "Might break her."

"You? Never. Here, take her."

Betty placed little Amy in my arms. She was weightless and nuzzled into the crook of my elbow as though she had been there since she was born. I cradled her and rocked her gently.

"You're a natural." Betty smiled, watching me with her child.

Amy began to wriggle.

"She needs a bottle," Betty said.

She made her way to the kitchen, and I felt as though instead of holding Amy, I was holding my own heart. Amy's cries grew louder as I began to shake with despair and guilt. I could not hold her any longer. I felt as though she knew that I had aborted my child, but how could a baby know?

"Would you like to feed her?" Betty asked, walking in with the bottle.

Gently, I gave Amy back to her mother. "No, I can't. I need to meet Brenda. See you later."

I ran downstairs to my room and shut the world out.

November came and the cold was setting in. Holiday decorations were cropping up all over Queens and New York City. I did not want the holidays to come. How could I celebrate Christmas without my child? I'd had no choice—my mother had tried to kill me once and would have done it again if she'd found out I was pregnant—but having that abortion had gone against every fabric of my humanity.

Meanwhile, my mother was going on and on about the Thanksgiving turkey. Since I worked in a supermarket, she didn't have to pay for many of the food items she needed, so all I heard was her daily shopping list for the coming holiday. But what was I thankful for? Nothing. Not one damned thing. My life was in shambles, and I hated every breath of it. I hated waking up in the morning, and the cold (which I usually loved) felt like knives digging at my flesh.

The Tuesday night before Thanksgiving, my beauty school teachers had planned a party for the students after class. I walked into a room filled with food, sweet treats, and a sparkling punch bowl. The food smelled wonderful, but my stomach was like a braided rope.

In the locker room, I replaced my coat with my white school uniform jacket and retrieved my hair dressing kit. Then I went to my station to set up for class. I was a senior and preparing to take my written and practical exam for my license.

An Asian lady walked in for a haircut, and since I was always the first prepared, my teacher, Anna, referred the woman to me. In those beginner days, it took me an hour to do a haircut, where years later it would take me twenty minutes. But I finished the lady and got an A. I was thrilled. I needed positive feedback that day as everything around me felt so negative.

After class, everyone mingled around the food, eating and having a great time. I could not even approach the table. The idea of having a good time made my heart ache. I instead went over to my station, cleaned and sanitized the area for the weekend, put my tools back in my kit, and returned to the locker to put them away. As I did, my straight-edged razor slipped out of the holder. I looked around the room at the small white lockers that lined the blue walls. One of the bulbs in the long florescent fixture overhead was burning out, and the light was flickering. I felt cold, and my eyes fell back to my beauty kit and the straight-edged razor. I took the razor out of its casing. Would the world be better without me? Everything about my life was wrong. Why should I live one more day?

I trembled, holding the razor. At least they would find my body after the party, I thought. I wouldn't ruin anyone's fun before then. I placed the razor against my wrist and pressed it into my skin. The steel was cold and woke me from my frantic state of mind. My hands shook so hard that I dropped the razor on the floor and could not pick it up. I stared at it as if I'd never seen it before.

The laughter from the classroom next door startled me. I picked the razor up, threw it into my kit, and closed the lid down hard. I placed my kit in my locker, put my coat on, and grabbed my purse. I did not want to cry in front of my classmates, so I held the tears in my gut.

I passed the stations where everyone was eating and having a great time. Mrs. Anna and the other teacher, Mr. Walters, came over to me. Mrs. Anna looked at me with alarm."

"Are you okay?" she asked, touching my shoulder. "You look pale."

"I'm fine," I said. "Just tired and want to go home."

"Aren't you going to stay?"

I wanted to yell at the whole room and tell them to leave me the hell alone, but I just kissed Mrs. Anna and Mr. Walters on the cheek and ran down the long wooden staircase out to the street level.

Now past nine, it was and dark and cold outside. The stores were closed, and I ran to the station to catch the 7-train for home. I stood alone at the station but for a Manhattan Transit Authority cop to the side of the pole. Tears began to swell in my eyes. I looked at the cop and thought, *No dead body to find tonight, hey, Officer?*

My train came and I rode home in silence, staring out at Queens passing me by. My stop came too fast that night. The doors opened to 61st Street and Roosevelt Avenue in Woodside. The Stop One Coffee Shop was still open; from the station, you could smell the fresh coffee brewing. I took in the aroma, then walked down the black steps and back to the station. The train came and I got back on. For the rest of the night, I went back and forth from Main Street to Roosevelt Avenue. I was cold, hungry, and wired, but I could not go home.

Finally, I read the time on an old man's watch: one a.m. For some reason, I felt threatened by the man, so I stood up and got off the train. The wind had gotten colder and it was now the day before Thanksgiving. I knew that I was going to walk into hell. It was late and I had never called home.

I walked the streets of Woodside alone, passing the coffee shop, the barbershop, the bank on Woodside Avenue, and the pub on the corner. I got to 61st Street and began walking down the winding road of private houses. Finally, I was at my block, on the corner of 44th Avenue and the six-story Winston Apartment complex. The lights were on in my kitchen and living room.

I sat on my front stoop and smoked a cigarette for courage. Then I opened the door, walked down the hall, and opened the door that led to my parents' apartment on the first floor. My mother was waiting, wooden spoon in hand.

"You were with *him,* that Greg guy! I know it!" she yelled, waving the spoon in my face.

"No, I wasn't." I pushed the spoon away.

"You're lying!" She thrust the spoon at me, but I managed to guard my head from the blow.

"Mom, please," I said quietly. "I'm tired and I want to go to sleep."

"Sleep!" She waved the spoon at me. "Sleep! I can't sleep knowing my daughter is out there slutting herself!"

"Is that all you think of me, as slut?" I wrenched the spoon from her hand and waved it in her face. "Well, you know, Mom, maybe it would be better if I were dead. Then you wouldn't have your slut of a daughter to worry about."

She stood there, aghast, as I took that fucking spoon and rammed it over my knee, breaking it in half. I dropped the two halves on the floor and walked away. For once, she didn't follow.

PART III
MARRIAGE
AND
FORGOTTEN
DREAMS

Chapter 22:
New
Beginnings

F our years later, I found myself married to John LoCascio.

No one was more surprised than I was when I fell in love with John. But after the trauma with Greg and my almost-suicide attempt, John was someone I felt safe with. He made me laugh, never looking for anything more than my friendship and love. The more time I spent with him, the more I realized I loved him; and the more I loved him, the more he matured into a man I knew would be a good husband and father.

John and I were married on September 13, 1980. Our first two years of marriage were typical: a couple working hard at the relationship while dealing with our respective jobs. John was a clerk accountant at Springs Mills Incorporated, working the usual nine-to-five shift. I was a full-time hairdresser and makeup artist in a high-style beauty salon in Jackson Heights called Dino's Hair Place. After many relentless jobs in the business, I had found this position, and Dino trained me to be a great hairdresser. As I gained more experience, I eventually became the manager of the salon, alongside Dino's sister. The downside of this career growth was that I often worked from eight in the morning until nine at night.

"Hey, what time did you leave work?" John asked as I strolled into our four-room apartment in Sunnyside, Queens, New York.

The house smelled great. John was preparing steak in our tiny kitchen. There were Birchwood cabinets that graced the walls for storage, and we had a small table right under the window. A narrow shelf held a toaster, can opener, radio, and cooking utensils. On the other wall was our full-size white refrigerator. The steak was sizzling on our stainless steel stove, and on the side were French fries and string beans—I was hungry.

"I left around seven thirty," I said, "but the bus was late."

I walked a few feet to our bedroom and placed my purse and coat down on my bed. I love blue, and our bedroom was furnished with a royal blue bedspread, blue satin drapes, and white Victorian lace curtains, with doilies to match. The carpet was a plush light gray, and the furniture was French walnut with a fan design on the bed's headboard and on my triple-mirrored dresser.

"So how was your day?" John asked as I went over to give him a kiss. He was as thin as he'd always been, able to eat like a horse and maintain his flat stomach. He was standing there in his gray sweats and Bermuda t-shirt; we had gone there on our honeymoon.

"Long," I replied, helping John bring our dinner to the table. We were saving for a formal dining room set. Until then, we ate at an old blonde wood kitchen table we'd bought secondhand. It was decorated with a green lace tablecloth, and I'd stolen four wooden folding chairs from my parents' basement, covering them with tan seat cushions I purchased from Woolworths. We didn't have a china cabinet, so we used our walnut bedroom bureau, lined the drawers with towels, and placed our fine china in them. On top was my French Wedgewood tea set. On the side wall, I used a bookcase from my bedroom to store my favorite books and figurines. I loved angels, dragons, birds, animals (especially wild ones), and knights and swords; the latter were on the shelves gracing and guarding my room.

"You look tired," said John, eating his French fries.

"I got my period today. I feel like crap."

"Ah. So go rest after dinner."

"Is that all you have to say?" I asked, agitated. "'Rest'? Hon, I want to have a baby, and let's face it—I am not getting pregnant."

All I wanted was to have a baby. I didn't want to have my kids in my thirties as both my mother and mother-in-law had. I wanted to be a young mom, but I was already twenty-five and my body was not complying.

"Hey, so we'll have fun trying," he said, grabbing my hand from across the table and smiling like a stud bull.

I pulled away. "You know it's bad enough that all my married cousins are parents already. Then your cousin Dennis gets his girlfriend pregnant and I have to hear *your* mother complain that *she* is not a grandmother—yet. I don't feel like hearing, 'We'll have fun trying,' okay?" I snapped.

"Relax. It'll happen!"

Relax, I thought after dinner. How could I relax? In the fourth month of our marriage, I had found out I was pregnant. I was ecstatic, but I lost the baby at the end of my second month. I thought about this as John and I cleaned the table and washed the dishes. *Fine,* I thought. *I'll try to relax.* I sat down for a while to read *The Once and Future King* for the twentieth time. When I began to yawn, I took two Midol for the cramps and went to bed.

But I couldn't sleep.

The shadows on the walls from the light outside allowed me to count the ceiling tiles, and my mind drifted back to my abortion, remembering my hospital stay. God was punishing me, I thought. The abortion was still my secret; not even my husband knew. In that moment, I felt that I would never have a child of my own. I turned over and cried myself to sleep.

A few months later, John drummed up the courage to see a specialist. A friend had suggested that maybe it wasn't my fault that I wasn't conceiving; maybe John's motility rate was the answer. As I put on my makeup in preparation to accompany him to the doctor's office, a rush of guilt ran through me. Could I really put John through this? I knew the exam would not be invasive, but to imply that *he* might be at fault seemed wrong. After all, I was the one who had had an abortion and the one who'd had the miscarriage.

After seeing the doctor that day, the answer was clear: John's sperm count and motility rate were superb. Sitting in a diner looking out the window toward Queens Boulevard, I sipped my wine and remembered Dr. Roberts smiling at us, saying, "Your husband could sire a hundred children at once— that is how fertile he is!"

I took the rest of my wine down fast. "Waitress, can you bring me another?" I called.

A round this time, some old ghosts began to resurface in my life. At work one day, I was cutting a client's hair when it felt as if a hot dull knife were slicing down into my side; instantly, I recognized the pain from my high school days. In less severe amounts, it had been going on for about a year, but when I'd complained to my doctor, tests showed nothing. This particular day, though, the pain was different: searing as it ran down my left leg. I could not stand and ran to the bathroom. I was bleeding heavily.

"Angelica!" Tina, one of the girls I worked with, knocked on the bathroom door. "Are you okay?"

"No, please finish off Diane for me—I need to go home."

Dino called me a cab, sent me home, and told me to call in the morning.

John rushed me into Boulevard Hospital in Astoria that night. It was the same scenario as back in the gym at Bryant when Mrs. Yanodious had come to my rescue. I lay on the gurney in the hospital, with John holding my hand. He was pale as a ghost.

"I'll be fine, hon," I said. "You'll see."

His hazel eyes were frightened. "I'm worried."

"What is going on with you?" said Dr. Carey, my gynecologist, as he strode down the hall.

"She came home from work in a lot of pain," said John.

"I'm bleeding heavily and my stomach feels as if I'm on fire," I said.

Dr. Carey felt my stomach, and I pulled up in agony.

"I'm keeping you overnight and doing some tests in the morning. In the meantime, I'm ordering some painkillers."

An hour later, I was up in my hospital room. John kissed me sweetly and left for home.

The next day, the orderly brought me down for an ultrasound. At that time, ultrasounds were a new type of X-ray. They used water, magnetic energy, and sound waves to see images of the uterus, cervix, and bladder.

The technician, a young African-American woman, gave me a quart of water and told me to drink the whole thing. I would not be able to use the bathroom until the test was over. So on the table I went, and she slathered an ice-cold green gel all over my belly. Then she began to roll a smooth plastic ball over my skin. It, too, was ice-cold, but after a few seconds, I did not feel it—I was too amazed by what I was seeing on the black and white computer screen before us.

"What is that?" I asked the technician.

"That cone-like image is your uterus, and that balloon there is your bladder; I can see that you really need to pee."

She rolled the ball over my left side, and I winced in pain.

"I'm sorry," she said.

"Not your fault—can you see what is going on?"

She smiled reassuringly. "Your doctor will tell you everything."

Before I was discharged the next day, my doctor gave me the bad news: I had a blockage in my left fallopian tube, with a cyst the size of a baseball on my ovary and some fibroids like small peas in my uterus. I needed surgery.

Standing by my bed, my doctor and my husband both looked down at me. John sat on the edge of the bed and held my hand.

"So will this surgery help me have a baby?" I asked Dr. Carey. In some ways, I was relieved the problem had a name and answers.

My doctor was a short, thin man with dark hair, light olive skin, and a Lebanese accent. "Yes, it can, Angelica, but it will require some reconstructive work."

"Will you do the operation?"

"Yes, I will. I'll give you a prescription to stop your period, and in a few weeks when you're stronger, we'll do the surgery."

"Thanks, Doctor," I said, and he touched my hand kindly before walking out the door.

Two weeks later, I was back at work. My doctor had given me Provera to stop my period and to keep my hormones at bay. Every one of my colleagues was worried about me. Dino and the girls didn't want me at the salon, but I could not stay home and think about the surgery—I needed to keep busy. Still, the girls were like a bunch of big sisters and mother hens; they made sure every day that I ate well and took a break so I would not overexert myself.

It was late October, and the holidays were coming; after the surgery, I would be off my feet for two weeks and out of the salon for six, so I wanted to make sure my mother had her permanent before the operation.

"Mom, sit here while I process your hair," I said.

Mom was sitting by the black shampoo sink, ready with rods in her hair.

"Angelica, dear, good luck with everything," said Dorothy, one of my regular clients. "I will keep you in my prayers." She gave me a hug and held me close to her broad frame, which was always well dressed for a woman in her mid-sixties.

"Thanks, Dorothy," I said, returning her embrace.

"Mrs. Marquise, I don't know what I would do without your daughter. She makes me feel special every time I am here." I was blushing, and Dorothy added, "It's true, and my hair is lovely."

"Well, so are you," I said.

Dorothy gave me a quick kiss on the cheek. "Dino and Tina will keep me apprised."

I began to process my mother's hair, squeezing chemicals on the blue and pink rods that were curled in her thick white hair.

"One of these days I'll be telling everyone I'm having a baby, Mom." My hands were soaked with white creamy lotion, carefully guiding the mixture in her hair.

She took a paper towel and wiped some excess liquid that was dripping down her cheek. "I don't know why you're in such a rush."

"Mom, you know how much I want a child."

She met my eyes in the mirror. "I can't afford to have a grandchild."

"You can't *afford* to have a grandchild? Mom, it will be John and I raising our children, not you." Her remark made me so angry that if I were not at work, I would have caused a scene.

She looked right at me. "Yes, you will, Angelica, but I am saving for a trip and don't have the money for a grandchild right now."

I finished the processing and went in back by the dispensary. There was a bottle of Clorox bleach sitting on the shelf. For a second, I imagined myself pouring that bleach in the processing bottle and squeezing it all over my mother's head.

One week later, I was in the hospital. It was the day of the surgery, which was scheduled for two that afternoon. I lay in bed watching a soap opera, trying to relax.

"Hi, doll!" My mom came strolling in my room and kissed me on the cheek. Every relaxed bone in my body cringed when she walked in.

"Mom, I told you that John would call after the surgery was over."

"You make me feel as though you don't want me around! I'm your mother and I'm worried about you."

I wanted to kick her out. Yes, I loved her. Yes, she was my mother. But after the remark she'd made at the salon, and what she had already put me through in life, I did not want her around that day.

A short while later, a young orderly came to claim me. He smiled, and he and an assistant helped me onto the gurney. They strapped me down and draped a blanket on me, and John came over to give me a kiss. My mother followed suit. I wanted to turn my cheek, but I was silently saying some Hail Marys and Our Fathers, asking God to guide the hands of my surgeon. What would those prayers mean if I wished malice on my mother?

I woke up in the recovery room. My vision was blurry from the anesthesia, and my doctor and my husband were at my side.

"Everything went well," Dr. Carey said.

"Thank God! Will I be able to have a baby now?" I asked through the cobwebs in my mind.

"Yes, you will, but first you need your rest."

A week later, I was home in my apartment. A WELCOME HOME ANGELICA sign greeted me from the arch between the dining and living rooms. It was so good to be home.

I was not allowed to bend, so John helped me put my pajamas on. I ate a bowl of cereal and then went to lie down on the couch. All I wanted to do was rest. I had not been home in almost ten days, but the doorbell soon rang; as if one set of parents weren't enough, two walked right through my dining room and straight to me.

"Hi, sweetheart!" Dad said, leaning to give me a kiss.

"What are you doing here?" I asked the group.

"Mom dragged me here tonight." Dad looked at my mother, who looked like she was itching to get to me.

"Hi, doll." Mom pushed through my mother- and father-in-law, showing that she was the leading lady of the evening.

I tried to pull up from the couch but had stitches in my lower abdomen and could not move quickly. "I asked all of you to come tomorrow night," I said, "not now."

"Well, I was talking to your mother," said Doris, my mother-in-law, "and she said that she and Adam were on the way, so Daddy and I thought we'd come over, too."

I dropped my head into the plush cushion of my couch. *Why don't people listen to me?* I fumed. *Go home already—just go the hell home.* I wanted to choke the bunch of them.

All during my wedding planning, the moms never listened to me. I said no engagement party, and my mother-in-law planned one without alerting my mother, so my mother got back at her by hosting a second party, inviting them but not allowing them to contribute. Then, once John and I had our apartment, I wanted to be alone to paint and do my own decorating. Both mothers showed up to "help." I didn't want to unpack my good china, but my mother grabbed the dishes out of the box, and Doris took them to the sink to wash them, only to almost break the whole stack. As for the dresses, Doris—an excellent seamstress—wanted to make my wedding gown, but Mom went ballistic; she was the mother of the bride, she said, and the groom's mother had no rights in this department. Finally, when we went on our honeymoon, I left my keys with my in-laws, and they brought cousins in from out of town to see my home without permission. When we returned, half our things were out of place. Now here they all were again, not allowing me a day of rest after surgery.

"Hey, hon, I thought we could get either pizza or Chinese food tonight," John said.

I shot John a death stare. "Did you know they were all coming over?"

"I wanted to surprise you."

"You promised me a homemade dinner."

"Yeah, but I thought you'd like some company."

I grabbed the arm of my couch and slowly pulled myself up. My abdomen was so tender that I could hardly stand. I looked at both mothers sitting across from me on the love seat, then hobbled into my bedroom to lie down.

The holidays came and went. I was hoping I'd be pregnant before St. Patrick's Day, but my body was not obliging. My doctor had me taking my temperature to monitor my ovulation cycle. If my temperature lowered to ninety-five or ninety-six degrees, I was ready to get pregnant. It made making love very mechanical.

Depression was setting in. It seemed like everyone around me—friends, cousins, strangers—were walking into my area showing off their springtime-pregnant bellies. It was all I could do to keep from convincing myself that

God still had it in for me and I was never going to see a child in my life.

Easter was on the horizon, and I decided that I was going to purchase my formal dining room set before another holiday passed. John and I scoured furniture stores until we found the perfect set in Huffman Koos. It was a simple yet elegant walnut china cabinet, table, and six chairs, just the right size for our dining room and for me to enjoy entertaining family and friends.

It was Holy Saturday, and John and I went to the Vigil Mass. He was tired from working overtime that day, so he went to bed as soon as we returned home. I was so excited about my dining set that I stayed up to set the table and place my good china, crystal glasses, and Lenox pieces—which were still boxed from my bridal shower—in the display cabinet. On television, there was a special about the Shroud of Turin, the shroud said to have the face of Jesus burned on it during his burial in the tomb of Joseph of Arimathea. The word "blood" was mentioned so many times on the show that a light went off in my head, and I suddenly stopped organizing my dishes on the glass shelves: I had not gotten my period in quite some time.

I grabbed the calendar off the kitchen wall and my temperature chart and counted the days since my last cycle. *One, two, three* . . . all the way up to forty. My finger shook as I turned the page of the calendar. *Forty-one, forty-two, forty-three* . . . I was shivering, hoping that what I was discovering at that wee hour was true. *Sixty, sixty-one, sixty-two,* until I arrived at Easter Sunday. I repeated the count three times. Three times the count came to sixty-two. My hands were shaking as I held the calendar and the chart. Could this be? Was I really pregnant? I had to be. And I had to believe that God wanted this for me, or else what was there to believe in?

"Hon!" I exclaimed, running into the bedroom. "Hon! Wake up, John!" Sometimes my husband slept so soundly a bomb could go off without him hearing it.

"Come on, hon!" I kept shaking him. "Hey, we're going to have a baby!" I finally screamed.

"A what?" He rolled over, looking at me as if a ghost was in our bedroom.

"I've been counting the chart and the calendar—look!" I pushed the calendar in front of his half-shut eyes.

John pushed me away and walked into the bathroom as though I hadn't just spoken. A couple of minutes later, he came back and took the calendar from me. "Okay, now show me!"

I gave him the calendar, sat next to him, and started counting. John, an accountant, looked at the first date, then the current date, and did the math in his head.

"Holy shit!" he said. "You're pregnant!" John grabbed me and kissed me so sweetly.

I was so happy I wanted to run out into the street and tell the whole neighborhood, but all I did was lie there wrapped in John's arms.

"Do we tell everyone tomorrow?" he asked.

I sat up in bed in my lotus position. "Not yet. I want to see Dr. Carey before we make it official."

John leaned against the headboard. "Why?"

"Hon, after everything I've been through, I need to hear it from Dr. Carey first. Then we can tell everyone."

"But what's the difference?" John said, his face twisting.

"Because that's the way I want it right now."

"So does this mean it's your way or no way?"

"Yes, John. It is my way or no way right now." I walked into the kitchen for a glass of milk, then went into the living room. This was my baby, and nobody was going to tell me how to do things. Not anymore.

CHAPTER 23:
A GIFT
FROM ABOVE

Right after Easter, I made an appointment with Dr. Carey. He took urine and four vials of blood. I felt as if he was a vampire collecting blood for his blood bank.

As I lay on the table waiting for him to return with news, a knot formed in my stomach. What if I wanted this so much and it was just another cycle gone wrong? I found myself counting the ceiling tiles—just as I counted the bricks at home when things went wrong. *Twenty-three, twenty-four, twenty-five ...*

"Angelica, please get dressed and join me in my office," Dr. Carey said, interrupting my count. He smiled and left the room.

"Oh, God, please let this be true," I said out loud as I pulled my clothes on.

John was already sitting in Dr. Carey's office. I sat in the chair beside him and held his hand.

Dr. Carey walked in with my chart in one hand and a cup of coffee in another. "Well, Mom and Dad, baby is due December 14," he said, lighting up my world.

I shot up from the chair. "It's true, Doc? It's really true? How far am I?" I was shaking from head to toe.

"You're nine weeks pregnant," he said, hugging me.

"Hey, Dad!" I said to John. We embraced, and he gazed at me with tears of love in his eyes.

Keeping my pregnancy a secret was hard, especially when my husband wanted to open his mouth every time he was on the phone or with either set of our parents. I wanted to tell everyone, too, but I also wanted to keep it to myself for a while.

It was coming up on Mother's Day, and John and I fought that week about keeping our secret. John was going over to his parents', and I reminded him to please not say anything.

"What the hell is wrong with you? Why are you acting like this?" John shouted at me while I dressed for work.

"Why? Because with everything I went through to get pregnant, your mother and mine both made me feel as though I was worthless!" I yelled across the hall.

"So I have to pay for it? Damn it, I'm the father!" His face was twisted with anger as he pointed to himself.

"Yes, you are, but I didn't hear you say anything to your mother or mine when they kept joking about me not getting pregnant or having to raise our kids." I could hardly zip up my pants anymore.

"They were just joking!" he said, as if I had been too dense to get their humor.

"I'm late for work." I picked up my purse and jacket and headed out the door.

Two weeks before, I had told my boss and the girls that I was expecting. I had to, as some of the wave lotions and hair dyes were making me sick. If I wanted to continue to work, my coworkers had to know about my pregnancy so they could help me.

It was the Saturday before Mother's Day, and during my break, I ran to the store to pick up a pair of pants with an elastic band. It was the first time since being overweight in high school that I needed a pair of stretch pants. It felt strange, yet comfortable—I could breathe!

After lunch, Dorothy, my regular, sat down and I began to comb out her hair. Standing behind my blue Grecian designer chair, I teased her thick brown hair and started forming her style. Dorothy always sported a French twist with a side French braid. Meanwhile, one of my other clients, Arlene, had paid her bill and was mingling with the other customers, wishing all a happy Mother's Day. Arlene was a fine blonde Jewish yenta—buxom, well dressed, and always smiling.

She gave Dorothy a kiss. "Mazel tov! Happy Mother's Day!" Then she looked at me.

Everyone in the shop knew how much I wanted to be a mom, but they were all discreet, respecting my desire to keep the pregnancy quiet. I could tell they were trying not to say too much when they looked at me that day. Dino was blow-drying a client's hair, and he stared at me in the mirror and smiled with a question on his face. I looked back at his reflection, feeling scared to say anything but bursting inside with the desire to tell everyone so I could celebrate, too.

Dino shut off the dryer, put it down, and placed his hand on my shoulder. He smiled like the big brother mentor he was. "Come in the back a minute."

I followed him, and in the dispensary, he touched my cheek. "Come on, Angeliki," he said, using his term of endearment for me—my name in Greek. "Let's open that bottle and celebrate today."

I wanted to so much, but I was afraid it would all blow up in my face.

Dino took the bottle of champagne out of the small refrigerator. "Shall I pop it?" he asked, again with that brotherly smile that assured me I was doing the right thing.

I nodded silently, and with a flick of his thumb, the cork popped.

Astra, Dino's lovely wife, grabbed some cups from the cabinet. "Angeliki is going to have a baby!" she shouted across the salon floor, pouring the bubbly in small paper cups and handing them out.

Jackson Heights was a diverse area. We were Greek, Jewish, Italian, German, and everything else, and blessings were bestowed on me in every language imaginable that day. It was the first formal acknowledgement of my child being in the world, or at least in my body. It was the sweetest celebration I'd ever known.

On Sunday, John and I went to church and then met our parents at Rinaldo's Italian Restaurant. The bistro was a cozy eatery with red and white checkered tablecloths and dark brown chairs. When we walked in the door, the aroma invited us to linger.

Our parents were there, along with my brother, Adam, and John's brother, Simon. We all kissed and hugged and took our seats. John and I sat next to each other, and the waitress came and took our orders.

I glanced around the table at my mom in her lovely pink dress and Doris, with her short blond hairdo and signature lavender ensemble. My dad wore his navy suit and red tie, and my father-in-law his green leisure suit. Adam, who lit a cigarette, sported his new Patrick Swayze haircut, designer jeans, and Ralph Lauren knit top. Then there was my brother-in-law in his wrinkled crushed cotton shirt and brown pants, his hair falling in his eyes. Our family—about to hear our secret.

The waitress brought over our drinks and appetizers. After she placed the food on the table and poured the first round of wine, I scurried to the bathroom and took a long pee. After I rejoined the group, I squeezed John's thigh.

"Let's do this," I said.

Under the table, I had a brown shopping bag. In it was a bouquet of flowers and a card for each mother. I took out the flowers and cards and gave one to my mother and the other to Doris, hugging and kissing them before returning to my seat.

"Well open your cards," I said, watching the scene unfold.

"I don't understand," said my mother after reading her card.

My brother took the card, read it, then read it again. "Am I going to be an uncle?" he asked, smiling at me with his big puppy dog brown eyes.

"More like a godfather if you'd do me the honor, brother." Chills ran down my legs as my brother rose from his chair and hugged me so hard I could barely breathe.

Then everyone began to realize what was happening.

My father shot up from his chair, and I smiled, saying, "Grandpa."

"Ah, sweetheart, I love you," he said, and he bent down and kissed my belly right there in front of a hundred people in the restaurant. Rising, he grabbed me and kissed me on the forehead. "I love you so much!"

My mother, looking at me taking in all the attention, pulled away from her chair and came over to me. "Grandma, huh?" she said and gave me a kiss on the cheek.

"Cara!" my mother-in-law exclaimed. The nickname meant "little kitten" in Italian. She gave me a wet kiss and added, "I don't want to be Grandma. I want to be Nonna."

I heard a pop: it was the waitress opening a champagne bottle. With a smile, she poured the bubbly for everyone.

"So, Uncle, how does that feel?" said my husband to his brother.

"All right, I guess."

"Do you know how long we've known?" John said, relieving himself of his guarded secret.

Guarded—now that was the word for it, and that was how I spent my next six months of pregnancy. At work, it was easy—I could be myself—but with both mothers, it was a fight to see who could get my attention.

My mother repeated things like, "You know I am more the grandmother to this child than Doris. After all, I am the mother of the mom-to-be."

As for my mother-in-law, one night during dinner she proclaimed, "We have to plan a baby shower."

"Nope," I said. I would not have another party from her or my mother. No baby showers, no parties. I was not going through the chaos that both mothers had put me through during my engagement. That kind of tension between the families was not happening with my child.

I spent my pregnancy building walls around me, trying to hold onto whatever respect I could and constantly telling two women who acted more like overgrown children to keep out of my business.

One day, my mother went with me to the doctor. Everything had been going well up until the end of my pregnancy. I was not dropping, and Dr. Carey was concerned about my delivery.

"You are three weeks to your due date, Angelica, and I'm worried. Your cervix and pelvis aren't opening properly to deliver your child."

My mom shot me a worried look. "So what does this mean, Doctor?" she asked.

"If her pelvis does not open, I may have to do a Cesarean section."

"Oh, no, I won't permit it," she said.

"What do you mean *you* won't permit it?" I asked, insulted.

"Having a C-section is not 'giving birth.' It's not natural in God's eyes."

There it was again, I thought. The same attitude she'd flaunted throughout my childhood.

"Mrs. Marquise, I don't know where you acquired your information, but I assure you, your daughter will give birth either by her body or with my assistance."

"No," my mother insisted. "That is a sin according to God—I know! I am Catholic!"

She was not doing this again to me, not now. It was enough that I still bore the pain of my abortion; she was not shoveling more into the pail. "Mom, go home," I said. "I don't need this now."

"I am your mother, and I won't have you sin in the eyes of God giving birth to *my* grandchild."

I looked at Dr. Carey and pulled up slowly but surely from my chair. "Mom, this is my child, not yours. Dr. Carey, I'll either see you next week or in the hospital."

With that, I walked out of the office. Instead of going home the usual way through Skillman Avenue, I walked up to Roosevelt Avenue and then down 49th Street. I promised myself that if Mom followed me home, I'd keep the doors locked and not let her in. She didn't follow.

Two weeks later, I was in the hospital in labor. John had called everyone and told them that the baby was coming. The grandparents wanted to come to the hospital, but I forbade it. I knew the mothers were not going to behave, and I was not giving birth while trying to mediate from the labor room!

After almost twenty-four hours of labor complications, my baby's heart rate was lowering, and Dr. Carey had to place an internal fetal monitor inside my womb. He also ordered an oxygen count, which meant they had to place a narrow scalpel in my womb, take a scraping of my baby's scalp, and test the blood for white and red blood cell count and oxygen mass. John was so worried and tired, trying to keep up with everything, including my yelling, screaming, and cursing through the labor. It wasn't fair.

"Get away from me!" I yelled at the nurse. "Please just cut me and get this damned baby out!"

I squeezed John's hand so hard for so many hours that it must have felt like a boulder was crushing it.

"Take deep breaths," he said soothingly, recalling the Lamaze lessons we'd taken to help with labor and delivery.

"Bite me already—get this baby the hell out of me!" I screamed again, so loudly they must have heard me in China.

Dr. Carey called John out to the hall, and a few minutes later, John came back in.

"Hon, listen to me," he said. "They are getting the operating room ready down the hall. Dr. Carey is going to do a C-section."

As he spoke, the nurses came in and removed all the monitors. I had been given an epidural and was numb from the waist down, so I was well prepared and relieved.

John held my hand as they wheeled me into the operating room where Dr. Carey greeted him, scrubbed and ready.

"John, go get something to eat," Dr. Carey said. "I'll call you when your baby is here." John gave me a big hug and kiss and left. I watched him walk out the door, and my heart began to race.

The anesthesiologist told me to take a deep breath and count backwards from one hundred.

I remember seeing a sheet divide my sight from right under my breasts. My whole body felt numb, as if I were floating, yet I was very awake. The next thing I recall was feeling someone's hands on me.

"Take a deep breath, Angelica!" I heard the nurse say.

I took a deep breath.

"Hold it until I say release!"

I did what she said, all the while looking at the circle of lights above me.

"Now release!" she shouted.

"You have a fine baby girl!" shouted Dr. Carey, with laughter in his voice.

The baby was wailing. "Is she okay?" I asked, straining to look over the sheet. "Is she okay?"

The labor and delivery nurse came over to me. She had blood on her gloves and gown, but her eyes were smiling as she looked down at me. "Your daughter is perfect! You did a great job, Mommy."

Those were the last words I heard until I woke up with my husband next to me in the recovery room. I was freezing, and my nurse rolled over a tall warmer light and blanket to keep me warm.

"This is normal after birth," the nurse assured me. "Your temperature will regulate with time. Do you want to hold your daughter?"

Shifting my eyes to John, I said, "Please bring her to me."

The nurse walked away for a second and returned with my child in her arms. "Here she is, Mom."

My baby was dressed in a pink and white receiving blanket with little teddy bears on it, and a small skullcap to match. She felt like a weightless angel in my arms. She looked up at me with half-shut eyes, and yawned and whimpered and cooed. Her little heartbeat rumbled through her back and against the fold of my arms. I took her very small hand, and she gripped my right index finger. I counted her fingers: *one, two, three, four, five*. All there!

I started to cry and held her close to my body. I was consumed in my daughter's face. She was mine, all mine. My heart and soul were overwhelmed. I kissed her face and every finger on both hands. I was a mommy, and no one could take this away from me, not anyone.

John kissed me, and I looked up at him. He was so tired and had tears rolling down his face.

"I love you," he said to me. Then he kissed his daughter on the cheek. "Love you, too!"

A miracle was born that day, and her name was Andrea.

CHAPTER 24:
THE JOYS OF
MOTHER
HOOD

After working every day of my life from the time I was ten, it was hard for me to adjust to being a stay-at-home mom. And as much as I wanted a baby, having someone depending on me twenty-four hours a day, seven days a week, was daunting. Yet there were days in the beginning where I would just watch Andrea sleep in her princess cradle. I had not wanted a bassinet, and when John and I were in Pennsylvania one day, I'd spotted the perfect blonde wooden cradle, an exact duplicate of those used during the Civil War. It stood at least three feet above the floor on a pedestal, which held the cradle on an axis. Above it, a gorgeous yellow lace veil crowned my daughter as my little princess. I would stand there and watch her sleep. Listening to every tiny breath she took, I couldn't help but be in awe of her. She was so beautiful.

Andrea was born just sixteen days before Christmas, and she was my perfect Christmas gift—my child, as Mary had hers in Jesus. John and I had invited the family for Christmas dinner, and I was not feeling that well the day before. I wanted to cancel, but John was eager to celebrate with his new child, so he helped me make spaghetti sauce and meatballs. We would keep it simple.

Christmas morning was hectic, but John and I wanted to take Andrea to eleven a.m. Mass. That week the temperature had been in the mid-thirties, and with Andrea's doctor's advice, I was able to take her out in her carriage for short walks, just to get some air. After being in the hospital for a week and then home, the cold air felt so good on my face. But Christmas morning it was only twenty-five degrees, and we dared not take Andrea out.

I was dressing Andrea when I heard a knock on the door. John went to open it. "Hi, Fran," he greeted our landlady.

"Where's the baby?" asked a little voice.

"In the bedroom," I heard John answer.

Little Heather and her younger sister Charlene walked right in to Andrea's bedroom. Heather, a wide-eyed nine-year-old, put her chin on the dressing table to watch me, while Fran played with five-year-old Charlene on the floor.

"Are you still going to church?" Fran asked. She was a long-haired brunette, beautifully shaped and in her early thirties.

"We were hoping, but I can't take Andrea out."

"Leave her with me," Fran offered. "The kids are itching to baby-sit."

I could not have asked for a better sign.

The phone rang, and John went to answer it. "Hi, Mom," he said, leaving me to wonder which mother was on the line. "No, that's okay. Fran is taking care of the baby while we go to church … Ang, what time do you want my parents over?"

I looked at Fran. "And so it begins," I said, rolling my eyes. "Three, I told her yesterday!"

A few seconds later, the phone rang again. "Hi, Mom" John said, letting me know by his tone that it was my mother this time. "No, Fran is baby-sitting while we go to church."

"Fran? Who the hell is she? I'm the grandmother!" I could hear my mother's voice from feet away. "Put my daughter on!"

John handed me the phone.

"What is this? I belong there taking care of my grandchild, not some stranger!"

"Mom, Fran is not a stranger. She is a friend, and I said it was okay!"

"Oh, so you don't love or trust your mother with your child?"

Just like that, I was no longer the twenty-eight-year-old new mom. I was sixteen all over again, being berated.

"Mom, this is how I want it today. As I said yesterday, come at three o'clock."

192

"I'm coming now!" she yelled.

"No, Mom, you're not." With that, I hung up the phone.

Fran took Andrea down to her apartment with the girls. John wanted to drive to church, but the walk felt great. When we returned, I noticed my brother's cowboy boots on the landing near my door.

Heather ran out to greet us and waved for us to come in. John and I walked into Fran's apartment.

"Beware, your whole family is upstairs," Fran said wryly.

"What the hell—are you kidding?" I was enraged.

"Yeah, your mother wanted to take Andrea from me and bring her up, but she and the girls were sleeping on my bed, and I would not allow her in." Fran pointed to her apartment door. "She told me that I had no right to keep her grandchild from her."

I looked at my baby sleeping peacefully on Fran's bed. With all the pillows around her, she looked like an angel.

"I told her that I have every right," Fran continued, upset for me, "as you did not give me permission to give your child to another person—grandparent or not."

"Do you want me to bring her up?" asked John.

I again gazed at my sleeping child. "No," I said, tapping my fingers on Fran's counter. "No, I am not going to take her up yet. I am going to walk into our house, take off my coat, and if it's a fight she wants, then let's have it. She is not going to ruin my daughter's first Christmas!"

"She really didn't mean anything, Ang," said John, thinking he was calming me.

"Oh, she means every thought, word, and deed, and I am not swallowing it."

In our apartment, my brother was sprawled on the couch watching television, with my dad across from him in the dining room reading the paper.

"Hi, doll!" Mom walked through the hall. "Merry Christmas." She came over with a smile and kissed me on the cheek.

I backed away. "Merry Christmas to you, too," I said back through gritted teeth.

"Hey, sweetheart." Dad came down the hall, giving me a big hug and kiss.

My brother walked right past us and into the kitchen. I looked over at him as he poured a glass of soda: my kitchen was a mess. Sighing, I went into my bedroom and took off my coat.

"I put the gravy back up and put the meatballs in the sauce," said my mom, following me into the room. She smiled widely, waiting for thanks.

Hanging my coat in the closet, I said, "I told you not to come until three, Mom."

"Thought I could help you," she answered innocently.

"Mom, it is *not* helping when I told you to stay home and you come anyway."

"Well, that Fran person would not give me my granddaughter," she shot back.

"And she was right not to. I left Andrea with Fran—not you." I walked away, back to my kitchen. "You could have at least cleaned the oven."

"You don't love me."

"You don't respect me," I replied.

"What gives, you two? It's Christmas," Dad said, looking first at Mom and then at me.

"Dad, I told Mom to be here at three, not noon."

Dad looked disapprovingly at Mom. "She told me that you wanted her here early."

A little voice interrupted us from the doorway. "Mommy sent me up to tell you that Andrea is crying," Heather said.

I followed slowly behind Heather, as my abdomen was still healing. I was met in Fran's apartment by the sound of sanity—the cry of my child calmed the rage that was brewing due to my mother's incessant need for attention. Fran was holding her and about to give her a bottle. When she saw me, she smiled and said to Andrea, "Here's Mommy!"

I took my child in my arms and cradled her on my shoulder, nuzzling her. She cried loudly in my ear, but it was the cry of my freedom to me. I sat down on Fran's couch and fed her there. Though Andrea was just sixteen days old, she had a good appetite. She took an ounce, burped, and then had two more ounces. After she was satisfied, I placed her on my shoulder and began to rub her back to see if I could get any more gas from her tiny belly. Andrea snuggled into my neck and fell asleep.

A few minutes later, I left Fran's family to their holiday. I had not even walked through the door before my mother was on Andrea like a fly to sticky paper. It was all I could do to close the door to Andrea's room and dress her. Mom opened the door without knocking, of course. As I began to change Andrea's diaper, Mom's hands brushed mine aside to take over.

"Mom, go back to the kitchen. I will dress my own child."

"But I'm her grandmother," she said, taking Andrea's dress from me.

I yanked it back. "Mom, go check on dinner, okay?"

"But I want to hold her." Her hands stretched out like Andrea was her prey, not her grandchild.

The doorbell rang just as the white wall clock decorated with a guardian angel read two thirty. I finished up Andrea, and there they were—the Lo-Cascio threesome. My in-laws were early, of course, with my mother-in-law trying to get in on the action before my mother did. Doris's expression when she saw my mother already there dressed in a Christmas apron was priceless. I was laughing so hard inside that my barely healed incision hurt, and I loved the way it ached. It let me know I had some control.

CHAPTER 25:
MYSTERIES
BEGIN AND
THE FAMILY
GROWS

Raising Andrea was a task at times. She was one of those babies who was a perfect gem at infancy, but once she found her legs and voice— look out! By the age of two, Andrea was bright, knew her words, and had a temper that could bring down the Empire State Building.

Even at that young age, Andrea hated the normal routine of her day being disrupted. She enjoyed her time with me, especially when we ate breakfast together before we went out for walks or visits to the park, and I'd read to her from *The Lost Kitten* and *Goodnight Moon*. Then, while I did laundry, she would play in the playpen or watch "Sesame Street" or "Zoobilee Zoo," dancing to the theme music as it played on TV.

One day during "Zoobilee Zoo," we were singing and laughing when I heard the doorbell ring. I was not expecting anyone.

"What are you doing here?" I asked Doris as I opened the door.

"Daddy and I parked the car around the block and thought we'd stop in," she said. *Daddy* was what she called my father-in-law.

"I see," I replied.

"How's Andrea?" asked John, my father-in-law, coming through the front door.

"Yoo-hoo, Andrea!" Doris shouted.

We all walked inside the apartment, where Andrea was sitting on the floor. "Hey, Cara, come to Nonnie!" Doris said.

Andrea picked herself up off the floor and waddled her little toddler butt into her room. Doris chased after her, scooping her off the ground. Andrea wailed long and loud, and Doris said, "Cara, what's wrong!"

Andrea stretched her arms forward for me to take her. My mother-in-law would not give her up. She kept bouncing her gently up and down, and Andrea wailed louder.

"Cara, Nonnie loves you. Why are you crying?"

Andrea pushed against her grandmother and again stretched her arms to me. I grabbed her, and she wrapped her arms around my neck, screaming in my ear.

"Bella Cara!" Doris stroked her face, but Andrea pushed Doris's hand away. My father-in-law walked in behind Doris, and Andrea wailed again. "Bella, bella, bella!" my mother-in-law started singing and reached again for Andrea.

I pulled my daughter closer to me. "Do you not get it? Andrea does not want to be held or touched right now, and what are you doing here, anyway?"

"We were parking and thought we'd come up," John said.

"Come on, honey!" Doris beseeched Andrea.

"We brought lunch!" John reached into a bag of cold cuts they'd purchased from the corner deli and took out a slice of American cheese, Andrea's favorite. He began to hand it to her and she wailed again, pushing it away. Her cries were becoming hysterical.

"Please, I don't mean to be disrespectful, but you have to leave," I said to Doris.

"We'll wait," said Doris in her little-girl voice.

"No. She is upset, and I need to calm her down."

"But we can wait!"

That day was an accurate depiction of my life at the time: my in-laws always coming unannounced, and Andrea rebelling against the intrusion. Neither of us liked people invading our space. I complained to John, but he saw it as his parents wanting to show their love, so I eventually kept my displeasure to myself.

Meanwhile, John was changing. He was showing signs of fatigue and had lost thirty pounds in less than two months without trying. This had happened before—once before our wedding when he dropped twenty-five pounds in a month and had to have his tux taken in at the last minute, and once right before Andrea was born. But now there were no major events that might trigger the sudden weight loss. And at over six feet tall, John was clearly unhealthy at only one hundred and seventy five pounds. I wanted him to see a doctor, but he waved it off.

Just as I was worried about John, I began to feel ill myself. I felt as though I had an early flu bug and was spotting. I went to see Dr. Carey, and he confirmed my hope: I was having another child. He was concerned, though, about the spotting and advised me to take periodic rests during the day so that I would not miscarry.

It was a Saturday when I found out about my pregnancy, and John was home with Andrea. On the way up the steps after my appointment, I heard John singing the alphabet with her: "A, B, C, D …"

"Hi!" I said, walking through the door.

"Mommy!" Andrea shouted.

"Hi," said John, getting up to kiss me. "So what did the doctor say?"

"Well," I said, all giggly, "Andrea is going to be a big sister!"

"What?" John's face was twisted.

"We're going to have another baby!" I beamed.

"When?" he asked in an abrupt tone.

"Dr. Carey said somewhere around June 4." I paused, looking at Andrea's small bedroom. "At least it won't be cold."

John sat back in his chair and sank into the cushion, a vague expression washing over him.

"Aren't you happy?" I asked, sitting next to him.

"Just wasn't expecting it to happen so fast."

I went to hold his hand, but he pulled away. I walked into the kitchen for a minute and looked out the window. *I should be off my feet,* I thought, but John's attitude was nagging at me. I needed to tell him the rest.

"Hon, we have to talk about something," I said, returning from the kitchen. Andrea came over to me and I lifted her on my lap. I gave her a big kiss and she gave me a big one back. I loved cuddling with her; she was my little cuddle bunny.

"What's up?" he asked, tickling Andrea.

"Since I'm spotting a bit, Dr. Carey wants me off my feet as much as possible."

"Is everything okay?"

"The baby is fine, but he doesn't want me to strain. It might cause a miscarriage."

"Can you lose the baby?" he asked, but the inflection in his voice was almost one of hope.

"I could if I'm not careful."

"Well, we'll play it by ear." He got up and turned on the TV.

It was easier to keep the special issues of my pregnancy a secret from the parents. I was not in the mood for meddling mothers, so I spent much of the beginning of my pregnancy on the couch, cuddling with Andrea, reading, or watching television. Sometimes I'd venture outside so that she could play for a while in front of the house.

Everything was going well until my sixth month, when I suddenly gained eight pounds and my blood pressure lowered. One morning in the bathroom, I was unable to stop urinating. I was lightheaded, though I'd eaten a good breakfast.

"John, come home, please—I'm not feeling well. I need you to take me to the hospital," I said over the phone. Then I called my mother at work and asked her to come to take care of Andrea.

"What is going on?" Mom asked, coming in the door.

"I don't know, but something is wrong with the baby—I know it!" I was quivering.

John came running up the steps. "Ready?" He helped me with my jacket, and we left.

Dr. Carey met us at St. John's Hospital. In an emergency examining room, he checked my vitals, noting that my blood pressure was low: one hundred and five over sixty. That was not good. He took urine and blood, then sent me up to maternity.

I rolled into the maternity ward on a wheelchair, watching all the pregnant women walking the floor. Dr. Carey joined me in a temporary room he had arranged so I could rest quietly.

I stood up from the wheelchair and stretched out on the bed, which felt like a dream.

"I want to keep you here for the rest of the day," said Dr. Carey.

A few hours later, I was taken for a sonogram. The wet gel and cold ball rolled over my belly, and in an instant, I heard my baby's heartbeat. It sounded like a locomotive rushing to its destination. As the technician did the exam, she asked John and me, "Do you wanted to know the sex of the child?"

I smiled. "Yes."

She rolled the ball again on my abdomen. "Look—see what looks like a finger digit?"

We looked at the screen.

"You're looking at your son!" She smiled at me with her hazel eyes and her brown cheekbones.

"It's a boy?" John said, beaming like a stud bull. "I have a son!" he laughed. It was the first time I'd heard him laugh in a long while.

Back in my room, Dr. Carey came in with a smile. "Your son is well and growing just fine."

"So what caused me to feel so lousy today?" I asked.

"Sometimes these issues are incidental or random, but if it happens again, we'll keep you longer," he said. "Now go home to Andrea."

It was a hot spring Monday morning a couple of months later. The heat was gaining on me, and my back was cramping, reminiscent of my labor with Andrea. Andrea and I had breakfast, and I felt a bit anxious before John left for work.

"Hon, can you take off today?" I asked as he was about to walk out the door.

"I can't. I already arranged with Richard to take off Thursday for the baby's birth." He kissed me on the cheek and walked away.

I had showered and dressed for the day. After dressing Andrea, I cleared the table and went into the kitchen to do the dishes.

"Mommy, play dolls with me!" Andrea stood by the door, cuddling her baby doll in her tiny arms.

"Are you going to hold your baby brother like that?" I asked, smiling at her.

"Ahum!" Smiling back at me, she cocked her head close to her dolly's. Her smile lit up my day.

Just then, a sharp pain seared through my back to my lower abdomen. I held onto the edge of the sink and doubled over. "Oh my God!"

"Mommy pee-pee!" Andrea laughed as my water broke, trickling down my legs.

Grabbing paper towels, I tried to bend to dry the floor, but another cramp pierced my back, and the rest of my water broke. I ran to the bathroom and sat on the toilet. As I wiped the water and urine from between my thighs, I saw blood on the toilet paper. "Holy shit," I gasped.

I wrapped myself in pads and put some clean pants on, then dialed my doctor. "Joan, hi," I said to Dr. Carey's nurse. "It's Angelica. I'm in labor!"

"When did it start?" she asked me, as I held the phone tight to my ear.

"My water broke a half hour ago, and my mucus plug showed itself."

"Let me tell the doctor. I'll be right back." There was silence for a few minutes. "Ang, the doctor wants you to time the contractions and get to the hospital as soon as possible."

I hung up and called my mom at work, then phoned John.

"Hon." My voice cracked.

"Are you okay?" he asked.

"I'm in labor!"

"You must be joking."

"No. My mother's on her way. John, please come home!"

The phone clicked, and I sat on the floor rocking back and forth. The motion seemed to lighten the pain in my back, and I took Andrea in my arms. "Remember I told you that Mommy would have to leave you to go have your baby brother?"

Andrea looked up at me with her radiant brown eyes. "Ahum!"

"Well, Mommy has to leave in a little while. Your brother is coming."

"No, Mommy, don't go!" she said, beginning to cry.

I held her as close as I could, but her weight on my abdomen worsened the contractions. She clung to me for dear life.

I did not want to leave like this; we were scheduled for a C-section on Thursday. Why now? Why so damned early?

My husband and my mother arrived at the same time.

"I had just punched into my time clock when Mr. Martin called me in the office and told me you were in labor," Mom said, taking Andrea in her arms.

I was always enamored with the way my mother handled Andrea. She had a calming effect on my daughter, who loved being with my mother in return. I often asked myself, *Is this the same mother that raised me?*

Mom kissed me goodbye. "I'll pray the rosary for you."

I reached for Andrea, but my contractions did not allow me to hold her long. I hugged her and kissed her, and then left her in the hands of my mother. In the car, I started to cry. I felt as if I had abandoned my little girl.

Dr. Carey greeted us in the hospital, examined me, and whisked me into the delivery room.

"John, we cannot wait another minute," Dr. Carey told my husband. "I ordered an epidural, and once that takes effect, I can do the Cesarean."

"Can't I give birth vaginally?" I begged.

"No, Angelica. It's too risky."

Then it was déjà vu as I was numbed, placed on a gurney, and taken into the operating room. The sheet was lifted and the overhead lights were bright; soon there was a hard push on my abdomen, and a wail resounded in the room.

"Hi, John, it's Mommy!" I shouted over the sheets.

Minutes later, the nurse pushed the lights away. She wrapped my son in a blue blanket with a duck on it, and he was placed in my arms. He was small, and his head barely matched the size of his nose. I swam in his blue-gray eyes, and he yawned loudly. I was holding him close when John walked in.

"We have a son," I managed through tears and a very dry throat.

"Hey, John, it's Daddy!" John kissed our son on the forehead.

"You did very well, Angelica," said Dr. Carey.

"Thanks, Doc!" I was exhausted.

"But you have to think about birth control," Dr. Carey added. He then looked directly at John. "I suggest you have a vasectomy."

I could see John was not pleased with the suggestion by the angered expression on his face.

"I will not tie her tubes," Dr. Carey said, as if anticipating John's argument. "Angelica has enough scar tissue in her, and I won't jeopardize her health. It's up to you now."

A few weeks earlier, I had told Dr. Carey that I wasn't sure if I wanted to tie my tubes after my son's birth. My hesitation was partly due to my Catholic faith—and the guilt that my mother had seared into me—and partly because I couldn't reverse it if I wanted another child. Dr. Carey had told me that once he opened me during the C-section, he would know more as to which direction to take. Now that he was suggesting a vasectomy, I knew I could not have any more children. I had two healthy children to raise, and they needed a healthy mother.

My husband looked down at our son and then at me. "We'll use condoms, but I am not having a vasectomy."

I closed my eyes to rest them from the bright lights in the room.

I had my beautiful son, John Anthony LoCascio, on May 23, 1988. He came in three weeks early at six pounds nine ounces. It was not until a week later, while Andrea was helping me feed him, that I realized his birthday was also another anniversary: one of my first days of life, when my grandmother and Uncle Thomas had raced to my parents' house after I'd turned blue in my sleep. They had rushed me to the hospital, and it was only because of their quick action that I'd lived. I couldn't help but wonder whether Grandma and God had known that on this day, thirty-one years later, my son would be born. I thought about this as I looked into the faces of my children. Their eyes and smiles quieted the rage that was always with me.

CHAPTER 26:
THIRTEEN
MONTHS

Living with two children had its comeuppances. When you are the parent of one child, you have all day to give that child attention. But having two ... that is another story.

"Andrea, please pick up those toys," I asked for the third time.

"Play with John!" she said, smiling at me and trying to climb into the playpen.

"No, your brother is sleeping. Leave him alone."

John was not the baby his sister had been. By the time he was a month old, I had taken him to the pediatrician thinking that something was wrong. He ate so fast and had so much flatulence at times, yet he would not cry. It scared the hell out of me. One month later, he had colic, and it was all I could do to get two hours of sleep a night.

Trying to blend Andrea's comfortable routine with a new schedule was getting harder every day. Complicating matters, my husband was falling back into a kind of melancholy state I recognized from my second pregnancy. By my eighth month, I remembered, I was so tired of him being worn-out and down all the time. He was also developing a mild temper, which reminded me uncomfortably of what I'd seen in my mother. I didn't want to relive that life, so I packed a bag for Andrea and me; we were going to leave him. But where would we go? Not with my parents or in-laws. With no other options, I unpacked and dealt with it as I did everything in my life—silently.

Now, after John's birth, I began to notice the return of my husband's mood swings. His nervous facial twitches and arm tremors were also getting

ANGELICA HARRIS

worse. They had started a bit before I got pregnant with our son, and I knew he was not happy that I had gotten pregnant again, but I was not prepared for anger and depression.

One night, I decided John and I needed some time for ourselves. I called my mother-in-law to take care of the kids, and John and I went out for dinner.

We went to Joe's Diner in Woodside, a great fish and chips type of eatery. Over dinner, John and I began to talk about the kids and the usual things.

"So, I paid the final bill for Dr. Carey today," he said, chomping down on his fries.

"That's good—we needed to get that bill out of the way."

I reached for his hand and he pulled away. This had happened several times in the past, but it was happening more and more, and I was getting frustrated.

"Are you okay?" I asked.

"Yeah, why?" He looked out the window, avoiding eye contact.

"You seem so quiet lately." I sipped on a glass of white wine.

He cleared his throat several times and asked, "Would you be mad at me if I asked you something?"

"Like what?"

He stared at his plate, then out the window and then at me, saying nothing for a few minutes. He cleared his throat again. "Do you regret having John?"

"What—no!" I exclaimed. "Not at all. I love my son! Don't you?"

John slumped forward in his chair for a second. Then he straightened up. "Yes, I love him, but I regret having him."

My heart stopped. "How could you say that? John is our son."

"Don't know, Angelica. I just regret having another child." His face was pale and he kept eating.

"Do you regret having Andrea too?" I dared to ask.

"Yes, at times." His face was cold and expressionless.

I felt as though I were under attack. "Well, we can't send them back now. And I would not trade my son or daughter in for the world. They are my diamonds—no, priceless gems!"

John said nothing for the rest of dinner. I finished my plate and looked across the street. It was the exact place where Greg and I had fought after a night at Finnegan's. The memory angered me, and my husband's revelations made it all the worse. A quiet rage began to boil in my blood. No one attacks my kids—not even their father.

For a time, it seemed as though John and I were separated while living in the same house. Then summer came. We went on vacation—we owned timeshare in the Pocono Mountains—and things lightened up. In October, we celebrated my son's baptism, and my father announced that he was retiring. My mother asked if I could help plan his party for after Christmas, and I was happy to do so. Retirement must have been contagious, because my father-in-law made his retirement announcement, too, and another party was planned for late spring, just before my son's first birthday.

All during these happy family plans, my husband's demeanor continued to change. At times, he came home sick from work, and a cold would turn into a case of bronchitis with a high fever. I was getting worried.

Meanwhile, my mother, a woman of boundless energy like me, was beginning to seem fatigued. Her beautiful full face was becoming gaunt, and her white hair showed signs of yellowing. What was going on?

Mother's Day was around the corner when my brother called me one afternoon.

"Hey, Adam, what's up?"

"What are you doing for Mother's Day?"

"Aren't you working?" I asked.

After years of struggling in school, battling his own private wars of abuse at home with our mother, my brother had found his niche in medicine. When he graduated from the LaGuardia Community College Nursing Program, he looked so handsome in his whites. I was proud of him, and he had become great at his job.

"No, I have the day off," he said.

"Well, I haven't planned anything yet, so what do you want to do?"

"Mom put me up to this—she doesn't want to be at your house; she wants to go out for dinner." His voice lowered. "Oh ... and are Doris and John coming with us? It's not me asking; it's her."

"Yeah, I know, Adam. She wants her day for herself, but it's not just hers anymore, is it?" I thought briefly of my first Mother's Day, when I had to make all the reservations, and my gift from my mother was a circular piece of wood with three sick-looking fake yellow roses carved into it. I hid it in the closet and, to keep the peace, set it out when she came over.

"Well, there's always Rinaldo's," I said.

That was May 2, 1989, and Adam called me back the very same night. "Angelica, Dad and I are in St. John's hospital. Mom has a very high fever and is in a lot of pain."

"Do you need me?" I asked, worried.

"No, she's in the emergency room. Ang, you don't need to come in contact with these people; you could get the kids sick. Stay home. I'll call you."

I knew I shouldn't worry. Adam would make sure that Mom got the care she needed. But still my heart raced.

Even with the phone next to my bed, I could not sleep that night. I tried to convince myself that my brother was right: I should stay home; the emergency room was a breeding ground for germs. Finally, just as I was dozing off, the phone rang.

"Angelica, they're admitting Mom," Adam said. "They think she has gallstones and need to do tests."

I looked at the clock. It was three thirty in the morning.

"She'll be in Room 319," he said.

"Okay," I said. "Thanks."

My husband woke up briefly. "What is going on?" he asked, half asleep.

"They're admitting Mom. Go back to sleep."

I pulled on my robe and went outside. Sitting on the brick stoop on 49th Street, I lit a cigarette and raised my eyes to the tall trees that lined our block. It was early May, and they were filling out nicely. As I smoked, a warning signal filled the pit of my stomach. Mom had not looked right for months now. She'd told me that her doctor had said she was fine, but as much as Mom had abused me, I *knew* her. I knew her demeanor, her voice inflection, her stance, and the look in her eyes when she was happy, sad, and feeling ill. She wasn't herself, and my red flag was up.

I went to the hospital the next day to see her. When I walked in the room, I felt as if time had stood still. I was the child again in my grandmother's room, IV pumps and antibiotics flowing, charts at the foot of the bed, bedpans on the side table. Mom was pale, drawn, and breathing hard.

"Sweetheart," Dad said, embracing me.

"Hi, doll." Mom's voice cracked as she raised her hand to me.

I went to the side of her bed and took her hand. It was cold, quivering like a feather.

Adam walked in with a doctor. "This is my sister, Doctor," he said, introducing me. The doctor nodded at me as he walked to Mom's bedside.

"How are you feeling today, Virginia?"

"Tired, and my stomach hurts a lot." Her voice sounded as if it were coming from a dark tunnel.

"I'll have the morphine drip increased," he said. "Can I speak with you, Mr. Marquise?" he asked my father.

"You can tell me, Doctor," Mom said, nearly under her breath. "What is going on?"

After a brief pause, the doctor said, "You have several tumors in your gallbladder, and we found a small one in your liver."

Dad looked at the doctor in disbelief, then turned toward my brother. Ever the nurse, Adam was reviewing her chart.

"Are you going to operate?" Dad asked.

"In a few days," the doctor said. "I need to control the infection first."

"She has an infection on top of this?" I asked.

"She does. That is what is causing the fever. It's in the gallbladder."

I wanted to ask, *Is she going to die?* But I didn't want to worry my dad any more than he was already.

A week went by, and the phone rang. My kids were still young, so I couldn't be at the hospital as much as I wanted. The phone had become my primary means of communication with my family. I could talk to Mom for a while, and then Dad would tell me what was really going on: Mom was not getting better. As always, I jumped when I heard the phone ring.

"Mom is being operated on this afternoon," Adam said. "She wants to see you."

"I'll be there."

I called Doris to baby-sit, and once she arrived, I left like a rocket, running up to Queens Boulevard to catch the Q60 to the hospital. When I got there, Mom was already being prepped for surgery. In the hallway, Adam told me the infection was under control enough that they could operate, but her stomach was swollen from the toxins in her gallbladder. He opened the door to Mom's room, and I saw Dad standing beside the bed. I had not seen Mom in a few days—her face was ashen and the whites of her eyes a bit pink. She reached for me.

"I'm here, Mom." I wanted to cry but held it back.

"I'm going to make it." She was trying to sound positive, but I could see the fear in her face.

"I know, Mom."

A nurse came in, asking, "Are you ready?"

Mom nodded, and my father bent down and kissed her sweetly on the lips. "Love you, honey," he said, his expression tense and fearful.

Adam was next. He kissed Mom on the cheek. "Love you, Mom. Knock 'em dead!"

Mom pulled her arm from under the sheets and reached for me. She was shaking and grabbed my hand for dear life. She was cold. "Take care of my grandchildren," she said.

I bent to kiss her. "I will, Mom. Love you."

Then the doors opened and she was wheeled to the operating room.

After seven hours in the operating room and six days recovering, Mom went home. She would not have been able to leave the hospital if her son weren't a nurse: she still had the drain bag in her where her gallbladder was removed, but since Adam knew how to clean it and her wound, the doctor sent her home.

It was Mother's Day weekend, and, of course, we cancelled our reservation at Rinaldo's. I promised Mom that I would cook and bring her Mother's Day dinner to her at home. That was about to change.

My brother called me Friday. "Mom is back in the hospital. The drain bag fell out, and they are replacing it."

"Is she okay, though?" I asked.

"For the most part," he said. "There really isn't a reason to keep her here."

Andrea was tugging at me. "Grandma!" she said.

"Yes, honey, we will go see Grandma on Sunday." I hung up with my brother and took my kids to the park.

The next day, I went shopping so I could make one of Mom's favorite dishes, which her own mother used to cook. Mom loved chicken, peas, and potatoes with garlic, onions, and oregano in the oven. It was a one-pot meal, and fifteen minutes before it was ready, Mom would add a can of Campbell's tomato soup for flavor. I decided that, with all the confusion, I would cook on Saturday night so that I would have Sunday (except for going to church)

209

to myself before going to Mom's. John and I gave the kids baths, ate dinner, and were about to turn down their beds when the phone rang.

"Angelica, how's it going?" Adam asked.

"Not bad, just getting things ready for tomorrow. Chicken smells great!"

My brother took a deep breath. "That's what I'm calling about."

"Okay, so what gives?" I asked, sounding like my father.

"You can't come over tomorrow."

"What do you mean?"

Andrea was tugging at my blouse. "Grandma's house," she said.

"Yes, honey, give me a moment," I told her. I sat on the couch and she sat near me. John was on the floor playing with our son.

"The hospital did some blood work while we were there Friday night to change the drain bag. Mom may have a staph infection and a touch of hepatitis," Adam said.

"Hepatitis? That's contagious," I said carefully.

"Yes, it is, and we are all on quarantine until further notice," Adam said slowly and decisively.

"All of you?"

"All of us—if we are exposed, we can give it to others."

"So we can't be with Mom at all tomorrow?"

"No," he said strongly.

I took a deep breath.

"Talk to Grandma," Andrea said.

Adam heard her over the phone. "Let me talk to her," he said.

I gave my daughter the phone and sat near her to listen. "Grandma!" she said, giggling.

"Hi, Andrea!" I heard my brother say.

"Uncle Adam! You coming over here?" she asked in her little voice.

"No, honey, Grandma is sick and I have to take care of her."

"I want Grandma," she said, now whimpering.

"She's sleeping, Andrea."

My daughter started to cry, and John came over to take her from me.

"Can I bring dinner over for all of you?" I asked, taking the phone back.

"John can bring it and leave it on the stoop." He paused. "Tell him to call under the kitchen window, and I'll come out to get it."

"Do you need groceries?"

"Yes, we do."

"Give me a list."

That night, John went shopping at our local Key Food, and the next day we went to church. I lit a candle and received communion for my mother, we picked up flowers, and as soon as I got home, I prepared a tray for my family and sent John to deliver it to them.

A week later, the coast cleared for my mother, and we went over to visit her.

"Grandpa!" Andrea said, jumping into Dad's arms the minute he opened the front door.

"Ah, sweetheart!" he said to his granddaughter and to me as he gave us both big kisses.

Mom was resting on the couch. "Andrea, come to Grandma." Mom reached out for Andrea, but my daughter pulled away.

"No, Grandma!" Andrea said, crying.

Mom had changed drastically in the days we hadn't seen her. She was pale, and her hair was now all yellow and needed a good washing. Lying on the couch, she almost looked like a skeleton with pajamas on. Andrea would not go near her.

John and the kids stayed for about an hour. After they left, I washed and dried Mom's hair. The texture had changed: it was no longer coarse and well bodied; it felt fair and fragile, and it slid out in clumps when I gently ran the brush through it. She was always so proud of her hair, feeling that it was her best asset, and now she was losing it. At that point, I was afraid I was losing her, too.

My son's first birthday came on May 23, 1989. We had close relatives and friends over, but my family wasn't there. Mom was not well enough to come, so my father and brother stayed home with her. Their absence was palpable.

The next day, my brother called me.

"Hey, so what's the good news?" I asked, trying to be positive.

"It's not, Angelica. Mom has lymphoma and colon cancer and needs chemotherapy."

I almost dropped the phone. "Is she going to die?"

"It's advanced, but some people do come out of it," he said, always reassuring.

I took a break that weekend and took the kids to the park. They had not been there for weeks, and we all needed to vent a bit. My brother and I were at our wits' end with each other. He was exhausted, going to work in the hospital all day, then coming home and taking care of Mom. I was going back and forth with the kids, cooking, cleaning her house, doing laundry, and helping Dad as much as I could. My kids' routines were long gone, and they were getting out of control. At times, Adam and I would yell at each other over a ketchup bottle left out of the fridge—stupid things like that.

At the park, a friend of mine introduced me to *The Mists of Avalon* by Marion Zimmer Bradley. It was good to return to an old friend. I had always found solace in stories about King Arthur, and I found myself wishing, as I read the book, that either Merlin or Lady Vivian would take away my mother's past abuse.

For five weeks, I was on the move nonstop, my mother's health issues taking precedent over my kids. Nagging at me was my family's lack of appreciation. Never did my brother or father thank me for making sure they ate a good meal every day and that they had clean clothes to wear. My mother thanked me after I washed her hair in the hospital, but not once had she said anything at home. I was tired and angry that she could not acknowledge what I was doing for her.

June rolled around and things were still the same. Dad and Adam spent most of their time at the hospital, and John stayed home with the kids while I went to see her at night. Then the three of us would go home for dinner. The kids were getting spoiled by having their grandfather and uncle around all the time. Meanwhile, I became increasingly worried for Dad. He was sixty-seven years young with a history of heart disease in his family.

On my brother's thirtieth birthday, he called me from an ambulance. "Ang, we are rushing Mom to New York Presbyterian Hospital. Her nose has been bleeding profusely all night and all day. We can't stop it!"

The next day, we found out that the lymphoma had gone to her blood. She had no control of the clotting factor and was losing platelets fast.

Father's Day came, and when I walked into the hospital to see her, she had blood marks that looked like red-brown freckles all over her body and a gauze bandage under her nose to keep the blood from dripping down. In my gut, I knew that she might not make it.

I stayed by her bedside for a while before taking a walk. I found myself in front of St. Catherine of Sienna Roman Catholic Church, an old Byzantine-style cathedral. As I entered the church and slowly walked down the middle aisle, I was surrounded by six-foot statues of the saints. The one that caught my attention was the Sacred Heart of Jesus. Towering above me, He was massive: brown-eyed, long brown hair to His shoulders, fully bearded, and wearing a white alb and red robes to that hung to his sandaled feet. On Jesus' chest was his heart, surrounded by thorns and fire. His arms were outstretched, and I wanted to be in them. My legs began to shake as I approached the statue. I stood under it, praying silently as tears streamed down my face. I knelt on both knees, holding the hem of his red robe, and I asked, "Please, Jesus, take my mother from her misery. She is so tired and so am I."

That week, we all kept watch by Mom's bedside, then returned to my house for dinner and rest before repeating the same routine the next day. Every time the phone rang, it was a member of my family or one of Mom's friends calling to ask about her. It was wearing on me, saying the same thing repeatedly—after a while, I just did not answer the phone. Exhaustion was setting in when my brother called to tell me that the hospital could not find a platelet donor for Mom. One of us, though, could be a candidate to help her. The hospital blood bank would call to make an appointment.

Sure enough, an appointment was made for Thursday, June 22. I woke up that morning with chills I could not ward off. My temperature, when I took it, was a hundred and one degrees. My body was telling me that after seven weeks straight of running nonstop to keep up, it was time to rest. Still, first things first—I wanted to call Mom.

"How are you feeling?" I asked.

"Not that great. How are my grandchildren?"

I shrugged, though she couldn't see me. "They're okay. Driving me crazy, but okay."

"Ah, yes. The joys of motherhood."

"Mom, I won't be coming to see you today. Andrea has a party to go to at a friend's, but I'll be there tomorrow." I had just lied through my teeth, but I didn't want her to worry about my health. "Get your rest," I said, preparing to put the phone down.

"Honey, don't hang up." Her voice was barely there.

"I'm here, Mom."

There was a long pause, and I thought she fell asleep.

"Mom, are you there? Mommy!" I said, loudly enough for her to hear but not so loud that I was yelling at her. I sat on the couch. My legs felt like weights, and I was shivering a bit.

"Angelica, I want to tell you something ..."

Again a pause.

"I'm listening, Mom."

She could hardly talk. "I do love you very much, and I am very proud of you."

I felt a peculiar chill run through my body, and a cruel sinking feeling as though I were being pulled down in a whirlpool. "You love me?" I asked. Tears flowed down my face. I was so tired I could hardly contain myself. "Mom, I love you, too. With all of my heart."

"Mommy, can I talk to Grandma?" Andrea asked, coming from her room to sit next to me on the couch.

I gave her the phone.

"Hi, Grandma, are you coming home?" Andrea asked in her little innocent voice.

"Maybe soon, dollface," Mom said.

"Miss you!" Andrea said.

I took the phone from her and moved over to my son, who was playing on the floor. "Say hi to Grandma." I placed the phone to his ear, and he made some baby noises.

I heard Mom say, "Hi, John, I love you!"

He laughed as though it were a game.

"Mom, I love you so much. I'll see you tomorrow, okay?" I held onto the phone tightly, feeling so guilty that I was sick. I wanted to be with her. I knew she might not make it, and I wanted to spend time with her, but I was afraid to make her even sicker. After we hung up, I went in the kitchen to make some tea and hoped to be able to see her tomorrow.

That night, I had strange, bleak dreams: a skeleton in a dark box, my couch on fire, me trying to get to my kids. In another dream, my mother was in my bed, telling me she was going to be okay. I woke up sweating and dashed to make sure the kids were okay and the house was not burning. After I calmed down, I tried to tell myself it was anxiety and that everything would be fine.

At eleven that morning, the door to the apartment swung open, and my husband came in, followed by my brother and my father. Dad's expression was grim.

"Is Mom dead?" I asked in a panic.

"Ang, sit down," Adam said.

Shaking, I obeyed.

Adam sat beside me. "Mom had a massive double stroke this morning. They're doing tests right now."

"What? Will she make it?" I asked, almost denying what I was hearing.

"We don't know," said Dad. He looked like hell. He hadn't shaved and his hair was a mess. His voice was low, as if he had to gasp to find it.

A half hour later, the hospital called asking for Adam. "Okay, we'll be there in an hour," I heard him say.

I called Doris and John, and they came over quickly. I got dressed and put on some makeup—I didn't know why. I was just going through the motions. The doorbell rang, and my in-laws walked in.

"We were there to see her last night, Tony," my father-in-law said to Dad. "We were laughing."

"I know," Dad said, confused and a bit dazed.

It was three when we arrived at the hospital. We could not go into the critical care unit right away, so Adam went to get the test results while we waited. He returned with Mom's chart in his hand.

"Mom is brain dead," he said. "They said it is a matter of minutes or whatever God wants from here on."

His word stunned me.

Dad began pacing, staring at the floor and walking in circles without saying a word.

A few minutes later, a bevy of doctors and nurses ran past us; there was a "code blue" in the unit, which meant someone's heart had stopped. We huddled together until a doctor emerged from critical care.

"Mr. Marquise," the doctor said, "may I speak with you?"

I did not have to hear the words. My heart already knew.

"Your wife just passed away."

It was a good thing there was a chair behind Dad because he fell into it. Adam and I rushed to him, and we all held one another.

Thirteen months to the day after my son's birth, my mother—Virginia Jenny Marquise—passed away at the young age of sixty-three.

The days that followed were chaotic. We planned her funeral and picked what she would wear: the gown she'd worn at my wedding. Hundreds of people from all of her societies came to honor and eulogize her. There were Catholic war veterans, politicians from the Democratic Club, and teachers she'd worked with at different schools. Everyone respected her. I sat there sobbing in Roth Funeral Home, wondering who this woman was they spoke of. I was angry through my mourning, wishing I had known that woman.

On Wednesday, June 28, 1989, we were to bury Mom at Calverton National Cemetery, where she and Dad had two plots. Mom left this earth just as she lived it: dramatically. I had fallen asleep in the limo on our way to the cemetery and awoke to my brother's scream of, "Holy shit!"

Our limo was engulfed with smoke from Mom's hearse ahead of us, and we slowly pulled to a stop behind it on the shoulder of the road. The hearse had overheated and the motor threw up plumes of smoke. Fearing the car was about to explode, the funeral parlor people opened the back, pulled out my mother's coffin, and laid it—with her inside—on the side of the road. The hearse could not be moved; the engine had blown. We were stranded there for an hour waiting for a second hearse to retrieve Mom.

We couldn't help laughing at the situation. Mom was always proud about how much attention she could draw, and every car that drove by us that day either honked or screamed, "Rest in peace!" It was weird. Hilariously weird, and I was so glad I'd left my children with my son's godmother.

Arriving ninety minutes late for her own funeral, my mother was finally laid to rest at Calverton. I cried all day and for days to come. My heart was broken. The day before she died, we had actually *spoken* to each other, even if for only a minute. I wanted more of that and felt as though I had been robbed of the peace she was trying to build with me. I was angry with her and angry with God at the same time.

CHAPTER 27:
TIME FOR
SCHOOL
AND THE
TELLING
OF TALES

I was always thankful that Dad did not become a recluse after my mother died. He continued to be active in the Catholic War Veterans Post, kept his membership with the Leisure Club at St. Sebastian's, and enjoyed meetings with his union; he even went on trips to Europe with them. But then again, Dad was like that—active and independent.

In September of 1990, my daughter started kindergarten, and my father came to our house on her first day of school. Andrea was excited and I was terrified—I was losing my baby. Dad walked in that day with a pencil case and a notebook for Andrea to place in her book bag.

"Thank you, Grandpa!" she said, giving him a big hug and kiss.

"Ah, sweetheart," said Dad, swiping her up in his arms and holding her close.

I picked up my son, Dad grabbed the carriage, and off we went to Public School 11. It was the same school my husband graduated from and I had attended for kindergarten. The school hadn't changed much since then, except for a coat of blue paint on the once tan walls. The kids lined up in the hall, and we met their teacher, a lovely young lady named Miss Friedenthal. I was afraid Andrea would be nervous to leave me, but as soon as her classroom door opened, an ear-to-ear grin formed on her small face. I gave her a peck on the cheek, and she walked away from me—no tears, no drama, just looked at me and walked away. I cried all the way home.

Dad lovingly laughed at me. "Now you know how your mother felt."

Deep in my gut, I knew that Andrea was going to love school. From the time she was six months old, that child enjoyed listening to me read to her. My son, however, was another story. I never wanted to compare my children to each other as my mom had done, but I was seeing a great difference between the two. I could cuddle up with Andrea and a good book, where my son would not have it. He threw toys around the living room and made noises that distracted Andrea and me from the story. Where Andrea picked up her toys and put them away without being asked, John would sit there among the mess. It took patience from me to finally train him to put just one toy away.

They say patience is a virtue, and I grasped as much of it as I could find. At the time Andrea started school, I was hoping she would grow out of the ear and throat infections that had plagued her since she was one year old. Meanwhile, my son showed signs of behavioral issues, and my husband's health problems escalated.

"Mommy, my ear hurts," said Andrea at eleven thirty one night, half-asleep.

"Come here, honey," I said, pulling her toward me.

She sat next to me on the couch. She was burning up. A quick thermometer reading showed her temperature as one hundred and three degrees. I gave her a dose of Children's Tylenol and cuddled with her until she fell asleep in my arms. Then John carried her back to bed.

Tuesday morning, I woke up as usual at six a.m., only to find my husband still sound asleep. John worked for an accounting firm in Brooklyn and was always up by five thirty. I touched his back to wake him, knowing he would be late; his skin was hot to the touch. Immediately I went to retrieve the thermometer.

"Hon, wake up," I said as loudly as possible without startling him. "John, come on, get up." I pressed his back again. "Hon, John? Wake up!"

He was not responding.

"John, wake up!" I shook him gently.

"Huh? What's up?" he said.

"Don't know. Put this in your mouth." I placed the thermometer in his mouth, then went to the kitchen to turn on the coffee pot before returning to my husband's side. The thermometer read one hundred and three degrees.

John nearly fell on his face when he tried to get up. Bracing himself on the wall, he slowly walked to the bathroom, took two Tylenol, and staggered back to bed.

The aroma of coffee permeated the house. I poured a cup and sat at the kitchen table, looking out my window into the shared driveway space. It was seven a.m., and I would soon have to call the school and my husband's job to let them know that both daughter and father would be absent that day.

I finished my coffee and poured another half cup, then moved to sit in the living room. I was worrying more about my husband than my daughter. This was the fourth time in six months that John had caught one of the kids' illnesses, but it always hit him more severely than it did them. Something was going on.

That afternoon, my mother-in-law came to watch the kids while my father-in-law drove John and me to the doctor's office in Astoria. Dr. Cosmatos was medium in height and build and around thirty-five years old. John and I liked his mannerisms; he was a people's doctor.

"Doctor," I asked, "is it normal for a man of John's age to be sick like this all the time?"

"Not likely, Angelica." He took his stethoscope and examined John, listening closely. "You are very congested. Have you been coughing?"

"No," John said.

Dr. Cosmatos listened again. "You are wheezing in your upper bronchioles."

"What does that mean, Doctor?" I asked. "He hasn't been coughing or sneezing like the last time he was sick."

John looked at me fearfully. We were both worried it was something serious.

"To be honest, I'm not sure. I'm going to take some blood and a chest X-ray, and we'll go from there."

Swiftly, this became our lives. While other couples and families were at the park or the movies or out for dinner on weekends, I spent my time in waiting rooms or at home taking care of Andrea or my husband. John's boss was not at all happy with the time he was taking off work and began docking his monthly pay. There was no helping it, though. It seemed every time I turned around, I was in the emergency room with a husband nearly delirious from fever as high as a hundred and five. I was at my wit's end and totally unprepared for what would happen next.

Andrea was in second grade, my straight-A student, when her teacher called me to her classroom.

"Mrs. LoCascio, are you noticing at home that Andrea is either not listening to you or is having problems hearing?" Mrs. Lasiter was in her early forties. She wore denim skirts and sweaters and had shoulder-length brown hair and brown eyes.

"Not really. Why do you ask?" I replied.

"In the past two months, I have noticed a decline in her energy and class participation."

I glanced back at Andrea and my son, who were playing with the blocks in the back of the classroom. "She's sick a lot with ear infections. That may be it."

"I agree with you, Mrs. LoCascio, but there is something else going on here." Mrs. Lasiter looked right at Andrea. "The other day she was playing in the back with her friends and I experimented."

"Experimented how?"

"I called each child by name with the same voice level. Each child turned to look at me, but your daughter did not. She continued to play with the dolls. She didn't respond to me at all until I moved to the middle of the classroom and called her by name from there."

"Now that you mention it," I said slowly, "it has been happening at home, too. I can call John from the kitchen and he will come, but Andrea just sits there near the TV as if I hadn't said her name."

"Yes, it's been happening here, too. During TV time, she sits practically on top of it."

My eyes were on my child, seeing her behavior in a new way; I had thought that she was acting contrary at home.

"Thank you for your kindness, Mrs. Lasiter. I'll let you know what her doctor says."

Right before Christmas, I was practically living at the different doctors' offices. My husband's health was not improving, and Andrea's ears had gotten so bad she could no longer hear me even when I stood right next to her. My pediatrician recommended an ear specialist, and we sought his care, medicines, and therapy for over a month. Nothing—not antibiotics, decongestants, or sound therapy—was opening Andrea's ears. She was going deaf.

"Have you made a decision, Mrs. LoCascio?" asked Dr. Arrigo, a tall man who wore a white jacket with three tiny stuffed teddy bears climbing up his stethoscope. "Would you like for me to place the O-tubes in Andrea's ears or the T-tubes?"

These tubes were to be used to keep Andrea's middle ear from filling with the dense fluid that was causing her to lose her hearing. The O-tubes stayed in place and would pop out by themselves as she grew; the T-tubes would need to be surgically removed.

"Remember," Dr. Arrigo added, "both tubes are good, but the T-tubes can remain in Andrea's ears up until she is ten and will keep her ear canals open to prevent further infection. The O-tubes can even fall out while she is playing, and you would not be aware of it until another ear infection showed up. Then they would have to be replaced."

"What about the surgical removal? How is that done?" I asked.

"She will not have to be hospitalized. We can do it here in the office with a mild sedative."

I contemplated. "Let's go with the T-tubes."

Dr. Arrigo flipped through his calendar. "January 31, then."

I nodded, though my first thought was that January 31 was my parents' wedding anniversary. I shook his hand and called a cab.

The phone was ringing when I arrived home. I picked up to my father's breathless voice.

"Dad, are you okay?" I asked.

"No, I'm not. Uncle Thomas is getting worse, and Aunt Carol asked if you could come to the hospital and cut his hair."

My stomach heaved at the thought of helping that man. This was his sixth round of hospital stays in the past four months. I had visited him once before and swore I would not go again. He was fifty-five and so obese that his weight had crushed his legs; they were now brown as tree trunks, his face almost unrecognizably bloated. He also couldn't breathe without oxygen, which happens after years of cigarettes, drugs, alcohol, and obesity.

"Dad, please, I'm so busy with the kids, I really don't have that kind of time," I said, shuffling for an excuse.

"Honey, I would not ask this, but I am so worried about my brother. Please do it for me," Dad begged. He never begged for anything.

"Okay," I said quietly, "but only out of respect for you."

Dad never knew why I hated my uncle. He only knew that my aunt called me a troublemaker and that I never respected her much.

Dad picked me up the next day, his face as worried as when my mom had been ill.

"Ah, sweetheart, why does God take all the people I love?" He held my hand tight with his right hand and drove with his left.

"I don't know, Dad, but I hate to say it … death may be better for Uncle Thomas." I did not know what else to say.

When we got to Uncle Thomas's room at St. John's Hospital, Aunt Carol was already there. My uncle's face was grey and yellow, his body so massive he could hardly fit in the oversized wheelchair. His arms were the size of car tires, and his legs were brown and black. As I looked at him, I only felt pity.

My aunt came over to kiss me, and I felt as though I were being kissed by Judas himself.

"Angelica." My uncle could barely gasp out my name.

"Hi …" I reluctantly bent down and kissed him on the cheek.

A nurse came in to disconnect the oxygen mask, giving me the go-ahead to cut his hair. As I placed my blue cutting cape around him, I wanted to scream, *Why did you hurt me? Why?* But I took pity on him, cut his hair, and shaved him. It didn't take long before he was gasping for air, and when I was done, the nurse secured the mask again.

Uncle Thomas reached for my hand and looked straight in my eyes. "Thank you," he croaked through tears.

I stood there silently. For a moment, I wanted to slap him, but then a calm ran through me.

"You're welcome," I replied.

On January 28, 1992, my uncle passed away. My husband and I went to the wake, though John was sick again with bronchitis and a high fever. Adam and I worried about Dad; he loved his baby brother. At the funeral home, I stood back and watched as my father's brothers and sisters stood around the coffin, a strong firm family.

I did not go to Uncle Thomas's funeral. Instead, I was with Andrea at her final checkup before the surgery. Dr. Arrigo gave the all-clear and Andrea was operated on at the New York Eye and Ear Infirmary the next day. My father had just buried his brother the day before but was there to be with Andrea and me because my husband was too weak. I was a nervous wreck, but Andrea kissed me and hugged me with her little arms before disappearing with the orderly like a trooper.

An hour later, she came out of the operating room half asleep. She looked up at my father. "Grandpa, can I have ice cream?" she asked, with a wide grin on her face.

"Sweetheart, you can have anything you want." Dad gave her a big kiss.

Dr. Arrigo beckoned me into the hall. "Everything was a success. The T-tubes were your best choice. Her hearing test after the surgery showed she was eighty percent back to normal."

"Will she ever have normal hearing?" I asked.

"She should after some of the swelling goes down. Bring her in a week from now."

A week later, I returned to Dr. Arrigo's office with Andrea in tow. The swelling had lessened, and her hearing was one hundred percent normal. Finally, it seemed, we were making strides in the right direction.

CHAPTER 28:
HOSPITALS
AND
HEALING

For a while, we saw life returning to normal. I took my kids to the park or a Disney movie, and John and I even went out for a few nice dinners alone. But by the beginning of the summer, my husband was getting worse again. Tests showed that John had polyps in his sinus cavity and upper throat, and we were soon back at the hospital for his surgery.

This time, all three grandparents were there for support. My in-laws took the kids, and Dad and I drove John to the hospital. The plan was to straighten John's deviated septum and scrape out the polyps that were causing the irritation and infections.

John was nervous that day. His facial twitches were rampant, and so were his leg tremors, which were showing themselves more and more. In the hospital, an orderly took John by wheelchair into the operating room while Dad and I sat together and waited.

"Sweetheart," Dad said, "I'm going to go for a walk."

Dad was again nervous for one of his siblings: his younger sister—my godmother—had been diagnosed with uterine cancer, and he would be going to see her over the weekend. I nodded and watched him leave the room.

Some time later, I heard a deep voice call my name. "Is there an Angelica here?"

I looked up to see an imposingly tall African American security guard. "I'm Angelica," I said.

"Is your father Anthony?"

"Yes, why?" Dad was not with him.

"He fell outside and is being examined by one of the eye doctors."

"What the ..."

I picked up my things and followed the guard. Dad was sitting in the eye doctor's examining chair with a large bump on top of his left eye.

"What the hell happened?" I demanded.

"I tripped over my own two feet. And landed on my head." Dad was almost laughing at the situation.

If not for his self-deprecation, I would have screamed. I couldn't take more stress.

"Okay, Dad, I have to go see if John is out of surgery. Are you going to be okay without me?"

He waved his hand. "Go!"

Back in the waiting room, a nurse called me just as I walked through door. "John is resting," she said. "He can go home in a couple of hours."

"Can I see him?"

"Down the hall, room twelve."

John was lying in bed, his face a bit black and blue from the surgery. He had a wide bandage across his nose and looked as if he'd been in a war.

"How are you feeling?" I asked, stroking his head.

"Tired. Just want to go home now."

I had been clutching his jacket, Dad's, and mine for about an hour, and I finally put them down and sat on a chair beside the bed. I, too, was exhausted and worried over my two men.

Two hours later we were home, and if there really is a hell, then it moved from down below to 49th Street in Sunnyside. Andrea was faring well for a time, going out to play and enjoying life without ear and throat pain. But my son had started making unusual sounds with his mouth. At times, it sounded like a machine gun or even a squealing pig. One day, while Andrea was in school, I took my son to the supermarket. He was in the shopping cart, and every time I turned around, he would reach out and take something off the shelf without my permission. I would take it out of the cart and replace it.

"Mommy, I want that!" he screamed.

"No, John, I did not say you can have that."

He again reached for the cookies on the shelf.

"I said *no,* John!" I grabbed the box and put it back.

He began to scream so painfully that one would think I was abusing him. As if that were not enough, out from John's mouth came the sound of a machine gun: "Put put put put put ..."

A lady in the aisle looked at me disgustedly. "You need to get a grip on your child."

On the last day of school, I rushed home with the groceries before going to pick up Andrea. There was a crowd around school, and all the kids were coming out, jumping and shouting, "Hurray!"

My girlfriend, Patty, whom I met at Andrea's school, was standing by me. Patty was a tall Irish girl with long red hair, green eyes, pale skin, and freckles all over. Her son, Josh, who was in Andrea's grade, was the male version of his mom. We had promised the kids pizza. It was Andrea's last day and she had received a good report card, so we followed through on our promise—even though my son had misbehaved. Going for pizza made me feel John was being rewarded for his actions, but I could not take Andrea's wins from her.

The kids were having a great time in the pizzeria. There must have been forty kids from the neighborhood playing pinball games, eating pizza and ice cream, and enjoying the first hours of summer vacation. I noticed that Andrea was picking at her food.

"Are you okay, honey?" I asked.

"No, Mommy, my tummy hurts." She pouted.

"Maybe you ate too fast." I brushed her long golden brown hair from her face.

"No, Mommy, my tummy hurts a *lot.*"

John was playing with the other small kids by the game machines, and I looked more closely at Andrea. There by her temple were two blotches that looked like overgrown mosquito bites. Andrea had the chicken pox. I felt bad for her because she worked so hard at school, had to deal with surgery that year, and now this. I knew my son couldn't be far behind with chicken pox.

Sure enough, for the next six weeks, it was insanity taking care of both children and my husband. My son ran a fever for five straight days, his body was ravaged with itchy oozing skin, and he looked like an alien with all the lesions. I wanted to take the pain from him, but we both had to weather this together. My husband, meanwhile, contracted a viral infection, and in between it all, my godmother passed away. I felt as though some strange entity had decided to use me for an experiment: how much worry and sadness could one woman handle?

Finally, when the kids had just about mended from their bout with chicken pox, John and I began planning a family vacation. We had that timeshare in the Pocono Mountains, and we were all eager for a break. We were about five days from leaving—and my bags were half packed—when my husband came home with a mild fever. *Please, Jesus,* I prayed, *I need a break. Let him feel better so we can go away.*

Two days later in mid-August, my husband began to cough badly. I had become accustomed to the sounds and the rhythms of his coughs, but this one sounded as though it came from deep in the wells of his stomach, not his chest. John went to the doctor and came home with word that it was just a respiratory infection. Dr. Cosmatos gave him antibiotics and said he could leave for vacation if all went well. We exchanged relieved smiles.

The day before we were supposed to leave, I woke up dazed and startled, thinking that my bed was on fire. My right hip felt as though someone had placed a hot curling iron on it. I shot up fast, not knowing what was going on. I raced to the bathroom and lifted my nightgown. Everything was fine except that my skin there was hot and the rest of my body was cool. Taking a glass of water, I calmed myself and thought it must be a bad dream.

It was two thirty in the morning when I lay back down. The whole bed felt hot, but the air conditioner was on and the room was comfortable. I reached over to pull the sheets over me, and my hand brushed over my husband's arm. He was on fire. Again, I shot up and reached to touch his back. It felt as though I had placed the oven next to him, with the door opened and the temperature set at four hundred degrees.

Every bone in my body went on the alert. This was no ordinary fever. Not even my children got this hot with a fever. I sat on the edge of the bed as John began to moan in his sleep. His face was contorted, and I carefully began to wake him.

"John, can you hear me?" Gently I rubbed his arm. He was as wet as if I'd poured water over him. "Hon, please wake up." I rubbed him with a bit more force. He was not responding.

Shaking, I started to dial 911 but hung up as John began to awaken, coughing so badly it sounded as if his lungs were pushing from his chest. I dropped the phone and went to him as he tried to sit up. His body nearly doubled over.

Quickly, I removed the thermometer from my nightstand drawer. "John, I know you're having a hard time, but please put this in your mouth."

John almost immediately coughed it out. I remembered that when my son's pediatrician could not get a proper reading from his rectum, the doctor placed the thermometer under his arm. I did the same with John and watched the mercury speed up the glass meter. It stopped just over one hundred and five. I could not believe my eyes. What was happening?

I was scared to pieces, knowing that I had to wake up the grandparents, call an ambulance, and get John to the hospital. He pulled up from the bed and stumbled into the bathroom. He barely made it back to our bedroom before falling on the bed.

"John, I am calling an ambulance."

"No, don't do that." His voice cracked.

"John, you need the emergency room."

"I won't go."

"John, I cannot fight this again. Your fever is too dangerous."

I did not know how he was talking with this raging fever. He got up and held onto my bureau, then walked back to the bathroom.

"When the kids have high fevers, do they take a bath or cool shower?" John asked, holding the wall. He was pale and sweating.

"I usually give them a lukewarm bath."

"Okay." He closed the bathroom door.

A few seconds later, I heard the shower door open and water running. "What the hell are you doing?" I asked, trying not to wake the kids.

"I am not going to the hospital. Maybe this will help," he said through the door.

I let myself into the bathroom and sat on the toilet bowl keeping watch over him. He was barely in the water five minutes before he came out, shaking. I wrapped a towel around him and helped him dry off. A few minutes later, in the kitchen, John sat at the table while I took his temperature again. It seemed the shower had helped the cough long enough for me to take a new reading. I withdrew the thermometer and it read one hundred and three.

The next morning, our primary care doctor sent us to a specialist for infectious diseases. Dr. Plokamakis was kind the minute we walked in. He did something I had never seen before: he drew down the lights and directed a beam of light at John's pupils.

"What are you doing?" I asked.

"The light checks for infections in the body," he said. "I can see the passages of blood vessels and mucus membranes."

John and I were both beyond exhausted after a long winter and spring of illness. Before long, John was being X-rayed for the tenth time that year, while I sat and waited. Afterward, Dr. Plokamakis placed his hand on John's shoulder.

"I am sorry to tell you," he said, "but it looks as if you have double pneumonia."

He showed us the X-ray and pointed to two masses on John's lungs that were filled with fluid. I was scared for my husband.

"I am sending you to the hospital from here Mr. LoCascio," said the doctor. "My biggest concern is that it might be tuberculosis."

I swallowed. "Isn't that contagious?"

"Yes, and if it is TB, you and your children will need to be tested."

John reached for my hand and grabbed it hard. We looked at each other. Just days ago we were planning a fun vacation with our kids, and now it was back to the hospital.

We returned home to pack some of John's personal belongings in a bag. My in-laws wanted to hug their son, but we were warned by the doctor to avoid physical contact with others until after the tests.

The kids were scared for their father, and John could not help but hug and squeeze them. I watched my husband try to hold back tears, but when our son held him around his neck and said, "I love you so much, Daddy," that was more than he could withstand. My six-foot tall husband cried like a baby in the arms of his four-year-old son.

D r. Plokamakis had arranged for John's room before we arrived; since he suspected TB, he did not want John in the emergency room.

It was after midnight, and I paced the hall floor for what felt like an eternity. As I finally sat down, John's attending nurse, Karen, called my name. She gave me a comforting smile and handed me an "isolation packet," which contained a gown, gloves, and mask. I had to wear all these things every time I entered the room and throw them out every time I left, even if it was just to go to the bathroom down the hall.

I was not prepared for what I walked into. John had intravenous tubes on both arms, one for saline and another for antibiotics. On his upper arm, there was a blood pressure cuff, and on his face, an oxygen mask.

"We gave him a nebulizer to help him breathe better," said Karen.

I reached for John and held his hand between the latex gloves I was wearing. I did not like how it felt, because I could not feel his flesh next to mine, but I knew it was a necessary evil. Soon, Dr. Plokamakis came in advising us that he'd scheduled John for surgery the next morning.

"I'm going to insert a tube into John's lungs to clean out some of the fluid and do a culture to see what we are working with," he said.

John held my hand hard. I wanted to cry, but I did not want my gentle husband to know how frightened I was.

"The operation is tomorrow morning at eleven," Dr. Plokamakis said and walked away.

I ripped off the isolation gown and ran after him. "Doctor Plokamakis," I called.

He turned.

"Is my husband going to die?"

"If we don't find answers soon, he may." He placed his hand on my shoulder. "But I am going to try very hard to prevent that from happening."

I returned to the room and stood in the doorway, watching John rest on the bed. "Dear God," I whispered, "we have two little ones. Please help us." Then I redressed and entered the room, trying to smile.

It was a week of trials. Though the kids and I were negative for TB, I was told that I had to disinfect my whole house. Every inch had to be sanitized so that my children and I did not catch it.

My brother came over with a powerful antiseptic cleanser that he used at the hospital where he worked. When we were done cleaning, my house smelled like a hospital, but I did not care. The kids were safe, and so was I.

In the evenings, my father came over to spend time with me. The kids loved having him there, too.

"More, Grandpa, more!" my son yelled.

I was in the kitchen cooking, and I walked out to see my son on my dad's back playing horse and cowboy. A memory washed over me of our house in Woodside, Dad on the brown carpet playing Cowboys and Indians with Adam and me, my mom sitting on the couch laughing so hard she was doubled over. I missed my mom at that moment, but I did not want to cry in front of anyone. I ran into the bedroom, sat on the bed, and the tears flowed. I was so afraid. I had watched my grandmother and my mother die. Was my husband next? What was I going to do?

"Ah sweetheart," I heard my father say as he came in. Dad sat on the bed next to me and held me. I cried for two hours in his arms.

"Mommy!" I woke up to Andrea in her Winnie the Pooh pajamas, sitting next to me. "I'm hungry," she said, giving me a big kiss on the cheek.

I looked at the clock. It was ten in the morning. I never slept that late, but I had passed out on the couch at nine the night before and staggered to my room an hour later. After that, I did not move, not even to go to the bathroom.

I tried hard to give the kids some normalcy while John was in the hospital. I made French toast for breakfast and then we dressed and went to the park for an hour. Watching my kids play was like watching angels on swings. Just the motions of pushing them back and forth felt as if I were lifting a ton of tension from my shoulders. Hearing them laugh was medicine for my soul.

I pushed John, and he screamed, "More, Mommy, more!"

He swung so high that the swing and the sky made him look like a bird in flight, a bird child, laughing as though nothing else existed in that moment. My heart felt so much love for both him and my daughter. They were keeping me grounded and sane.

Two weeks later, my husband's arms had weird brown lines weaving through his skin and veins. They frightened me. He was losing weight, and his face was gaunt. I kept thinking that he was not going to come home at all.

I was still not allowed in without the isolation gear, and I was so tired I could not hold my sobs back any longer.

John grabbed my hand.

"I am so afraid," I said through tears.

John began to cry, too. We were both at our wits' end, and no one could tell us what was making him so sick. Finally, it was deemed that John had an extremely deep bacterial pneumonia, and after three weeks and countless antibiotics, nebulizers, cortisones, decongestants, and procedures to clear his lungs, things began to look up.

"Mr. and Mrs. LoCascio, I have good news," Dr. Plokamakis said, walking into the room toward my husband's hospital bed. "First, you don't need that gown anymore, Mrs. LoCascio. Your husband is no longer contagious."

I stood from my chair and tore off that ugly yellow gown, mask, and gloves. "Can I hug and kiss my husband? Please?"

The doctor smiled, and I gave John a great big hug and kiss.

"When can he go home?" I asked anxiously.

"Once his final blood work comes back and his chest X-ray looks clear, he'll be good to go."

A few days later, the phone rang while I was making dinner for the kids.

"Hi!" John said, sounding more jovial than I'd heard him in weeks, maybe months.

"Hi, are you okay?" I asked.

"Guess what?" he said playfully.

"What?" I tried to hold on to the phone and turn the omelet I was making.

"I can go home." John's voice was positive, loud, and clear.

My legs gave way and I sat on the kitchen floor, lightheaded with relief. "What? Really?"

"Yup. The doctor just signed me out."

"Holy shit!" I said, brushing the hair from my face. "Thank God!"

"Hon, please stay home tonight. I'll see you in the morning."

"Are you sure?" I asked, feeling almost guilty for the reprieve.

"Yeah, I'm just going to relax and watch T.V."

"Okay, then. I love you so much," I managed through tears.

"Love you too, hon," said John.

The next day, my father-in-law and I went to pick him up. The kids and I had made some special treats the night before and set them on the table at home. My father-in-law, John, and I walked into the house, and the kids shrieked, "Welcome home!" and nearly knocked John down with hugs.

John scooped his children up in his arms and kissed them a hundred times. He was home and safe with his family. We were whole again.

I clung to that tenuous feeling of joy for the next several months, during which John had two more bad bouts of pneumonia. Only this time it was a strain of pneumonia associated with AIDS. In the hospital that winter, we went through a battery of questions as a couple. The doctors were trying to determine whether John did, indeed, have AIDS or was HIV positive. They asked us about our past sexual partners, and I kept silent about my rape. John did not know about it, and I decided to await the outcome of our tests before saying anything.

For the week that we waited, I was in hell. I was terrified that Greg had given John and my children AIDS and that I had never known it. I didn't know how we would cope if that were the case. Thankfully, we were both clear of the disease, and I thanked God a thousand fold.

As the dust from this panic began to settle, a specialist for immune disorders was called in. I watched my poor husband go through another battery of tests before doctors finally discovered that John had Common Variable Immune Deficiency (C-VID), or what had been known as HIDS (Hidden Immune Disorder Syndrome) before AIDS was discovered. C-VID is a deficiency of the "T" cells that fight infection. Because John's cells had died off, he could die from the smallest cold or allergy attack.

The diagnosis was horrifying, but at least we finally knew what we were dealing with. From then on, we went on a quest to find the right medications and treatment for John's illness. It took some time, but a doctor at Montefiore Medical Center found that if he could infuse John with a blood product called Immune Globulin Intravenous Gammagard every three to four weeks, John could have some semblance of a normal life. I hoped that meant we all could.

CHAPTER 29:
TIME
AND
WOUNDS

Two years passed before John was able to handle the treatments at home rather than the hospital. Finally, we would no longer need to leave the kids with their grandparents. Instead, a visiting nurse named Lisa would be coming to give John his meds.

The day before the first at-home treatment, we received a rather large box. Inside was a folding intravenous pole, a box for the used needles called a "sharps container," an IV pump, needles, gauze pads, and the plastic bag that contained Sandoglobulin, the blood product that was helping John.

"Mommy, is the nurse coming for Daddy today?" asked my son.

"She is, John."

"*All* right!" he said, excited to watch the process.

I was not the type of mother who held things back from her children. When John was in the hospital, I explained everything to them in terms I knew they would understand. I used the description of their pediatrician's office and what they remembered seeing in emergency rooms to explain what their father was going through in the hospital.

The doorbell rang and little John ran to the door. "Hi, are you my daddy's nurse?" he shouted when he saw Lisa. Andrea was looking down from the stop of the stairs, quietly assessing the situation.

"Yes, I am."

Lisa was a young lady in her mid-twenties, with long brown hair pulled back in a ponytail. She wore white scrubs and smiled at both my children. I liked her.

"You must be Mr. LoCascio," she said, noticing John in his chair.

"I am." He rose to greet her.

"Did everything come for me?" Lisa asked.

"It did." John led the way to the dining room table.

"Can I help?" asked little John.

"No, you cannot help," my husband said, a bit annoyed.

"But, Daddy, I want to help," my son whined.

"Go to your room." John's curt inflection let me know how anxious he was, and my son's face went from joyful to crushed in one second.

"John," Lisa said, leaning down. "Is that your name?"

"Yeah, that's my name!" said my son.

"How about we make a deal? If I need you, I'll call you from your room."

"Okay." Resigned, John dragged his teddy bear with him to his room.

I was surprised that my son had given in so easily. That was not at all like him.

Andrea stood next to me, gawking at all the medical supplies on the table. She watched Lisa open up the sterile gauze and needles, and hook the IV pump to the pole.

"Mommy, I had the same thing at the hospital!" she exclaimed.

"Yes, you did when you had the operation on your ears," I agreed.

Lisa hung the IV bag on the pole, then wrapped the tubes inside the pump.

"What does that do?" asked Andrea.

"It counts the amount of drips per minute that will go into your daddy's arm."

"Oh, okay." Andrea nodded and then joined John in their room.

From the reflection on my small china cabinet, I saw my son standing by the door, itching to come out and see what was going on. He was still holding his blue teddy bear he lovingly called "Oh We Oh" from the song in *The Wizard of Oz*.

I beckoned him to come out, and my husband said, "Ang, please. I don't want him around right now."

My son gave me a dejected look. I went over to him and gave him a kiss. "Proud of you," I whispered in his ear.

Lisa took the IV needle out from its sterile casing.

"Is that going to hurt my daddy?" asked John.

"Maybe a little."

"Can I watch?" he asked, all excited.

"John, just go to your room," my husband snapped.

"He can stay," Lisa offered, looking between us.

My little six-year-old moved right next to his dad, but my husband moved him away from the table.

"Daddy!" said John. "I want to see."

"John, if you want to watch, go around the pole to the other side of the table," I said.

My son walked around his dad, and my husband followed him with his eyes. "Leave me alone, John," he said.

"Daddy, you can hold my hand," my son offered.

"I don't think so."

"It's okay," Lisa said.

"All right!" said little John. My son's small hand got lost in the larger one of his father.

Lisa tied a tourniquet on my husband's arm, then pricked his hand with the needle.

"Daddy, you can squeeze my hand," my son said, his jaw clenched.

John squeezed his son's hand, wincing.

"Yucky!" shouted little John. "Look at all that blood!" He pointed to the blood pooling in the tubing coming out of his father's vein.

Lisa took the heparin needle to flush out the tube.

"Does that tickle when it goes in, Daddy?"

"It feels funny is all," John answered.

Lisa set the timer on the pole for the amount of drips per minute that would eventually push into John's veins. I watched the gentleness of my son as he stood beside his father, with his head barely going over the edge of the table. He did not flinch once as Lisa applied her skills to helping my husband. I could not help but remember John saying he regretted having his own son. I wondered if he still regretted it. Today, in my eyes, our son was a hero, and his father didn't even seem to notice.

By this time, John and I had been married fourteen years and had seen more than some couples who'd been together for fifty. As we'd battled through the health issues together and raised our growing children, it seemed our home had shrunk around us. The kids' room was only six feet long by four feet wide; it could barely hold the two twin beds, let alone one bookcase for books, toys, and VCR tapes. Andrea, now in fourth grade, was becoming a young lady. Her body was changing, and I knew it was time to move on.

"John, we can't stay here too much longer," I said.

"Why?"

"Look at our daughter. She needs her own room."

"She's just a kid, for cryin' out loud!" John argued.

"Yes, but not for long."

"She is still a child!" John yelled.

I was grateful that Dad had taken the kids to the park down the block; at least Andrea did not have to hear this.

"Yeah, she may be a kid today, but before you know it, she is going to be a teenager," I said, trying to make him understand.

"A teenager? Hell," he pointed at himself, "I shared a room with my brother until we got married!"

"Holy shit, John," I said, exasperated. "You two were brothers and boys. We have a girl who will be becoming a young lady and a boy who is getting mighty inquisitive."

John brushed me away, placed his hands in his pockets, and walked out the door.

This was not the first time John left while we were fighting or after a fight. I sat on my couch and looked around. No longer was my apartment a place to come home to and relax; my living room, dining room, and bedroom had become extensions of the kids' bedroom. I had moved the coffee table in the living room so my kids had a place to play and shoved it by the long wall in the dining room as a place to store my stereo, speakers, records, and the new CDs that were coming out. Their old wooden changing table was in the corner of the same room, holding toys and some of Andrea's clothes. The outside door of their bedroom had shelves, which I'd created from cardboard, that held Andrea's Barbie dolls and John's action figures. In my bedroom, an old white bureau we had purchased from a Salvation Army store held the kids' winter wear. The floor and wall space were gone. John and my father-in-law were supposed to build a storage shelf above the doorway in the hall, but it never happened. John was always too tired.

Despite my husband's refusal to move, I decided to start looking for either a nice condo or our own home. I had grown up in a house and wanted to own one, just as my parents did.

While the kids were in school, my father went with me to look at houses. Some were so beautiful and expensive. Because John was sick for so long, we didn't have much money saved. But there was something I had been keeping from my dad, and he had a fit when he found out.

"He did *what?*" shouted Dad.

We were in the park, the kids were playing, and I was trying to explain to him why we could not afford the house we'd looked at that morning. I wanted to bury my head in the sandlot the kids were playing in.

"Why did you not tell me this long ago?" Dad asked.

"I was embarrassed." I swallowed hard.

"I taught you better than that!"

I felt like his little girl learning my lessons the hard way. "I know, Dad, but when I turned my back for one minute, John cleaned out our savings accounts to pay the bills."

Dad took my hand. "Did he take everything you saved?"

I kept quiet and he held my hand tighter.

"Did he?" he pressed, voice raised.

"Dad, I saved just like you showed me when I was a kid, but the bills got out of hand when John was sick, and he wanted to get them off his shoulders real quick." I paused. "I told him we could wait a bit longer and pay them as we were doing every month, but he didn't listen. One day he just went to the bank and took out the money."

I felt my fingers curl into a fist. I had held in my anger for so long I could have knocked someone unconscious right then.

"How did you find out?" Dad asked quietly.

"I went to Astoria Federal to deposit money I had left over from the week. When I got there, I opened my savings book ..." I unfolded my hands as if I were looking at the book. "... to place the deposit ticket and I was shocked— no, Dad, I panicked—because there was only fifty dollars left in the account."

"How much had you saved?"

I looked at the trees rocking in the wind. "Eight thousand dollars."

My father folded his hands and tapped them on his lips. "What gives, honey? You should have told me."

"Maybe, but I'm a big girl and can take care of myself."

"Ah, sweetheart, I know. But you are still my daughter and he is not taking care of you." My father grabbed me and hugged me hard. "Do you want me to talk to John?"

"No, Dad, just leave it be. Leave it alone."

About two weeks later, John and I had looked at a few apartments and four or five houses in the area, two of which Dad and I had already seen. I knew deep down he was only appeasing me, but still I asked coyly, "So what did you think about the last house?"

John wrinkled his nose. "It's okay."

"What does that mean?"

He shrugged. "It's okay, that's all."

Hopeful, I pressed on. "So do you think we can do it with a good loan from the bank?"

"I don't know, Ang. I don't know what to say." He placed his hands in his pockets, and I knew the subject was closed again.

I walked around for the next few weeks wondering what to do. It was getting harder and harder to put the kids in bed. My son's behavioral issues were getting worse. Night after night, he tormented his sister, not letting her sleep.

"Mommy! John is jumping on my bed again," cried Andrea.

John jumped off his sister's bed and onto the floor with a loud thump.

"Get back in your bed—now!" I yelled from their doorway, hands on my hips.

John mimicked my motions, pointing to me and then putting his hands on his hips.

"John Anthony, get in your bed now!" I shouted.

"*Now,* Mom said!" shouted my husband, coming into the room.

John just laughed at his dad. He jumped from his bed to Andrea's, and my husband picked him up, placed him over his knee, and smacked the hell out of his butt.

"Daddy, stop!" he cried, but John kept hitting him.

I grabbed my husband's hand. "Enough!"

"You're right. Enough is enough. I've had it with you and with them." My husband pulled up from my son's twin bed, shoved him onto the mattress, and walked out—again.

My son pulled the covers over his body and cried in the sheets. "Daddy hates me," he sobbed.

I didn't know what to do. I tried so hard to control my son, especially when my husband was around, but this night I could not. My son was out of hand, and my husband did not have the patience for it.

My son's kindergarten teacher was Mrs. Friedenthal, and she called me into class one day. It was the same scenario as at home: my son would pick on the kids, make fun of them, and act out, always looking for attention. I told his teacher I would have a talk with him at home.

"Do your homework!" Standing by the stove, I was making hamburgers and trying to help the kids do their homework.

"Mommy, John keeps throwing my books on the floor," complained Andrea, who was still a straight-A student and loved school.

"John, pick up those books now," I said, entering the dining room.

My-six-year-old son stood and looked up at me defiantly. "John, pick up those books now," he mocked.

I'd had it. I felt my hand go up and smack him hard across his left cheek. He screamed and began to cry. My hand felt like dead weight as it lowered to my side. I was shocked. I'd never once hit my kids like that—not ever. Yes, I smacked their hands for touching the stove and once swatted John on the butt for running in the street after I had told him not to, but I never hit them hard. Never. He was doubled over on the floor crying, and when I bent down to grab him, his little face was red with tears.

"Oh, no, please, God, no, I did not do that. Please, God, please!" I begged, rocking my son in my arms and holding him close to me.

Andrea stared at me, stunned.

"Oh, God, no …" I could not breathe. I had just left my finger mark on my son's face… In my head, all I could see was my mother standing over me, yelling and calling me names. "John, I am so sorry." I hugged my son for dear life.

B etween my husband's health issues and now my son's behavioral problems, I could not think straight anymore. I was having a considerably hard time dealing with both of their psychological head games, but I was still loathe to forgive myself for what I'd done.

A week or so later, my brother called and asked me to join him for lunch with his wife. He had married a pretty lady, and while we'd had our differences in the beginning, we now had mutual respect for one another. It was my birthday, and we had lunch at an Italian restaurant called Alberto's while the kids were in school.

"There's a house on our block for sale," Adam said. "Thought you'd like to go see it."

"How much do they want for it?"

"The owner died and the sons want to get rid of it ASAP," said his wife.

"Ah, so it's a fixer-upper, huh?" I remarked.

"It is, but it's a good house, and I think you might like it," Adam said.

"It would mean getting to know a new area. Glendale is pretty, but I'm not sure." At that time, I was feeling ambivalent about a lot of things.

"Why don't we go see it and find out?" Adam's wife suggested.

We finished our lunches and drove to the house. I wondered the whole time if my husband would go for it even if it did turn out to be perfect. Adam parked right in front of his house.

"Be right back," he said.

A few seconds later, he emerged with a set of keys. To my surprise, the house was right next door to him. I immediately liked the front porch; it reminded me of an old house out west, with a high flat-top roof held up by three columns.

"So why are *you* showing the house?" I asked. "Shouldn't there be a realtor or something?"

"I grew up with the owners," Adam's wife explained. "They asked us to show it while they were out of town."

"Oh, that's good," I said, walking through the door.

I was immediately hit with twin doors; one led to the first floor and the other to the second floor. Adam opened one door, which led to a long hallway that led to a small galley kitchen, the living room, and a dining area off the side. The rooms were a nice size. The only things I did not like were that the living room and dining area were paneled with dark wood, and there were only two bedrooms.

"You know I need three bedrooms," I said.

"Well, there *is* a basement," teased Adam. "And upstairs ..."

We went upstairs first, and it was the same layout as downstairs except there were three bedrooms—I did like that. Heading down to the basement, I thought how nice it would be to take my Christmas ornaments and other things out of Dad's basement, not that he minded storing them for me. With some paint and a good cleaning, I thought, this house could be our new home.

We had coffee and cake at my brother's, and then they drove me home.

That night, before my husband came home, John and Andrea were fighting over toys, space, and everything else brothers and sisters fight over. I kept thinking that if we bought the house, I would take the first floor and give Andrea either the master bedroom upstairs or build one for her downstairs in the basement. On nice days like this one, the kids would have access to their own yard, which was right out the back door of the kitchen.

"John," I broached when my husband arrived home. "Adam showed me the house next door to him today."

"He showed you a house?"

"Yes, it is right next door to him."

"How much?"

I took a deep breath. "One fifty-seven."

"I don't know if I want to move away from here, Ang," he said again.

I was beginning to realize that part of John not wanting to move was because his parents lived three blocks away.

"It's a good house," I said.

"Maybe. I don't know."

With that, John walked away from me and turned on the television.

For a week or more, I kept thinking about that house. I brought it up one more time to John, but he simply walked away.

My dad came over one day, and he and I had a chat while the kids watched television.

"Sweetheart, what are you going to do about that house?" he asked.

"Still not sure, Dad."

"Well, if I could help in any way, would you think about buying it?" Dad smiled at me with that grin that made me feel that things would be okay.

"How can you help?" I asked, curiosity piqued.

"Your mom and I had been planning a month in Europe and planned to see Africa after that. Remember?"

"I do. Mom got really sick, and you had to cancel." My heart broke for him as the memories came back.

"Please, honey, I miss Mom, too." Dad's eyes welled with tears. He cleared his throat. "So here's the deal. Mom and I saved for that trip and never took it. In fact, we saved a lot toward retirement and trips. So ... what if I gave you the down payment for the house?" Oh, he grinned at me like a schoolboy in a candy store.

"Dad!" I held my chest for breath. "Are you for real?"

"Ah, sweetheart, you can't keep going like you are. You need help, and I am here." Dad pushed from the table, came over, and wrapped his arms around me. "Come on. Let's buy a house."

CHAPTER 30:
CRUSADER

Convincing my husband to buy a house, let alone move, was a task in and of itself. John was rooted to our apartment in Sunnyside and the area in which he'd grown up. I, too, wanted to stay near to Woodside, especially since my dad was still there, but I knew that the change would be best for us all.

As much as I wanted my own home, however, I did not want to take my father's money. I pined over the idea of taking ten thousand dollars from him. There were times I would just sit on the stoop watching my children play and wonder if we shouldn't stay. Then one day I arrived home from a meeting at my son's school to find a letter from my landlord. Apparently, they wanted our apartment for my landlady's aging parents, and they wanted us out in sixty days. That was the kick in the butt we needed.

Life in Glendale took some getting used to. Growing up in Woodside, then living in Sunnyside, had been an adjustment, too, but the two areas held the same rhythmic flow: the areas were closer to Manhattan, so we felt the vibrations of the city fall our way. Glendale was slower paced, which the kids had trouble getting used to. In addition, both Andrea and John had gone to public school in Sunnyside, but due to district borders, they could not go to the school I had hoped in Glendale. The schools we *were* zoned for did not have enough room, so one child would need to go to the school around the corner and the other to one in the designated annex. Andrea and John were out of their element enough and did not want to be separated. So I did what I felt was best and placed them in St. Pancras Catholic School.

Of course, Catholic school came with a hefty price tag. Doing hair on the side would no longer be enough to pay the bills *and* tuition; I had to find another job. My husband, who didn't like the idea of our children in Catholic school—public school had been good enough for him, he said—was happy with the idea of my salary picking up the cost of tuition. So the kids began attending Catholic school in our new neighborhood, and I began working for the district manager of Avon for four dollars an hour. I filled reps' kits and called reps to remind them that their orders were due. Still, the need for money only increased, as my husband's health issues were getting worse and he could not work the long hours he was accustomed to. I took a part-time hairdressing job in a few shops before I started working at a shop called Sal's Coiffures. It was a great location, three blocks away from St. Pancras, and my boss let my kids come straight to the store and stay with me until I left at five in the evening. Sal was great, and I enjoyed working in my field again, but something was going massively wrong with my son.

It was my day off, and I walked over to the school to pick up my kids. The red door of the main entrance of the school opened, and John's second grade class was dismissed.

"Mrs. LoCascio!" I heard his teacher call me.

Crossing the street, I could see my son standing next to Mrs. Bromley, tears rolling down his cheeks.

"John, what's wrong?" I cried.

"Mommy!"

"Mrs. LoCascio, your son needs to be punished tonight," Mrs. Bromley said. She was a full-bodied German-Irish lady in her early thirties. She had short, layered hair and green eyes and wore oversized blouses to cover her weight.

"May I ask why?" I answered, taken aback.

"He is constantly making noises, getting up from his chair, and not doing his work."

"What gives, John?" I asked.

"Mommy, I don't know," he said, crying and almost laughing at the same time.

"As you can see," Mrs. Bromley said stiffly, "he does not care."

John stood near the manicured hedges. It seemed he was crying with one eye and laughing with the other, but how was that possible?

"I gave him an additional homework assignment as punishment. It's in his bag."

"He'll do it, Mrs. Bromley." I grabbed John's hand and said sternly, "Please say you are sorry to Mrs. Bromley, and that you will behave tomorrow for her."

"I'm sorry," he said rudely.

"I accept, John, but only if you start behaving. You can't go on like this," his teacher replied.

"I agree. I'll take care of it," I answered and walked away with John.

John's behavior in school and at home only got worse. There were days that I did not have to wait until I got to school to find out about his behavioral issues because the phone would ring at home or at my job.

One warm spring day, I was standing in front of the school with some friends of mine, talking to Jill, one of the mothers. Jill was a lovely German girl with sandy blond hair, brown eyes, and the body of a teenager, though she was in her mid-thirties. I, on the other hand, had gained a lot of weight after two children and dealing with my husband's issues. I was not happy with myself, and standing next to Jill reinforced those negative feelings.

"Jill, I don't want that door to open," I said, watching the kindergarten kids stream out of the building down the block.

"Yeah, I know the feeling. Karen is always getting into some kind of trouble."

"How so?" I asked over the music from a Mister Softee ice cream truck parked behind us.

"She's having a lot of problems in class this year."

"Same here with John," I said. "I don't know what to do. I even spoke to the principal. She suggested that when John misbehaves, we should place him in a lower class for the day. She said that maybe if he's treated like a baby, he won't act like one."

"She gave me the same song and dance about Karen, but that isn't the answer," Jill said firmly. "I don't know about John, but my Karen will retaliate."

"Same here. John has a lot of rage in him."

"When Karen is punished, so am I," Jill said. "She doesn't take punishment as a lesson. It just becomes another wall to climb over."

The younger kids and their parents lined up to buy ice cream. They were making a lot of noise, and Jill and I moved across the street to hear each other better.

"That sounds like you're describing John. But, Jill," I said, hesitating, "your mom told me the other day that you're taking Karen for testing for learning issues and neurological disorders."

Jill nodded. "Her pediatrician thinks she may have ADHD. She may even fall on the autism spectrum," she added heavily.

I nearly gasped at the idea that Karen could be in this much trouble. Did that mean John could be, too?

As if reading my mind, Jill said, "If you want, District 24 will test John for free at their Metropolitan office."

District 24 was John's school district. I hadn't known they performed such services. "How can I make an appointment?"

"You need to write a letter explaining his problems and they'll send a date for you to bring John."

At that moment, I felt some kind of relief. "Where do I send it?" I asked.

Over the next few months, writing and waiting became the same daunting tasks that my husband and I had lived through during his two years of treatments in the hospital. I found that writing these letters brought back skills that had lain dormant since college. I had to hone my words and refine my vocabulary to correctly express what I needed for my son. As much as I knew how to write and form the ideas, I was also afraid that maybe he would not be accepted. Finally, in late spring, I received a letter that we had an appointment for the end of May.

My husband, son, and I walked into the District 24 building where children with special education issues went for testing.

"Can we go home now?" my son asked. It was raining hard that day, and he pulled at my coat.

"No, honey, we're here to help you," I said, nodding at the security guard who greeted us.

"Daddy, I don't want to stay." John stamped his feet in front of his father.

"You have to. That's it," my husband said.

"But Mom!" Again, John tugged at my coattail.

I said nothing but signed in, took the clipboard the security guard gave me, and walked my son into the waiting room on the left. It was a pleasant-looking room, with soft green paint and Disney characters on the walls. There was a table and chairs where the kids could color, and John went over to the table and joined two children already sitting and coloring. I began to fill out the thick sheaf of paperwork. It was the usual questions—medical history, school grades, etc. But then there were other questions I had never read before, such as whether I had taken drugs during my pregnancy and whether my husband or I were alcoholics. I checked 'no' for all of them. Then another set of questions addressed my son's behavior at school and home. I answered them as best as I could, handed it back to the guard, and sat there nervously playing with my wedding band. My husband picked up a magazine and started reading.

We had waited for about a half hour, and as I grew more anxious, so did my son. "Mommy, I want to go home," he said.

"So do I, but we have to see the teacher." I grabbed John and gave him a hug. "You're being a good boy, playing with the kids over there."

"I'm bored."

"Yeah, so am I," said my husband, who had dozed off while reading his magazine.

Ten minutes later, a small-framed Asian lady approached us. "Hello," she said. "I'm Mrs. Shu. I will be evaluating John."

"Hi!" said John.

"Hi! So you must be John," she said.

"Yup, that's me." He smiled at her.

His smile relieved me. I picked up my things, and my husband and I followed Mrs. Shu to a small room furnished with only a round table the size of a bar stool and four black chairs. We all sat down quietly, and she placed her clipboard on the table and looked at the pages I had just filled out.

"Do you like school?" she asked John.

John shrugged. "Not really."

"Why?"

"Teachers don't like me." His smile turned to a frown.

"Why do you think that?"

"Cause he doesn't listen, that's why!" my husband broke in.

Mrs. Shu looked him, seeming a bit annoyed with the tone of his voice.

"I do listen, Dad," John said. "I do, but you don't believe me."

"No, I don't." My husband pointed to himself. "Because you don't listen to me at home, either."

"Mr. LoCascio, why don't you leave the questions and answers up to me?"

Mrs. Shu suggested.

My husband was getting fed up with our son, just as he did at home. I knew he was concerned, but he just did not have the patience with John that I did. My patience was quickly running out, too.

"I'm going to take John into the other room," Mrs. Shu said. "We'll be back in a few moments." She took my son by the hand and led him away from us.

My husband stood from his chair and cracked his knuckles. "I don't think these people are going to help John. He's lazy."

I watched my husband pushing his fingers back from his palm. The noise from his joints cracking was irritating me. "I agree with you, hon—there are times when he's lazy, but is it all the time?"

"Look at his room, Ang! He doesn't clean it or do any chores, for that matter. He's lazy."

"Maybe Mrs. Shu can find something for us to work with." I folded my arms around my torso, trying to keep calm in the face of John's relentless fidgeting.

"I don't think so." John took his seat again and rolled his neck back and forth, making it pop.

Forty-five minutes later, Mrs. Shu and John walked into the room.

My son was smiling. "We played games!"

"You did?" I smiled back and breathed deeply. Somehow, I felt as though the winds were changing.

"We had fun," Mrs. Shu said. "John, go into the playroom for a bit while I talk to your parents."

I looked at the clock. We had been there almost four hours. We took our seats at the small round table, and Mrs. Shu began.

"I am seeing tendencies of ADHD," she said.

"ADHD? What is that?" My husband's face twisted into the strange expression he'd acquired lately: his nose and the side of his mouth pushed down and his head cocked to one side.

"Attention Deficit Hyperactivity Disorder is a neurological disorder, where an individual has trouble keeping still and paying attention for long periods of time."

"Could that be why he moves around in school and fails his tests?" I asked.

"I think so, but I would like to have him come in a few more times to test him further," Mrs. Shu said.

"What tests will be involved?" I asked.

"We'll do a series of reading comprehension, writing, and auditory and movement tests." Mrs. Shu placed a workbook on the table, flipping pages. "I want to see how developed his motor skills, memory, and attention spans are during the process."

"How long will each testing session be?" I asked as I sifted through the book.

"About ninety minutes."

"Is after school okay? I don't want him to lose another day."

"That's fine," she replied.

Throughout the conversation, my husband was notably silent.

Every Tuesday after school for the next four weeks, we went to see Mrs. Shu. On our last meeting, Mrs. Shu diagnosed John with ADHD and suggested we see our pediatrician for a referral to a neurologist. I called Dr. Chris, as his patients lovingly called him, and he gave me the name of a Dr. Monette Basson in Woodside.

Dr. Basson's office was on 37th Avenue and 62nd Street, in a private house. Her office was somewhat old-fashioned with paneled walls and wicker chairs. Both my husband and Andrea had come with us, and the four of us waited together. As usual, Andrea—who was already ten and so ahead of her brother in almost everything—brought her books, so she settled in a corner and did her homework.

"John, take out your spelling book. We can work together," I suggested.

"Do I have to?"

Andrea rolled her eyes and sighed. "John, shut up and do what Mommy tells you."

"I don't have to listen to you!" he yelled at his sister.

"You know, John, if Mommy had a baby-sitter today I could be *home* doing my homework, but I am here—"

"So what?" John cut her off.

"If I can do homework here, so can you." Her words were absolute and clear.

"Enough! Both of you do your homework!" shouted their father.

"See? You're getting me in trouble again!" Andrea yelled at her brother.

John stuck his tongue out at his sister.

There were times when I felt as though I were looking in a mirror backwards, and through some bizarre time warp, Andrea was me and John was my brother. There were the good days when my children would play and get just as dirty as my brother and I used to, and I would laugh, remembering how my mom loved those days. But when John, especially, tried my patience, it brought back memories of my mother's temper. The mere thought of *understanding* it frightened me so much that I choked back my anger and held it securely in my gut.

Dr. Basson emerged from her office. She was a tall stately woman in her late fifties or early sixties, with shoulder length white hair that reminded me of my mother's.

"Hello," she greeted us. "Come in."

In Dr. Basson's office, my husband, son, and I took seats at her desk while Andrea remained in the waiting area with her homework. The walls were covered with the doctor's certificates and degrees.

"So, what is going on with John?" she asked, looking at my son.

"Don't know." John shrugged his small shoulders.

"Do you know why you are here?" she asked him.

"Yeah, something the lady told my mom about . . ." Again my son shrugged. His face twitched. "She said I had ADHD or something."

"So you *do* know why you are here." Dr. Basson smiled at John.

"I think so," he said, twisting his lips to the side.

"Doctor, I took John to District 24 for evaluation," I said. "After five sessions, a social worker named Mrs. Shu told us that John has ADHD and suggested we see you. I have her assessment here in front of me."

"Why don't I do some motor assessment and see what we have?" Dr. Basson said, leading us to the room next to her office. "Can you jump up here?" she asked John, patting her hand lightly on the exam table.

John climbed on the step stool and onto the table.

"I am going to check your arms and legs and eyes and see how everything works," she said. "Is that okay with you?"

My husband sat on a chair and folded his hands together. It was getting harder and harder for him to come with me, as he was still seeing his own doctors, too.

Dr. Basson took a small rubber hammer and tapped John's knees to see how he reacted. She continued on his elbows and hands, and she moved his neck and arms as well as his legs. Then she took a light and aimed it into his eyes, asking him to follow the movement of her finger. John did everything he was told, and she then had John walk back and forth across the floor to watch how he balanced himself.

"John looks pretty healthy to me," she said, "but he has some facial movements and a bit of exaggerated rapid eye movement."

"What does that mean?" I asked.

"Rapid eye movement out of sleep shows that his brain is working faster than the rest of him. That is what I feel is keeping him from paying attention."

"So do you think it's ADHD for sure?" I asked.

"I do." Dr. Basson was unhesitating in her response.

Here was my perfect little boy, I thought, looking at John. How could she be so sure? Yet I knew there was a problem here. My husband quietly watched his son, allowing Dr. Basson to complete her examination. I was quiet as well. As much as I'd hoped Mrs. Shu was wrong—that my son *didn't* have ADHD—I was relieved to know his problems had a name. I could work with him now.

"I was told about medication that could help." I looked at John sitting on the floor, playing with a toy hammer on his knees just as the doctor had a few minutes ago.

"Yes, there is medication, but I prefer to work with diet," she said.

"What do you mean?" asked my husband.

"We have to monitor John's sugar intake, and some preservatives in foods can cause kids with ADHD to lose concentration and act up in school." Dr. Basson handed me a pamphlet. "Take that home," she said. "We are going to work on his foods, sugars, and other related issues before we think about medicine. Also, I want to see if you can find a good resource center in a public school."

"But he's in Catholic School," I said, thinking, *Oh, please, not more work to do for him.*

"You'll need to write to your district to get permission for John to take a resource class in a public school near home."

"What is resource?" I asked, with a knot growing in my gut.

"It is a special room with a qualified special education teacher who can help John learn to stay on task," Dr. Basson said. "The teacher will work one-on-one with him, and also in a small group of kids his age, with tutoring."

My head was spinning. I looked out the door at my poor daughter waiting again for me to be with her. She, as I, had learned the waiting game. But I had no choice. If John was going to be a good student like his sister, I had to learn the ropes for him.

Collecting my son's things, I asked Dr. Basson, "Will you write a letter of recommendation so I can send it to the district with my request for resource?"

"I'll have my secretary work up a letter and mail it to you right away," she said.

"Thank you, Dr. Basson."

Together, my family walked out of the doctor's office, and as much as we were together, I sensed that my son's issues were strapped to my shoulders. I would have to lead the crusade.

CHAPTER 31:
A DEMON
REVEALED

"Helen, I don't know what to do with John anymore," I said.

It was six months later, and I was running ragged from taking my son to school, resource, and his various doctors' appointments. Helen Boyansky, a young woman with a mild Russian accent, was the social worker assigned to John at Queens Child Guidance Center, a non-profit program for children with special needs, where Dr. Basson had referred us. Helen pulled a tissue out of a box of Kleenex and gave it to me.

I wiped the tears from my face. "He hates going to resource room."

"What is he telling you?"

"He hates being pulled out of St. Pancras just to walk into public school in his uniform." I blew my nose. "He screams halfway down the block."

"Is there a reason? He told me the last time that he liked resource," Helen said.

"He hates the idea of being in a different school, and he also hates being the only kid in a uniform."

Helen slid a chair my way. I sank into it heavily, as though my body were deadweight.

"He hates it, Helen. And I'm losing it." Every bone and nerve in my body was spent, and I could not think straight anymore.

While I sat in the chair, I observed my son through the two-way mirror that was between Helen's office and the room beyond. Another social worker, a young woman named Lois, took the kids in a group setting and tutored them in subjects they needed immense help with, and in behavioral modification.

Helen poured some water from a cooler and handed me a cup. I sipped, and the water hit the knot in my stomach like a brick.

"Can I ask you something?" asked Helen.

"You've asked me so many questions already. Are there any left?"

Helen smiled.

"Go ahead," I said.

"Do you have any siblings?" Helen walked over to the window, observing the group.

"A brother. Why?" My legs wanted to give way, but I stood and joined her in watching my son play with the building blocks with another boy on the ABC fun rug.

"Did he have any issues with school?" She looked over to me.

"He did, but not like John."

"Like what?" Helen took her notepad and began scribbling about the kids in the other room. "Most times children who have learning disorders have either a parent or other family member who had similar problems," she explained.

"There are times John reminds me of my brother, but it was more behavioral with Adam; my brother had some serious anger issues." My neck was so tight I was holding onto my shoulder.

"What about your parents?" She turned from the window and looked straight my way.

I found myself unable to look at her. For years, I had hidden my family's issues from everyone, and now this stranger wanted to know about my parents.

"Are they alive?" she asked.

"My mother died a while ago." I still could not move my eyes from my son. The secret of my mother's abuse had died with her. I twirled my ring on my finger. "Dad is very much alive. John loves him."

"What is your relationship like with your father?" she asked.

"We have a good relationship. He's my dad."

"Rather vague," she said lightly. "'He's my dad'?"

I wrenched my eyes from the window. "My father worked very hard raising his family. He worked two jobs to make ends meet." I clenched my hands. Helen was bringing up ghosts that I did not want to think about.

She changed the subject. "When we talk about your husband's illness, you are quite educated in matters of immune deficiency."

"My husband is sick," I said. "I need to know how to care for him. But I'm here to learn how to handle my son."

"Are you a stay-at-home mom?" Helen was again scribbling.

"I'm a hair dresser and work part-time. Why do you ask?"

"I thought you had a college education."

"I did go to college but had to bow out when my dad took sick. Why all the questions, Helen?"

Helen placed her notebook on her desk. "You seem defensive today," she said.

"I'm here to learn how to handle my son, and you keep asking about my family," I said, my voice slightly raised.

"Angelica, I am not trying to make you uncomfortable, but sometimes in order to help me understand a parent, I need to know about their background." Helen sat back at her desk.

"I understand—"

"Mommy, we had fun!" said John, interrupting my sentence.

"You did?"

John ran over and gave me a big kiss on my cheek. He was beaming for the first time in months. "Yeah, we played blocks, and Lois had us count all the balls in the basket."

"Mrs. LoCascio, may I speak with you in the other room?" Lois waved her hand to show me the way to the playroom where John had just been. "John can stay with Helen."

Lois was a young Puerto Rican girl in her late twenties. She volunteered at Queens Child Guidance Center, working toward her Masters in Special Education.

"I notice that John learns more from visualization than with books," she said, confirming what I was learning at home about my son.

"I agree." I said, looking around the playroom from the other side of the window. "When I help John in math using coins or his own building blocks, he gets it. But he hates the workbook."

"Did you ever ask him why?" asked Lois.

"I have, but he just rambles on about how hard the work is."

Lois opened the door, and there was my son on the floor playing with the Tonka Trucks in the toy box.

"What concerns me, Lois, are the noises he's been making lately."

"What kind of noises?" she asked.

"You mean you haven't heard them?" I was shocked.

"Not really."

"Lately, especially in church or even at the movies, it's like he's sneezing or hiccupping."

"But he's not?"

I struggled to explain. "It's like when your mouth is dry after eating, say, popcorn, and you're moving your tongue around and get the hiccups. But he hasn't been eating. This sound starts out of the blue."

Lois was listening intently. She folded her arms. "When did this start?"

"It actually started when John was about three or four, but then it disappeared. Now it's back—but louder."

"I see." Lois looked at me. "Are there other noises?"

"Yeah ... on and off, since summer of last year, he makes this sound like a machine gun is going off. He does it in the street and in stores, and there are times he catches me off guard." My hands were beginning to shake. "The other day he ran into the kitchen making that noise, and it frightened me so much I dropped a cup of hot coffee all over the floor."

Lois grabbed my hand, and I began to cry.

"I don't know what to do anymore," I whimpered. She held me as my cries deepened.

"Mommy, are you okay?" My son's voice broke through my tears.

"Just tired, John." I forced a smile, looking down into my son's worried face.

My little boy hugged me hard. "I love you, Mommy."

"I love you, too, honey." I wiped away my tears. "Go play for a few minutes. Then we have to leave."

A few weeks later, my husband and I walked into the office of neuropsychiatrist Eugenia Guz. Helen and Lois had arranged a meeting with her, and I was glad the day had finally come. Home was getting more and more tedious, and the tensions were rising. Between my husband's issues escalating and me trying to mediate between the kids and their dad, I was at my wit's end.

"Hi, John," Dr. Guz said.

"Hi!" John looked curiously around the office. It wasn't much more than a little box, painted boring beige. The only decoration, besides her diplomas, was one picture of a tree on the one wall.

Dr. Guz shook my hand. She was medium height with pixie cut blond hair, a lithe waist, and piercing blue eyes.

"Helen tells me that you are having difficulties with your son." Dr. Guz sat down behind her desk and looked kindly at my son.

I looked to my son, then to my husband, and again to the doctor. "We are, Dr. Guz. I am at my wit's end with him."

"Tell me about the noises," she said.

"He can be as quiet as a mouse, and then it starts out of the blue." I folded my hands as if in prayer. "He just hiccups or makes this machine gun sound. It's gotten so scary lately. The other day, he made this squeaky mouse noise that just—" I covered my mouth with my hands, unable to continue.

"Mr. LoCascio, what are you observing?" Dr. Guz asked my husband.

John shrugged his shoulders. "I think he's doing it to get out of doing his homework and chores."

"Why do you say that?" Dr. Guz glanced my son's way. John was playing with the blocks, but he was pouting his lips and blowing out like a fish. It had a rhythmic sound to it: *hew, hew, hew, hewhewhew, hew, hew, hew* ...

"Doctor, we've tried everything possible. Nothing works. Personally, I don't even think *this* is going to work," my husband said.

Though I always felt my husband was detached from our son's issues, his remark took me by surprise.

"John, come here." Dr. Guz beckoned my son. "How do you like school?" she asked with a smile.

John cocked his head. "It's okay. Sometimes."

"Only sometimes?" She was writing her notes.

He frowned. "Yeah, you know, my teachers think I'm lazy."

"Do you think that you are lazy?" she asked.

"Nah. Just don't like school or some of my friends."

My son sat on the floor and stared at the ground. He looked so dejected. This was not my happy boy anymore. Where was he?

"Do you think you can do better in school?" Dr. Guz got down on the floor with John.

"If you ask me, I don't think so—he's lazy and needs to concentrate on his work," my husband said.

"Dad, I *am* trying, but I just don't get it," my son said.

"You can do it if you try," my husband countered.

"Is John on any medication?" Dr. Guz asked.

"No. Helen did recommend it but only if John really needed it."

A part of me was begging for the meds, maybe some miracle drug to cure him, but, deep down, I really did not want it for him. I had watched an Oprah show about kids with learning disabilities, and doctors spoke candidly about the long-lasting side effects of the meds used to treat them. John was so little. Was I about to give him meds that could possibly hurt him in the long run? What was right and what was wrong? My head was splitting.

"Okay," Dr. Guz said. "I'm going to start him on Tenex. It's a blood pressure medication that could help him with his concentration."

I looked at my baby. "How can a blood pressure medication help John concentrate?"

Dr. Guz placed a pamphlet in my hand. "The beta blocker that helps bring the pressure down has other uses, including slowing down the activity in the brain to help kids like John concentrate at a more normal level. Right now, his brain is all over the place and cannot stay on task."

"Are there any side effects?" I asked.

"It could either make him tired or stimulate him more. That we will have to see."

That night I went home with the pamphlet Dr. Guz had given me. As much as it all made sense, this was my son. How could I give him drugs that adults take for high blood pressure? I sat quietly in my kitchen reading the uses and side effects. I was so torn. I did not want this for my son. He was only eight years old. But the hope that this might *finally* help won out, and I was soon giving John his first pill.

At the end of the school year, John's teacher recommended that he be held back. Helen was not happy with this decision. She was afraid that holding him back would only drag his already fragile self-esteem further down. She and Dr. Guz wrote letters to Sister Jane, the principal of St. Pancras, recommending that John be placed in the grade ahead with the rest of his class. The Sister was not happy but, with the letters from Helen and Dr. Guz, she reluctantly pushed John forward.

John's noises only worsened that summer. By the time he started school, they were getting him in more and more trouble, and by the following January, his fourth-grade teacher called me into the classroom.

"Mrs. LoCascio, I cannot have your son in my class," said Mrs. Xeneon.

"He is disruptive with his noises, and he is a class clown."

"Please, I understand, and I am doing everything possible to help him." I had become a beggar for my son.

"Well, it's not good enough!" she practically yelled at me.

"I *am* trying. I just don't know what to do anymore."

That was it for me that day. I made an appointment to see Dr. Guz, and she recommended that we see Dr. Basson again.

A few days later, my family and I were in Dr. Basson's office. It was at that meeting that John's noises finally showed themselves.

"Put-put-put-put-put!"

"Doctor, this is what I am talking about!" I exclaimed. "It doesn't stop!"

"John, can you stop that, please?" Dr. Basson asked gently.

The noises got more frantic. "Putputputputput—" My son placed his hand on his mouth, crying, "Ppppppppputtt!" The noises got louder, and he wailed, "I—I—can't—putputput!" He dropped on the floor and sobbed.

Dr. Basson bent down and picked John up. He was making the noises through sobs, and as I looked across the room, my daughter was crying with him.

"What is wrong with my brother?" Andrea was just one step away from falling apart.

My husband watched, his expression unreadable. "I don't know what to say."

Dr. Basson gave my daughter a tissue to wipe her tears. "I'm going to help you and your brother. I promise."

Dr. Basson observed John another minute. His hands trembled through the noises, and she took his hands in hers. But John could not stop shaking, and the noises got louder. I almost wanted to cover my ears, but I was there to find out what was going on and could not silence what I was hearing.

Finally, Dr. Basson let go of John's hands. "Mr. and Mrs. LoCascio, I believe that your son has Tourette syndrome."

I swallowed hard, recalling what little I'd seen or read about the disorder. "Tourette's. I've heard about that. Are you saying my son is going to start cursing, too?" All I wanted to do was crawl under the desk. In my heart I was begging, *Dear God, not this, oh, please, not this.*

"No, not all cases curse, but I can tell you it is Tourette's, and I am going to send you to the Tourette Syndrome Association for help."

That night in the car, my husband and I didn't say two words to each other. We were both trying to digest what Dr. Basson had told us.

For the next few days, every time I brought up the subject, my husband just sat there—either watching television or eating. I sat down on the couch next to him.

"Hon, please. What do you think about what Dr. Basson said about John?"

He shrugged, his eye on the ball game. "Don't know."

"John, please. This is all scaring me."

John turned and looked at me square in the eye. "Scaring *you?* It is scaring me, too, but I'm tired of him not listening and you being tired all the time. I can't deal with it."

He turned his attention back on the game.

"Tired? Is that what you call it, John? Dear God, I am more than tired," I said. "I am *spent,* but we have to find out what to do for our son!"

My husband's expression was blank. "I don't know if I can handle it."

I swallowed my tears, walked into my children's room, and sat on the floor watching them sleep.

Dr. Basson had given us some literature about Tourette's, and everything I read seemed to confirm that my son had this disorder. The information gave me the name of the social worker for the program at the Tourette Syndrome Association. It took me almost a week to call them. I was having trouble dealing with the fact that my son had these tics, or neurobiological involuntary movements, but finally, when the courage came, I picked up the phone. I remember how I felt as I heard the phone ringing: *My son is in trouble, and the problem now has a name—Tourette syndrome. If that is your name, then I can fight and fight hard for my boy.*

"Hello," I said when someone answered the phone. "May I speak with Emily Kelman-Bravo?"

CHAPTER 32:
THE
TOURETTE
SYNDROME
ASSOCIATION

In the middle of John's fourth year at St. Pancras, I had to take him out of parochial school. His teachers simply could not handle his issues. I was lucky to have Helen Boyansky, his social worker at Queens Child Guidance Center, to advocate for me, as John was zoned for Public School 68 around the corner from us. Unfortunately, the school did not have the programs John needed, but Public School 91 did. It was with Helen's help that we attained a variance, and John got into the school with the program he needed.

John was in and out of school for almost two weeks. He had developed a new neck tic, and our pediatrician started him on a medicine called Migrazone. I don't know how many forms I filled out just to allow the nurse to give my son a combination of his meds. I needed one for the Tenex—the blood pressure medication—and now one for the Migrazone. But there was a catch, always a catch: a form such as this, which allowed the school nurse to give a child his medication at school, took four to six weeks to be approved. In the interim, I had to go to school at the times he needed a dose and personally administer his medications. It was a blessing for me to have a boss who knew about and understood my child's issues. Sal was a kind man who loved my kids. Until the forms came through, I had to go to the school twice a day to give John his pills. It became quite a task, but if they were go-ing to help my son get well, I had no choice. I would be at that school twice a day, no matter what.

The social worker with the Tourette syndrome program was booked, and we had to wait two weeks to see her. The day of the first visit, I was called to school to pick up John because his neck tics were so bad. I marched up to the nurse's office two hours early to pick him up.

"Mommy, Mommy." John was lying on the couch in the nurse's office, crying.

"He is in a lot of pain," said Mrs. Dwyer.

I sat next to my son, who placed his head on my lap. He was sobbing. "Mommy, my head hurts." His face was pale from the pain, as I had seen before, but his eyes were red and swollen—not just from crying but from the headaches.

Mrs. Dwyer handed me the little red pill. I took it and gave it to John. He raised his head from my lap, took the pill with a sip of water, and lay back down.

"I don't know what to do," I said. "We have an important meeting at the Tourette Syndrome Association this afternoon. But I'm not sure if he can make the car ride." I stroked John's head. As I caressed his temples and neck, it felt as if he had one big knot that was compressing on his nerves. His head began to move uncontrollably even as he lay on my lap. It was all I could do to hold his head against the force of this new damned tic.

About a half hour later, John fell asleep. He was still and silent, and I watched my angel slumber. I hated that I had to wake him. "Mrs. Dwyer, can I use your phone?"

"Sure thing, Mrs. LoCascio."

She placed the phone on the table next to me so I would not disturb John, and I dialed the Tourette Syndrome Association. Mrs. Bravo answered her three-digit extension, and I was relieved that I did not have to leave a message.

"Mrs. Kelman-Bravo," I said, "I don't know if I can bring John in today. He is in terrible pain."

"What is going on?" she asked, concerned.

"He's been having such headaches lately. He is in so much pain." I couldn't help but repeat myself.

"Is he having one now?"

"Yes." I was holding hard to the phone. "Mrs. Bravo, his head would not stop moving in my lap." I wanted to cry but held my composure so as not to wake John.

"Don't cancel," she said. "I need to see him right away."

"I'll be there." I hung up the phone and called my husband to ask him to pick up the folder I'd left on the dining room table and bring it to the Tourette Syndrome Association.

Mrs. Dwyer was good enough to let me take over her couch until John woke up. My son awakened like a storm, going from sleeping peacefully on my lap to moving like a caged tiger. His head and neck twitched from side to side, reminding me of Regan in *The Exorcist*. I managed to get him into the car, and we drove down the block and picked up Andrea from St. Pancras. She had Girl Scouts that day, but I did not know how long we would be at the Tourette Syndrome Association.

The office was in Bayside, and the ride took us about a half hour. It took all I had to help John walk. His head was moving from side to side again.

"Mommy, I'm dizzy!" he cried.

My husband, who had met us there, scooped him up in his arms. "We should have stayed home."

I opened the door to the lobby. Andrea took her brother's backpack from me and we all walked into the elevator. The doors opened on the second floor, and we walked down the long hall to an office with a little child logo on the door.

The office was pleasant enough with light blue walls, gray carpeting, black end tables, and cranberry comfort chairs in the waiting room. On the walls were pictures of flowers and, on one wall, a country scene. I sat down, and my husband placed our son on the chair next to me. John drooped on the chair and placed his head on my lap again.

A young African American lady emerged from one of the offices. She was short and a bit overweight, with tight cornrows and pretty yellow eyes. She smiled. "Who are you here for?"

"Mrs. Emily Kelman-Bravo," I said.

"She is in session. She'll be with you shortly."

"She'll be with you shortly," I repeated to myself. By now, I had heard those words more times than I could count. Between my husband and my son, I lived by those words almost every day.

A half hour later, a full-bodied woman came through the door. She wore a brown and beige pantsuit. "You must be the LoCascios."

"We are, Mrs. Bravo," I said.

"Are you his big sister?" Mrs. Bravo asked Andrea.

"Yeah, I am," Andrea said. She sounded tired and annoyed, and I could not blame her. This was her life just as much as it was ours, but she was young and it wasn't fair.

We followed her into an office with a large window through which I could see a huge tree, the backs of houses, and some of the storage yards. We occupied the four chairs in the room.

John could not hold his head up. "Mommy, I want to go home," he cried, his head moving without his control.

"Mrs. Bravo, it has never been this bad. I don't know what to do."

"Please call me Emily." She rose from her chair and sat on the floor. "John, come down here and lay on my lap."

Shocked, I nearly gasped and looked at my husband. She was actually on the floor. I nodded to John. "Go, honey. Emily wants to help you."

"No, I don't want to go," he cried again. "My head hurts."

"Where does your head hurt?" asked Emily.

"All over."

"Does this happen often?" she asked.

"It started a few weeks ago and won't go away," my husband said.

Emily rose and took out the folder she had sent to me to fill out before our meeting. "You stay with Mom for now," she said to my son. She perused the page, then looked up. "I see you have an immune disorder, Mr. LoCascio."

"I do," said my husband.

"How long ago were you diagnosed?"

"About three years ago now."

"How are you dealing with it?"

My husband shrugged. "Okay, I guess."

John was calming down on my lap.

"And you," she said to Andrea, smiling. "How are you in school?"

Andrea pulled her shoulder to her head. "I'm in the gifted class," she said softly, holding back her pride. I hurt every time she did that. She was withholding from the people around her how wonderful a kid she was, just to keep from making her brother feel bad. She did not have to say it; I could see by the fear on her face how afraid she was for him.

"Do you and your brother get along?" asked Emily

Again, Andrea shrugged one side of her body. "I guess. But sometimes we fight."

"Really, about what?" Emily questioned.

"John and I share a room, and he doesn't clean up after himself." Andrea looked right at John on my lap.

"I do, too!" he yelled and then grabbed his head.

"All he does is complain, and he gets away with everything," Andrea said. I could not help but feel she had turned into another me. Her father had promised her over and over again that he would build her a room in the basement, but he made one excuse after the other; it was either a lack of money, time, or patience, but he would not let anyone come in and build it. Andrea's frustration was almost palpable.

"Is John ready to talk to me?" Emily asked.

He raised his head. "Mommy, my head hurts."

"Emily, this is all we get from him," I said.

Emily scanned the paperwork I had sent her. "I see he is on Tenex and Migrazone. Do you see any improvement with the Tenex?"

"I did see some, but then these headaches and neck tics—that is what Dr. Basson called them—showed up and everything went haywire." I took a deep breath, trying to hold myself together. "Emily, can you help my son?"

She picked up the phone, pressed a button, and said, "Sue, can you come to my office?"

She hung up and then explained. "Sue Levi-Pearl is an expert on tics relating to the upper nervous system. She is coming in now."

The door opened and in walked a short lady with cropped gray hair wearing a stunning gray pantsuit. She took one look at my son and knelt down next to him.

"Hi, my name is Sue. What is yours?" she asked, stroking my son's shoulder.

"I'm John." His voice, wracked by sobs, resonated down into my chair. He lifted his head for a second before his neck jerked so fast he could not contain it.

Sue stood up and gently removed John from my lap. She and Emily sat on the floor and lay him across their laps. John's head kept moving, and Sue held it between her palms. My son wailed in pain.

"Mrs. Pearl, this is what happened at school today," I said. "I almost didn't come here."

"That hurts you, John, doesn't it?" asked Sue.

My daughter looked as though she was about to break. "Andrea, why don't you go into the waiting room and relax there?" I suggested.

Andrea picked her things up and left the room.

"I don't get it," my husband said. "What the hell is going on here? I can't take much more of looking at him this way."

"Mr. LoCascio, your son is having severe neck and head tics—" Sue began.

"Squueakkkyy!" John squealed, with the sound that scared the hell out of me. He trembled on the floor, and Sue pulled him close to her, rocking him as he screamed, "My chest hurts!" Hysterically, he kept uttering the high-pitched mouse noises, sounding possessed.

"What the hell is that?" I asked frantically.

"This is called echolalia," Emily said. "It is a form of vocal tic, along with his head and neck tics. This child is suffering."

It was six thirty by now, and I felt comfortable giving John another pill. I had grown accustomed to carrying a bottle of water and his meds in my tote bag. I opened the small prescription bottle, took out the red pill, and sat on the floor with Sue next to John.

"Here," I said, giving him the pill, and Sue helped him lift his head to drink some of the water.

Sue took the prescription bottle from me. "He's on twenty-five milligrams a dose, I see."

"Yes, and I don't think it's enough," I said.

"I'm going to send you to Dr. James Liguori at North Shore Hospital. He is a neurologist who specializes in severe Tourette syndrome in children." Sue touched my shoulder. "He will help your son."

Dr. Liguori's diagnosis included more than Tourette syndrome. He eventually diagnosed my son as having Obsessive Compulsive Disorder (OCD), as well as rage and defiance disorders. By now I was beyond exhausted from caring for my husband and son, as well as trying to keep Andrea's life as "normal" as possible. How could I go on?

At the advice of Emily at Tourette Syndrome Association, I started writing letters. I wrote to the district office of the Board of Education. I wrote to politicians about community services for children like my son. I wrote letter after letter. My writing skills that started in high school returned by necessity, and my letters were getting responses. Senator Serf Maltese, a kind man with a formidable reputation in his community, answered my letters and saw me in his office. After we spoke, he told me that John needed more than a public school setting and his social workers in both the Queens Child Guidance Center and Tourette Syndrome Association. He explained to me that there was a program right in my own neighborhood. He referred me to the Greater Ridgewood Youth Council, a non-profit organization in Glendale. It was there that Bob Monahan, president and founder of the organization, met with me.

The office was just around the corner from my house. It had a small storefront atmosphere with a long table, some chairs, and lots of boxes and file cabinets around the room. There were some young adults sitting at the table, along with kids I recognized from my area. In the back was a tall, broad man who walked around his desk and approached me, introducing himself and shaking first my hand and then my son's.

"Good grip on ya, kid," he said to John, grinning. Looking directly at me, he said, "So I hear from my assistant Rose that John needs help."

"He needs so much help with everything, sir," I said.

"Leave the 'sir' part for my dad. Just call me Bob." He smiled again.

I handed Bob and another man, whom Bob introduced as Joe, my son's school progress report. I explained that he had Tourette's and other co-morbid issues and that Senator Maltese had referred us here.

Bob and Joe looked through the report. "This is a daily afterschool program," Bob explained. "The young adults at the table are high school kids and college interns who volunteer to tutor kids with subjects they need help in."

"John goes to his social worker at Queens Child Guidance Center on Thursday and Emily at the Tourette Syndrome Association on Tuesday afternoons," I said.

John zeroed in on a box of toys near Joe's desk. "Can I take them out, please?"

"Go ahead, but you have to earn playing with them," said Joe.

"Okay," he said reluctantly, and out came Optimus Prime, his favorite Transformer.

Joe folded his arms. "So bring John over on the other days. The kids here will help him with his homework."

"He can do his homework here?" I repeated, so surprised and relieved that a lump rushed to my throat. Then I braced myself. "How much is this going to cost me?"

"This is a non-profit organization," said Bob. "We just ask for a donation to help us help John."

"A donation? How much of a donation?" My salary had to pay for Andrea's tuition, my son's medication, and cab fares to all his special needs doctors. I could not afford much more without worrying about taking Andrea out of St. Pancras.

"Mrs. LoCascio, you give what you can afford. That is all I ask." Bob stood next to me, so tall that I felt like an ant among spiders.

I was so relieved, yet my soul was crying out for help for myself. Could either Helen or Emily help me with the issues of my past? Both of them had asked about my life at home and whether any of my family had issues similar to my son's, and I wanted so much to tell them about my mother. There were times I could see her in my son, especially when his rage got out of control. I wanted to tell them everything, but I always thought that talking about *me* would take away from my son's needs. Now I dared to hope that I could find a new home here for John at the Youth Council. I knew it was time to deal with the abuse I'd endured. I needed to be able to drop John off here, let Andrea go home, and then go see someone to whom I could release the ghosts in my closet. Life has a way of drawing circles around us, and it seemed my own circle was returning to a point where I needed to care for myself.

Part IV

Return to an
Old Love

CHAPTER 33:
MERLIN

T hings were starting to settle down for me. My husband continued with his treatments, and though I was constantly watching him, I was finally able to focus more on my work and my kids.

"Mommy, there's a great movie on tonight called *Merlin*," Andrea said, making herself a snack.

At thirteen, Andrea was a fantasy geek just like me. We loved stories about magic, wizards, and dragons. The more spells conjured in the story, the better for both of us.

That night, Andrea and I tuned in to the TNT special starring Sam Neill as Merlin and Isabella Rossellini as Merlin's lifelong love. The movie opened with Merlin on horseback riding through the lake in Cornwall with magical music in the background.

I could not help but immerse myself in the story. I was flooded with memories from my teenage years, when I escaped the painful realities of my life by reading any Arthurian book I could find. Before I knew it, Andrea was cuddling up against me. We had not cuddled in such a long time, and I had felt so guilty about it. Somehow, it seemed as though Merlin had conjured some magic for us that night.

The movie ended past Andrea's bedtime. She had fallen asleep on my lap, and I stroked her hair and kissed her on the cheek. As she slumbered there, she reminded me of the baby I had brought home from the hospital, my little girl who would suck her thumb and cuddle on my shoulder after she drank her bottle. Yes, Merlin did conjure some magic that night. We had bonded for the first time in months—or what felt to me like years. As I watched my oldest child sleep on my lap, I thought about how much she had endured in her short life. Andrea's brother and father took so much attention from her, much like my own mother had taken it from me. I always thought how unfair it was to both of us. It was too much for a little girl to deal with.

The next day, Andrea helped me set the table while I made dinner after work. "Honey, what do you want with the chicken cutlets?" I asked while breading them.

"Rice and corn is okay," she said, taking the corn out of the freezer. "Can't wait to see part two of *Merlin* tonight," she added, pouring the frozen corn in a pot to steam.

"Oh, honey," I said. "John and I have a meeting with Emily tonight."

Andrea's face fell.

"I'm so sorry, sweetheart." I went over to touch her, but Andrea pulled away from me. She finished setting the table and went down to her room.

I stood there heartbroken. I wanted more of last night, and I knew she did, too, but again John took center stage, and I had to leave her.

My husband, son, and I went to our meeting after dinner. By then, my husband and I had joined a parents' support group at the Tourette Syndrome Association, which Emily led with another social worker in the program named Evan.

The group met every other Tuesday evening, and I was still not accustomed to going. Emily would make a pot of coffee and snacks for the parents, while Evan Michaels took the kids into another room and worked with them. They talked about how Tourette's alienated them and how they could learn to live with it in a very normal world. In the conference room, we parents talked about general issues, the doctors we saw, medicines our kids took, side effects, and the like. I found it rewarding, and once I began to work with this group, I never felt alone again.

Andrea was old enough not to need a baby-sitter. I would let my brother know that I was going out, and if Andrea needed him she could always go next door to spend time with her aunt and uncle. But Andrea was independent, a feature she'd developed out of necessity: being the daughter and sister of special needs family members.

Andrea was watching television when we arrived home later that night. "You're not watching *Merlin?*" I asked, noticing that she was watching a new show she liked, "Buffy the Vampire Slayer."

"It's still on, Mom. Just taping it."

I sat beside her and gave her a kiss. "You could have watched it."

"Nah. I wanted to watch it with you." She looked at me with those brown eyes that could pierce my heart with one glance.

"You waited for me?" I asked.

She shrugged her shoulder, the way she always did when she felt a bit low and needed me with her. "No fun watching it by myself."

"It's late now," I said. "Let's plan to watch it this weekend."

It was Saturday night, and I had worked all day at the shop. John picked me up with the kids, and we went to the five o'clock Mass at St. Pancras before returning home to Chinese food and Carvel Ice Cream.

"Mom, are we watching *Merlin* later?" Andrea asked, eating her fried dumplings.

I scooped some lo mein onto my plate. "Oh, yeah, honey. We'll have ice cream while we watch."

"Dad, are we going to play a game?" John tore apart a barbeque spare rib.

It was good to see him out of pain. Between the new meds and the many specialists he was working with, my son was almost himself again.

"What do you want to play?" asked my husband.

"Chess!" John chomped down on his food with gusto.

"Chess?"

"You promised you would teach me, remember?" My son looked at his dad with beaming eyes, itching to learn the game.

"You got it," my husband said. "We'll play chess while the girls watch TV."

After dinner, we cleaned off the table and Andrea helped me wash the dishes. My husband took out a chess set his parents had given him years ago and placed the board and pieces on the dining room table. Meanwhile, Andrea took the VCR tape out of its sleeve and placed it in the entertainment center.

"Mom, movie's ready when you are!" she shouted from the living room.

I finished drying the dishes and put them away. "Be right there!"

John and his dad were already at the table. I sat next to Andrea, who gave me the biggest grin she had. As I sat back, she cuddled next to me and nuzzled into my chest. For the next couple of hours, I was all hers. Nobody, not even her brother, had dibs on me. Andrea pressed play on the remote. The music started and there he was again: Merlin, the wise wizard of King Arthur.

"A good sword for a good king," said Merlin on screen, as the young Arthur took the sword Excalibur in his hand and began to extricate her from the stone. Every man, child, and knight bowed to him, recognizing him as their king.

"I'm gonna get your king, Daddy!" I heard over the television.

Both father and son had pieces on the board and a few on the table.

"See, I'm taking your king!" My son took the king piece off the board and ran out of the room with it. John ran after him and they laughed in the hall. I got up for a second to look at them, my heart warming when I saw them on the floor, my husband tickling my son. Just hearing that boy laugh was music to my soul. The laughter was contagious, and Andrea and I couldn't help joining in.

It was almost the end of the movie, and Arthur and his son Mordred were in high battle. Mordred had never known his father and was brought up to hate him, but as I watched the story, I felt as though there were underlying issues to his hate and rage. I couldn't help seeing my son and his father in Mordred and Arthur.

Andrea buried her head in my chest as Mordred and Arthur slew each other—it was a bloody scene. We were on the edge of our seats as Merlin returned to Cornwall to find his lover, who was locked away in a secret forest by his evil mother, Queen Mab. Every time Mab came onto the screen, belittling her son, I saw my own mother in the guise of the dark queen.

"Mommy, do you think Merlin can free Nimue?" Andrea asked.

"Don't know. Let's watch."

Andrea and I gazed at the screen while Merlin, with his magic, opened the wall to a secret cave. He and Nimue ran to each other, and they embraced and kissed. They had both changed; they were older, sadder, and with one sweep of his hand, Merlin turned back time and transformed them back to when they were young and in love.

"There," he said to Nimue. "There is no more magic."

After the movie ended, we joined my son and husband at the table, where they had returned to their game. I noticed that as my son concentrated on the board, he did not tic once. Not one head move or vocal sound. He was quiet the whole night, and I made a mental note to ask Emily about this at our next meeting.

The week passed as usual, with work, school, and medical treatments. It was actually a good week for all of us—no incidents at school for John, and Andrea excelled on her class exams.

It was Friday, and the day was busy at the salon. It had rained so much recently that it seemed as though everyone who had cancelled earlier in the week came in without an appointment that day. I worked feverishly, but for some reason the end line from *Merlin* kept jostling me: "No more magic." In between clients, I kept thinking, *No more magic? What would be left to believe in?* It gnawed at me all day.

I stood behind my chair cutting a client's hair. Eleanor enjoyed sporting a long layered look, and I enjoyed cutting it for her. As I took my scissors and blended the layers, I again found my head on that line.

"No more magic indeed," I whispered.

"What did you say, Angelica?" asked Eleanor.

"Oh, did I say something?" I laughed, embarrassed.

I looked up in the mirror to check the line of the style. I saw Eleanor and the spider plant on Sal's desk behind me. I saw the coat tree on one side of the salon and two ladies waiting for shampoos and sets. But I also saw something else: there, in the far corner of the mirror, I watched a woman dressed in riding clothes in a forest near a lake. She was digging for something.

A chill ran down my back, and my hands shook as I tried to recall myself to Eleanor's hair. I was questioning my own mind!

"Ouch!" Eleanor said. I had pulled her hair.

"I am so sorry."

Apologizing again, I brushed and prepared her hair for blow-drying. I began to section off her hair, and the blow dryer blared. I could not keep my mind on my work. There in the mirror I watched a woman that I knew was only in my mind's eye lift a sword from the soil. She took the sword, strode over to the lake, and washed it clean of dirt. The sword sang in her hand, and in a loud voice she proclaimed, "You're Excalibur!"

I dropped my good brush on the floor. What the heck was going on?

I finished Eleanor's hair, and the strange vision vanished. I was so shaken that I could not take on my next client. I hid in the bathroom and, on a clean paper towel, jotted down what I had seen in the mirror. I kept thinking I was dreaming, but the words wouldn't stop flowing. As I wrote, the name of the lady was revealed to me: Arianna Lawrence. She had my initials, but who was she and what was she telling me?

What I did not realize at the time was that I was writing my first book, *The Quest for Excalibur*. Subconsciously, I saw my son as Mordred, the insane son of Arthur, and I formed a kindred bond to the king and his wizard, Merlin. My character, Arianna, would go back in time to meet Arthur, and the two would connect for the sake of their sons. And I would reveal a secret, a secret so silent I had buried it, just as Excalibur had been buried for over a thousand years.

It took me three days to write a chapter called "The Lady of the Lake." Every time I wanted to write, I would put my pencil down and go do something, anything but reveal what my soul was dying to let go. It took all I had to finally sit on the stoop of my house on a cold day and write the words, "No, I don't want to remember!" But there, in a tapestry of clear lake water, was Arianna, ravaged by her boyfriend.

After twenty years, I had found my voice. On the page, I told King Arthur and Lady Viviane that I had been raped. It was the hardest thing I had ever done—and the bravest. My voice was released, my guilt cast away, and the bonds broken. No one could bind me again.

CHAPTER 34:
WRITE IT
DOWN

"You know, Mom, you should start writing that in a notebook," suggested Andrea, looking at all the paper towels, note papers, and copy papers strewn across the dining room table. "Where did the name Arianna come from, anyway?"

I shook my head. "I don't know, honey. Do you like it?"

"Yeah, it's pretty," she answered.

My story came to me in pieces. The way it started was the way the words filled my mind each day. I'd be doing a haircut, coloring a client's hair, or sitting down doing a manicure, and as my hands were kept busy in one form of art, the other flowed like milk and honey.

To my surprise, my father, too, was becoming invested in my book.

"Write it down, before you forget it," he'd say, his voice urgent. He slapped a pencil into my hand one day and handed me my notebook. "Go on. Write it."

He sat across from me at the dining room table, creating his own art. With beads and wire, Dad handmade the most beautiful rosaries. He fashioned one for every member of his family and friends, each rosary unique. Dad seemed to have one eye on me and one on his beads. I pretended not to notice, but by the expression in his eyes, I knew he was proud of me.

I placed my pencil down to go make coffee.

"So how are you going to open the time gate?" Dad asked about the book.

"I'm working that out right now," I answered, the aroma of coffee permeating the house.

"Be careful you don't go against the church when you write your spells."

I took Dad's advice to heart. "I won't, Dad. That's the last thing I want."

He nodded.

"How does this sound?" I said, thinking out loud. "Arianna takes the sword Excalibur and raises her point to the sky. The light of the moon refracts like pieces of crystal off the blade ..." I trailed off, noticing Dad had his eyes closed. "Dad, did you hear me?"

He opened his eyes and gave me that big smile of his. "Yes. And I like what I am hearing."

Reassured, I smiled back and put pencil to paper.

It took me two years to complete *The Quest for Excalibur*, two years of writing in between doctors' visits, research, and taking care of my husband's increasing needs. Arianna was me, and I became stronger and wiser as I created her. Somehow, she was restoring the faith in God I had begun to lose. I was tired of sacrifice, weary of being a constant caregiver. In the book, I was myself but different. I could hide from my real world and yet keep fighting my battles.

Dad and I had the best times talking about my work. Although there were days that I was angry with him for not supporting me with college years ago, I was happy that he was supportive of my writing and, most of all, my family and all our problems.

When I finished my first book, I sent the manuscript out to several publishers. However, because I could not afford an editor and it wasn't yet finely tuned, it was rejected. I had been rejected too often in life to sit back and take the blow, so I began looking into self-publishing. I decided that if I was going to get out there, I had to control my own future.

I published the first book under my real name, but my real name was doing nothing to push me forward. At the advice of my author rep at AuthorHouse, I decided to adopt a penname. At first, I was going to take the penname I'd had as a kid: Octavia Greer. It was the name I'd used for the poetry I wrote in my basement, poetry that helped me fight my mother's abuse. But I did not want to be that girl anymore. Instead, I tweaked my first name and, for my surname, thought of my favorite actor, Richard Harris. He was my very first King Arthur in Camelot, and I loved watching him perform. So I became Angelica Harris. A new name can change a path in life. As Angela

Marquise-LoCascio, I am my parents' daughter and my husband's wife. As Angelica Harris, I am my own invention.

Even as I careened down what felt like a magical journey, mundane daily life had to continue. In December 2003, my doctor sent me a card reminding me that it was time for my physical. I was so tired of doctors and nurses, but I went anyway. After all the routine tests, I waited with my usual silent impatience for someone to say, "Everything looks good. You can go home now." Instead, my doctor asked me into his office.

I walked in, and on an X-ray monitor was a picture of a person's lungs, with a shaded area at the top right side. *Poor guy,* I thought. *Glad it's not me.* Then my doctor looked from me to the X-ray, and alarm buzzed through my chest.

"Is everything okay?" I dared ask.

"Are you in any pain right ... here?" Dr. Hinz—tall, broad, and balding at the top of his head—touched me about two inches above my right breast.

I shook my head. "No, not at all," I said truthfully. "Why?"

"Do you see this area here?" He pointed to the shaded area of the X-ray. "Yes."

"This is a mass of some kind. It could be an infection or a cyst, but we have to address it."

"I don't understand," I said. "I'm in no pain."

Dr. Hinz nodded, looking again at the X-ray. "I'm going to give you an antibiotic in case it's an infection. Take it for five days. Then I want you to go for a CAT scan to make sure the mass is gone."

That Friday, a dose of Zithromax later, I was in Doshi Diagnostics for a CAT scan. On Monday afternoon, I met Dr. Hinz in his consultation room, where I'd never been before. He waited for me in a brown suit and white open-collared shirt.

"So what's up?" I asked him.

Dr. Hinz didn't mince words. "Angelica, you have a tumor on your right third rib. You'll need to see Dr. Wong, the oncologist, for blood work."

"Oncology." I swallowed the word as I said it. "Why oncology?"

Dr. Hinz came to stand beside my chair. "Ang, if it is cancer, I need to know right away."

"When do I see this Dr. Wong?"

"Lorraine will make the appointment for you."

On Christmas Eve, I met Dr. Wong, a short Asian man wearing a navy suit and purple tie. He asked me one question after another:

"Did your mother have cancer?"

"Yes."

"Has any other relative?"

"Yes."

"Is your father alive?"

"Yes."

I must have answered fifty or more questions until, at last, he took six vials of blood. My Christmas present that year was the waiting game, and I swore my husband to silence about the whole thing. My dad was getting on in years, and I worried he'd have a heart attack if he knew I might have cancer.

A week later—though it felt like an eternity—I found out that my white and red blood counts were within the normal range, but Dr. Wong concurred that I had a tumor and we needed to keep an eye on it.

I visited a slew of doctors, all saying that I could live with this tumor as long as I got a CAT scan every three to six months to check on it. I knew better—I was not living with a loaded gun in my chest. I could not go through what I had gone through with Mom. If this could become cancer, I was going to beat it on my own terms.

In late February 2004, my husband and I met with Dr. Lajam, a cardio-thoracic surgeon at Lenox Hill Hospital. He was tall, lean, and very French in his accent. I sat in his office while he looked over all my tests. When he was done, he asked me to lie down on his examining table.

"Pain?" he asked, touching my chest.

"No, Doctor, not at all." That was always my answer.

"Did you ever have an injury in this area?"

"Injury like a fall?" I asked.

"Yes. It would have had to have been something that caused a bruise here on the rib."

"Doctor, what do you mean?" asked my husband, sitting next to me.

"I think your wife may have had a blow to this area in the past," said Dr. Lajam, "and the scar tissue on the bone caused a tumor."

"Do you remember anything like that, hon?" John asked.

"A fall or injury? Not that I recall," I answered.

Dr. Lajam stood over me and fixed his eyes on mine. "This mass has grown and it must come out." He opened his little black book, shuffled some pages, and announced, "I am operating on March 18."

Trying to find courage, I said, "I'll be there."

In the following days, I restricted myself to a light workload, yet the question about an injury kept gnawing at me. There was a secret about my son I was keeping from everyone—a secret I have not revealed until now.

In 2004, my son's needs were still casting a shadow over my family. John was a teenager, and his rage attacks hit like a mallet. He was outside playing when one of his friends called him names. It was late afternoon, and I was writing quietly to the hum of the air conditioner. Suddenly the front door flew open.

"I'll kill him!" shouted my son, his voice raging through my peaceful thoughts.

I was down in the basement and ran up the stairs. As I approached the kitchen, my son, my thirteen-year-old child, stood by the kitchen drawer with a steak knife in his hand. His face was bloody, and the hand bearing the knife was torn with a wide gash. In my mind, I did not see John, but my mother. I was sixteen years old again, paralyzed with fear.

"I'll kill Aaron!" John's voice shook me into action.

"John, what are you doing?" I asked, trying to stay calm.

"I'll kill him!" he kept repeating. "I'll kill him, him, himmmmm!" His neck was twitching, his rage triggering the echolalia.

I held the fear in my gut. "Kill who? I don't understand."

My son wielded the steak knife in both hands, rigid and in attack mode. *This is your son,* I told myself. This was a boy I loved with all my heart, and I knew he loved me. He had a heart of gold; someone had just tripped it. *Hold on, girl,* I thought. *You can save him.*

"John, look at me," I said. "Look into my eyes, John."

He didn't move. I took a step toward him, but he moved back. "Stay away, Mom. I—am—going to kill him!" He raised the knife higher.

"Okay, what happened?" I asked.

"No!" he screamed, walking toward me.

"John, put the knife down!" I shouted, desperate for both of us.

He moved again.

"John, put that damned knife down before you kill me or yourself." I noticed the broom was leaning on the wall by the refrigerator. Could I reach it and use it to knock the knife out of John's hand?

"I want him dead!" he yelled, long and loud. His eyes were fixed and dilated, a look I recognized, and fear seeped within my veins.

Get a grip! I told myself. *This is your son, not your mother!* I breathed deeply, trying to find the calm I'd found with Mom that day. I lunged to the left, grabbing the broom and thrusting it at my son's hand. The move caught him by surprise, and one swat knocked the knife away. The force was hard enough for me to fall up against the refrigerator handle, right smack down on my right side.

"Why did you do that?" he yelled, going to retrieve the knife.

Like a ball player trying to make first base, I slid on the floor, grabbed the knife, and threw it toward the living room. "You could have killed me, damn you!" I screamed at the top of my lungs. Through hard coughs I said, "I—am—your—mother!"

John fell into my arms, crying. "I'm sorry, I am so sorry!" he sobbed over and over again as we held each other.

He'd had a similar rage attack before, and I'd needed to take him to Schneider Children's Hospital, where his psychiatrist practiced. The phone number was always on the inside of the cabinet. I called them and they came quickly, taking John to the hospital. The next day, my chest was black and blue. Was that what had caused my tumor?

The evening of March 17, the night before my surgery, I went to see my priest, Father Fullum. I am a practicing Catholic and asked for the Sacrament of Extreme Unction—otherwise known as The Last Rights. I was not going to die without being in a state of grace with my God. The priest heard my confession and gave me communion. Whatever happened the next day, I was ready.

At home, we had a quiet dinner. My husband made a dish my mother invented—chicken, peas, and potatoes in the oven, a tasty one-pot meal that always brought the family together.

"In the name of the Father and of the Son and of the Holy Spirit," John said.

"Amen," the kids and I replied.

"Bless us, oh Lord, and these they gifts, which we are about to receive through thy bounty through Christ our Lord."

"Amen!"

I added, "Yes, Lord, and I thank you for my good doctor and for my family. Please take care of them and take care of me."

Andrea shot me a look of worry, and my son came over to me and gave me a big hug and kiss. "You'll be okay," he said.

We ate dinner, Andrea did the dishes, and I packed pajamas, toothbrush, and a book to read while I waited to go into surgery. Then we gathered together again to watch a movie, but I became more and more agitated as night fell. Seeing my nervousness, my husband brought me a glass of merlot, and I cuddled up with him and sipped my wine.

I had to be at the hospital by ten the next morning, and it was time to leave before I knew it.

"Love you, Mom," Andrea said, embracing me before I walked out the door.

My son enveloped me in a big bear hug, kissed me, and gave me that reassuring look he always does when he knows I am nervous. My husband picked up my bag and we left for the hospital.

Right before the doctor gave me the anesthesia, I looked at the light above me and said one word: "Jesus."

What was supposed to be a routine ninety-minute surgery proved to be otherwise. Three hours later and before I was awake, my doctor told my husband that he had not only removed the tumor but my whole third rib, my chest wall, and some of the tissue from under my right breast. The tumor was the size of an orange and would have killed me in a month if he had not removed it that day.

The nurse in the recovery room woke me up at ten that evening. Through blurred vision, I noticed that Dr. Lajam was right behind her.

"Angelica, you are going to be fine," said the doctor.

I tried to lift my head but excruciating pain seared the right side of my chest. It was a pain I welcomed—I was alive!

Tears began to roll down my cheeks, and as my tears wet my pillow, my skilled doctor placed his hand on my left forearm. "Your guardian angel must have been watching today." Dr. Lajam placed something in my hand. "This is a morphine drip. Push this button as often as needed."

My husband came in with a great big smile on his face. He bent down to kiss me. "Hey, you made it!"

I smiled back, barely.

"I just gave your wife a morphine drip," Dr. Lajam told John. "The pain from this surgery and the chest tube are going to be unbearable for the first forty-eight hours."

"Understood," John said.

I was flying high at the time, but I remember that, as happy as I was to be alive, something was eating at me, and it had been there from the minute I'd found out about the tumor: maybe I was better off dead. I was so tired of everything, of being strong for everyone else. Could I face being strong for myself?

CHAPTER 35:
A NEW
LEASE
ON LIFE

My recovery from my surgery was a lengthy one. The pain was more intense than I could have predicted being able to endure. But one factor that helped was that I had recently lost forty pounds through Weight Watchers. Three years earlier, my weight had escalated to two hundred thirty pounds, and my blood pressure was so high my doctor was afraid I would have a stroke. He warned me that I had to lose one hundred pounds or I could die. Losing the weight saved me, as it made the surgery less invasive. Dr. Lajam agreed that if I were heavier, I may not have made it out of surgery alive.

It was a good thing that John and I had purchased a brand new living room set six months earlier. I could not sleep flat in my bed, so I spent days and nights in my plush recliner for two months after returning home.

Oddly, I had already written a good amount of my second book, *Excalibur and the Holy Grail*, in which there is a scene where Arianna is impaled through her shoulder, piercing her rib and almost killing her. I wrote that scene two months before the tumor was found. Coincidence?

After a week of rest at home, I strapped a sling around my right arm and sat by my computer. I had begun editing my first book, *The Quest for Excalibur*, with a lovely young lady by the name of Andrea Howe, who owned a company called Blue Falcon Editing. However, that day I could not sit for more than fifteen minutes at a time without the pain searing straight into my back. I hated taking painkillers, but my body did not want to fight. I took a Percocet and fell asleep.

The phone woke me up some time later, and I answered groggily.

"Sweetheart?" Dad asked, concerned. "Are you okay?"

"Yeah," I said, but I turned the wrong way and wailed in pain.

"I'll be right over," I heard over my own tears.

My in-laws and father had wanted to visit me, but I had told them the surgery was to repair a tendon in my shoulder and didn't know how to explain the painful state I was now in.

I got up from the couch and almost fell, dizzy and crying. That was how Dad found me when he let himself in with the key I'd given him.

"For cryin' out loud, now tell me the damned truth!" he yelled at me over my tears.

"What do you mean, Dad?" I sobbed.

"Don't give me those words. Your mother said them to me enough." He handed me a tissue. "What gives, honey?"

Dad looked right into my eyes, straight on like a beam of light, blinding the truth out of me. I spat it out in one breath. "Dad, I had a massive tumor removed from my chest wall last week."

That beam turned into a red-hot flame. "Do you have cancer?" he asked.

"Don't know yet, Dad. The culture hasn't come back yet."

Dad's hand was rotating in circles the way it did when he was trying to process his thoughts. "What the hell? Why did you keep this from me?"

My vision was blurred from tears. "I didn't want to worry you," I squeaked, feeling like a little girl.

"Worry, *worry!* I worry more when I don't know anything, you hear me?" Dad gently pulled me to him. "Ah, sweetheart, don't be like your mother. She hid her pain from me, and now she is gone."

"I know, Dad, I had to do this my way." I leaned my head into his shoulder. "I was so scared. I still am."

My dad held me, and for the first time in months, I felt relief from this burden. From the day the doctors told us that I might have cancer, there was a wedge between my husband and me—one that would only build in the days to come. He couldn't handle this, and it was worsening his temper with my son; at least four walls in my house had already been punched through.

If I weren't so sick I would have walked out, but I had to see this through.

After we received the bolstering news that I did *not* have cancer, my husband invited his parents over for dinner. They made no secret of the fact that I was not recovering as quickly as they'd hoped from my "shoulder surgery."

"So where's the girl?" my father-in-law asked of his granddaughter.

"At school." I replied. Andrea was already in her first year of Southampton College. She could not have made me more proud. She was truly my "Alexis," the strong, stable, independent daughter of Arianna in my books.

"Why isn't she here to help you? My son can't do all of this," said my mother-in-law.

"Well, Andrea is not my personal Cinderella," I shot back.

"How are you feeling?" my father-in-law asked. "Shoulder any better?"

My father had been down in the basement helping my son with a science project. He came upstairs and stood by the living room door, wiping paint from his hands with a rag.

I decided a head-on answer was best. "I did not have shoulder surgery," I said. "I had a tumor removed from my chest wall."

"A tumor?" my father-in-law asked, obviously stunned.

"Yeah, Dad, a tumor," my husband said, sitting across from them.

"What kind of tumor?" asked my mother-in-law.

"It is called a benign chondroma. And it is not cancer," I said confidently, thinking back to the recent test results.

"So how long you gonna be like this?" asked my father-in-law.

"The recovery period is long. I lost my third rib and part of my chest wall."

"Well, thank God it's not cancer," he said. "My son needs you to take care of John and him."

I decided right then that I would try my best to keep my in-laws out of the loop of most of my struggles with my son and husband.

And struggles, there were.

My son, now in the beginning of high school, was still having major issues. When he was in middle school, I had been able to procure a paraprofessional, Jodi, who was with him all day. Jodi and I worked together to help John attain the grades he needed to get to high school. However, the high schools near home did not have the programs John needed, so I met with a special education teacher who helped me work with John's Individual Education Plan (IEP). I had attained the IEP with the help of Evan Michaels, social worker with the Tourette Syndrome Association. Evan advocated for me with the district directors to make sure John attained his goals.

With or without an IEP and partners in the fight, there was always trouble of some kind. John was getting older and did not take his meds the way he was supposed to. I'd find them on the floor, in the bathroom sink, and in the mailbox.

"I hate taking these," he'd say. "They make me tired."

"I know, John, but you need them," I'd argue.

For years, he'd been on various combinations of Risperdal, Adderall, Orap, Tenex, Ritalin, Haldol, and Wellbutrin. He looked like a zombie in his school photos. I hated making him take the pills, but I knew they were what he needed. Still, the arguments were frustrating, and my husband was losing patience.

"Take your fucking pills!" my husband yelled one school morning.

"Dad, they are making me sick. I don't want them anymore!" my son shouted back, his voice deep now.

My husband lunged at his son, pinning him to the wall, and tried to force-feed the pills to our son.

"John, what the hell are you doing?" I screamed, coming down the hall. I pulled him off my boy.

"I'm tired of this, Ang! I want him out of here."

My husband raised his hand to our son, but John ducked and he rammed his fist into the wall, making a hole and gashing his hand. My son ran for cover in his room. I saw myself in my son and hated it. I hurt so badly for him. In that moment, I wanted my husband out of my house.

That day, I received a call from school. I had not noticed, but my son was marked by his father under his chin, and the school counselor asked him about it. By then my son was so tired of his father's tirades he told the counselor about it. The school warned me that they were going to call Child Protective Services.

Panicked, I called Evan Michaels at the Tourette Syndrome Association. After explaining to him what had happened, nothing more came of the situation. But I decided I'd had enough—we all had—of living with my husband.

"Mom, if I were eighteen years old, I would punch the lights out of Daddy." My son's face was stoic, and it seemed to confirm my decision.

"I know, honey, but before you even think of that, I plan to have Dad removed from this house," I said. "I am going to call the police so he does not take his temper out on you again."

My son began to cry. "Don't do that. Please don't do that."

"Dad is getting worse, honey. We can't live like this anymore."

John wrapped his arm around my shoulder. He was growing to be a big teddy bear of a young man. "Mom, I have put you through more hell then you deserve, and you didn't throw me away. How can you throw Dad away? He is just like me."

"But, John, he has hurt all of us."

"Mom, look at me. I am not a child anymore. I can take it."

I looked at him, wanting to cry. Here was a handsome young man with a big heart of gold that he wore so generously on his sleeve. My boy, my son, my John. He was a knight in my eyes, a knight in shining armor for his family. With all his quirks, I would not replace him for the world.

As I began to develop my third book, *Excalibur Reclaims her King,* my writing became the only sanity I had to get through taking care of my two special men.

At the time, I belonged to an online writers group and enjoyed interacting with fellow writers through e-mail. We shared our ideas and thoughts about writing and helped critique one another's work. I was learning that a good writer needs a great editor to make her a great writer. Enter Corey Michael Blake.

Corey was a participant in one of my online groups. One day we were talking about adapting novels to screen. He caught my attention when he explained some of the details, such as that a twenty-page chapter in a book can become six pages of script for the screen.

"Six pages? How is that possible, Corey?" I asked him by e-mail.

"A lot of the copy is not needed," he said. "The description is used on the set instead of on the page."

Within Corey's e-mail were links to Elevation 9000 Films and LA Film Labs. My head spun. He was a film writer—wow!

I soon told the group that I had written these fantasy novels, and Corey was intrigued. I sent him synopses of both books, and he asked to read them in their entirety. I sent him the books, and he read and reviewed *The Quest for Excalibur.* I was thrilled with what he wrote:

With courageous strokes, great passion, and a fire for honor, Arianna Lawrence fights for her family from the present by journeying back in time and fighting for the people of Camelot. A beautiful story for people of all ages, "The Quest for Excalibur" takes us back in time to the legend of the Sword in the Stone, the Knights of the Round Table, Arthur, Galahad, and Merlin. Our favorite figures are reborn in the telling of this magical tale that unites answers from the past with questions of today. A book for mothers in need of adventure, husbands who wish to awaken the spirit of their wives, and young audiences that love the thrill of the Arthurian legend, "The Quest for Excalibur" is a book to be revered for its courage, and Angelica Harris, a writer to be honored for having the courage to expose her truth. —Corey Michael Blake

I already had written at least fifteen chapters of my third book, *Excalibur Reclaims Her King,* and Corey was eager to know more. As well as working in film, he provided writing and editing services and asked if I wanted to work with him. I was strapped for cash and hesitant to send my work to a fellow writer, so I decided to give him a little test. By e-mail, I asked, "If there was an evil in this world, what would it look like and what would it do?"

Corey wrote back, "This evil would be a hideous monster that would seep within the core of the earth, bleeding it dry of every good the earth holds. It would castrate humanity, killing the life force of each and every individual …" He ended the e-mail with, "Now that I feel so dirty, come play with me."

I was blown away by Corey's description. It was creative and dark, as if he had already read my book. Though I still had misgivings, we set up a time to speak on the phone.

"So how can I help you?" asked Corey after we'd chatted for a few minutes.

"I don't know," I said honestly. "I've worked with an editor before, but not one like you. Why are you special?"

Corey gave a hearty laugh I would come to know well. "Some editors just edit the work for you, such as Andrea did with your first book. What I do is help you build your characters using character bibles, scene descriptions, location research, plot outlines, and so on."

"What are character bibles?" I asked.

"I'll send you a few things to read and you'll know," said Corey.

"What will you charge me for all this?" I was preemptively bracing myself. *Here goes the damage, and there goes the dream,* I thought.

"Ang, I'll send you a cost-effective list and will work within your budget," Corey said.

An e-mail later, Corey sent me a list of his costs. Slowly, I read through them and did the math. To my own surprise and dawning excitement, I realized I could do this.

I began to work with Corey in earnest, and it soon became obvious what he most needed from my writing: more. More character development, more research, more conflict, more description—more, more, more! There were times I wanted to scream when I saw his trademark comment: "I want more from you." But I came to understand that he wasn't telling me I wasn't *enough*; he was trying to take me from good to great.

Over phone and by e-mail, we had long, detailed conversations about my story and characters.

"What if we gave Arianna a tool?" he asked one day. "Maybe a brooch. What does it look like, and what does it mean to her?"

"Yes," I said. "The brooch is a gift from Merlin. It has a gold crescent moon, a pentacle carved in a red stone, and on the pin is a sword much like Arianna's Gwydion. It is engraved with the figure of a woman."

"I love it!" he responded.

In this way, we began to take my third book to a depth my first two books had aspired to. I was in heaven, living in my stories.

Meanwhile, though, my dad's health began to fail. He had just turned eighty, and instead of him taking care of me and supporting me with my son and husband, as he had for years now, I was a twenty-year-old girl again, giving up my time and work for my dad. I remember thinking that as much as I wanted to be there for him, years of hospitals and doctors for my son and husband had worn me down—could I do this again?

As Dad began needing more medical attention, I let my brother Adam carry much of the burden. Adam was hurt, I knew, by how I seemed to step back, but it wasn't that I did not want to be there for Dad. I simply knew that Dad had Adam, and I needed a break from doctors, shrinks, and the mayhem my family had wrought on me.

Still, I found that I was stronger than I thought and could spend the hours I needed with Dad. My issue with that was that my brother, who had moved to Florida with his wife, was Dad's health proxy. Each time I went to the doctor with Dad, I had to set up a call with Adam so the doctors would talk with me. It was disempowering.

During this time, my son was growing into manhood and still having issues at school. Now a high school kid, he should have been sailing through his classes with the help I had procured for him, but he was falling behind again due to homework issues and playing that game we all play in our teen years—the one where we become bigger than our own britches.

"So, John, Mom tells me you're not doing what you're told." Dad folded his arms and sat back in the dining room chair.

"I listen to my teachers," John answered.

"From what Mom tells me, you are not doing your homework, and you are failing again—what gives?" My father was not one for yelling if he didn't have to, and he reached for his grandson's forearm. "John, you are not a child anymore. You have to start thinking about what you want to do when you're an adult."

"I know, Grandpa. I just can't wait to get out of school."

Dad sat quietly, listening.

"I'm tired of school," John said, his voice cracking.

My father looked at him. "Don't do what I did. I quit school at thirteen and never went back. John, your mother will tell you that Grandma and I struggled for a penny for a long time." He kissed my son on the cheek. "It is hard, but try. Your mother is sacrificing a lot for you. Look at her face. Look at the worry she has for you—for her family."

My son turned his gaze to me and, just like that, wrapped his arms around me and cried in my embrace.

Not long after this, Dad's health took a turn a turn for the worse. I caught little innuendos, such as him struggling to hold the tweezers as he made his rosary beads. I would watch him rub the pain from his hands or struggle as he came up staircases, not only holding onto his cane but also guiding his steps with the handrail, taking one at a time, only to be winded when he got up the fifth step. It was hard to watch.

When my brother moved to Florida, he gave me all of Dad's doctors' information and any records he had pertaining to my father's medical history. It was all too familiar to me, as being a caretaker was what I'd done for my husband and son for many years.

By the end of 2006, Dad was on a walker full time. I was so mad at him; I wanted him to have a hip replacement, but he was afraid of the surgery.

I tried to encourage him, but my brother made the choice. When Dad refused the surgery, it made me crazy.

"Tony, while you are in reasonable health, you can do this. The surgery would increase your quality of life," said Dr. Kleinman, Dad's new doctor.

We were sitting in the doctor's Manhattan office, discussing what we could do about Dad's health issues. In addition to having mitral valve regurgitation, thyroid problems, and major arthritis, he needed a new hip, yet I could not get him to consider the surgery. Maybe Dr. Kleinman could.

"How long would he be in the hospital?" I asked.

"About six days if all goes well. Then, depending on how well he heals, two to six weeks in rehabilitation." Dr. Kleinman looked at Dad and smiled. "Tony, you will feel like a new man."

"Dad, I know you can do this." I took my father's hand and squeezed it.

"I want to talk to your brother first. My son is my health proxy," he added, nodding to Dr. Kleinman.

Dr. Kleinman looked at me. "Aren't you his daughter?"

"I am."

"And where is your brother?"

"He lives in Florida," I said.

"Sir," he said to Dad, "not to impugn your judgment, but she should be your proxy."

The doctor's words validated my anger. "Dad, *I* am here, not Adam. I know everything about you, every smile, every body movement. Why do you insist on listening to the one who's far away?"

Dad waved his hand at the doctor, and it was all I could do to contain my rage. I loved him and wanted the best for him, even wanting him to move in with me, but my voice didn't count. It brought back the feelings of unworthiness I'd had living as a child in his house. It was driving me nuts.

Though I couldn't influence Dad in matters of his health, the time I spent with him in and out of doctors' offices was a time of love for both of us. We would spend hours at a time in waiting and consultation rooms. After his exams, he and I would go to a kosher diner called Mendy's in Manhattan, where we'd order the chicken soup and share half a turkey sandwich. Those meals were filled with conversation about the doctors, my son and husband's issues, and my writing. Dad was often my sounding board, and I have to give him credit—he was the one who helped me raise King Arthur from the dead.

"Sweetheart," Dad said, "remember only God can raise the dead."

"I know, Dad, but it has to be real. I mean, it is fantasy but has to *seem* real."

Dad was a religious man, but he was not the mad fanatic Mom had been. He expressed to me that raising Arthur just like Jesus raised Lazarus or as Christ was raised from the dead would teeter on heresy, so the two of us went back and forth working on ways to raise the king from the dead. I said to my father one day, "If Arthur is both Christian and Druid, what if I raised him in a Druid ritual?"

Dad gave me a huge smile of approval, and I began my research on pagan ritual resurrections. While waiting again for the doctors to see Dad, I would bring in my books and pore over them. He began to realize how much I truly loved history and learning about everything in my genre. Together, Dad and I read about dragons and the meaning of the phoenix in many religions. He found a new awareness to his own faith through mine. We talked for hours about my findings, and he looked at me in a new light—I remember him grabbing my hand and telling me how proud he was of my writing but encouraging me to stay true to my given faith as a Catholic and a Christian. He did not want me to ever deny Jesus in my life, as the books I was writing were about the Holy Grail, the cup of Christ.

One day, I looked up from my books buzzing with excitement—somehow I just knew I'd found the solution.

"Dad," I said, "what if I used the blood of the dragon, since Arthur is the son of the dragon, and add in the tears and ashes of the phoenix? We can mix these elements with the earth and raise him from the dead."

"How did you reach this conclusion?" Dad asked.

"Well, you know I've been looking at the symbols in church. Do you know that in at least four churches I have gone to in the past three months, two had a phoenix on the altar? And I found a unicorn on one."

Dad smiled and folded his arms in his thinking mode. "So how are you raising Arthur?"

"You know the scene where Arianna places Arthur's ashes on the pyre?"

Dad nodded.

"Well," I said, knowing my eyes must be sparkling, "we are going to do a reverse cremation."

"I'm listening." Dad closed his eyes, which he always did when he was working hard to envision something.

"Imagine Arthur's ashes are on the pyre," I said. "The dragon flies over-head and gashes himself with his talon, sending three drops of blood to soak into the ashes."

"Sounds good so far," Dad said, eyes still closed.

"Then the phoenix flies over, crying bitter tears, and sends three teardrops into the ash. The dragon then breathes fire on the pyre, Arianna says her prayer, and Arthur comes back to life." I beamed, excited that I'd found the answer without going against the teachings of my church.

Dad opened his eyes and grinned. "Now that is a resurrection I would respect."

Dad was my sounding board, and I loved talking with him about my book. As much as I resented not being his proxy, I was glad we had that time to-gether. He and I grew inseparable. He would talk about his childhood, and I my work. Somehow, without ever saying the words, I forgave him for not believing in me when I was younger, for saying, "One day you are going to get married and have a husband and a family, and your husband will provide for you. You don't need college." It was Dad's words *now* that counted—that made me realize God had given me these books to stay strong and to never be separated from His son. I learned to finally understand the death of Christ, not just through my own faith but through others as well and from the history of Christianity, Druidism, and Judaism. I wanted Arthur's resurrection to be recognized and revered as much as I revered my work and my own faith. I wrote the resurrection chapter with the support of Dad and Corey's con-stant demands of excellence. It was Corey's edits and my dad's love for my work that allowed Arthur to be raised with dignity for all faiths.

CHAPTER 36:
A BROKEN
HEART

"I'm moving to Florida!" said Dad over the phone.

Shocked, I almost choked when I heard the words. I knew my brother had broached the idea with Dad, but I never expected Dad to take it. We had talked openly for a while about him possibly moving in with me.

"How did this happen?" I asked.

My brother, who was also on the call, explained. "Dad and I looked at some great assisted living homes, and he fell in love with a place called Summerville."

"But so soon? What about the house?" I asked, thinking of my childhood home.

"We're taking care of it already," Adam said. "Dad spoke to my lawyer in New York, and the paperwork is getting done."

I sat in my dining room, staring at a painting of St. George the Dragonslayer. Everything inside of me wanted to blow. I had offered my home, my family, and my love to my father, and he was settling for an assisted living facility.

The months ahead were long ones. Dad was already on a walker, so he needed someone to help clean out the house. Being the dutiful daughter, I obliged, and my husband and children helped clean the house and pack Dad's belongings. But his health was worsening, and I was getting scared.

"Tony, you need to have that operation," said Dr. Davidson, another one of Dad's physicians. "You cannot stay on that walker the rest of your life."

"Dad, I agree," I said. "When do we do this?"

"Ah, I have the house I'm selling and too many things on my mind," said Dad.

"So you go into the hospital and I'll sell the house."

Dr. Davidson nodded, agreeing with me.

"Ah, your brother is handling that for me," Dad said from his perch on the examining table.

"Tony, your physical says you're a go. Let's get you healthy again," said Dr. Davidson.

"You all don't understand. I have the house," Dad said curtly.

I handed Dad his shirt. "Dad, you can't keep putting this off."

"Doctor, I want you to talk with my son." Dad turned to me. "Call your brother."

Seething, I dialed Adam. "Hi," I said when he answered. "We're with the doctor."

I put him on speakerphone. "So Dr. Davidson agrees that Dad should have the surgery."

"Adam," Dr. Davidson chimed in, "your dad is getting worse. I'm afraid if he waits too long, it's just never going to happen."

"Dad, how do you feel about this?" Adam asked.

"Adam, I have the house to take care of. I'm not sure."

"Adam, we can't wait any longer," I blurted. "Dad needs this!"

"It has to be Dad's choice," Adam said.

By then I wanted to throw my father's walker across the room or cram it down my brother's throat.

"Well, I don't want the operation right now," Dad said.

And there it was: my brother's ambivalence and Dad's decision all at once, and I had nothing to say about it.

It got to a point where, in respect for an old man who just happened to be my father, I stayed the course and continued to take him to the doctors, clean and pack his house, and get it ready for people who had bought it. I asked my dad one day, "So what gives, Dad—why are you not having the surgery?"

He folded his arms. "Your brother has some great doctors lined up for me in Florida."

"Oh, so you are going to wait until you get to Florida!" I grabbed his walker, wanting to throw it against the wall. "Look at you, Dad. You are a slave to this damned thing and you hate it! Don't tell me you don't!"

"Enough!" he yelled, putting his hand up to me.

"Dad, you have the best doctors here at Beth Israel Medical Center—the *best*. You have no idea how much they care about you. And with their help, you can be that independent man again—the man I know."

"Ah, sweetheart, enough," Dad said, somewhat sullenly. "What's done is done."

In July of 2008, my brother arrived, and we took Dad to my mother's grave. We had not been there together in quite a while. Calverton National Cemetery is at least a two-hour drive from my home in Queens. We stopped at the florist first and picked up some flowers; Mom loved her roses.

Calverton is spacious, with trees that line the entryway. As you drive up, the road opens to the burial area and then takes you to the gravesite. We parked and walked about a half block to Mom's grave. The flat landscape gave way to the many grave plaques on the ground. We found her and—just as I did every time I saw her grave—I missed her fiercely. I felt as though she had been robbed of old age.

We held hands, and Dad took his rosary from his shirt pocket and we prayed. It did not matter if it was a sunny day or it was raining; when we visited Mom, we stood and prayed the whole rosary. To Dad, the prayer was sacred.

Afterward, Dad placed his beads back in his pocket and gazed down at his wife's resting spot. It may have been a long time since her passing, but I could see he missed her, missed her still.

Dad grabbed our hands, and I knew in my heart it was the last time we would be together there. We hugged each other silently and got back in the car, driving home to Queens.

After visiting Mom's grave, we returned to my father's house for the last time. The day of the closing was hard for me. As much as my memories of abuse lay in those walls, so were the proud, strong moments I'd shared with my dad. That day, Adam and Dad stayed outside talking with a neighbor, so I walked in alone.

"Mom, I'm home!" I yelled, coming into the hall pretending I was a child again.

The house was bare. I went through the six rooms upstairs and then descended the steps onto the main landing of my parents' first-floor apartment. The beatings I had taken from my mother shot through me like arrows. I watched them in my mind and realized they were only memories. Taking a hard breath, I walked to my old room, remembering where I placed my records and posters. My room had always looked so pretty, but now the walls were peeling from age and neglect.

In the kitchen, I stopped cold. It was there that Mom and I had fought over the knife; in that very spot years earlier, I had feared her rage, her madness, would kill us both. Yes, it was there, like a mirrored image refracting all over the room. I watched, allowing it to play out as though it was happening in front of me, but I stopped it where I pushed the knife out of my mother's hand. I knew what came next—I held her and she hit me—but I couldn't allow myself to relive it. Instead, I looked my mother in the eye and whispered, "I love you, Mommy, and I always will." I threw her a kiss and walked away.

CHAPTER 37:
INTUITION
RECOGNIZED

After Dad moved to Florida to "live a better life," his health became increasingly poor. He had a pacemaker put in that first December and ended up in multi-organ shutdown. I flew down to Florida with my husband, whose depression was in such a landslide during our stay that I almost placed him in the psychiatric ward. Dad, however, proved he was Dad and fought the good fight; after five days, he began to recuperate with the help of my brother and the good nurses in the kidney dialysis ward. I wanted to stay, as Christmas and Dad's birthday were approaching, but my husband was not fairing well psychologically and I decided it was time to go home.

Christmas that year was rushed, but my husband and I welcomed some peace of mind being home—if there was peace of mind with Dad still in the hospital fighting for his life. And in the middle of all this, I feverishly continued working on my book. The journey, which Corey supported me through, seemed endless. Page after page of rewrites, draft after draft, research upon research, but finally, in April of 2009, *Excalibur Reclaims Her King* was finished.

It's funny, but the only celebration I had was receiving a congratulatory call from Corey and opening a bottle of my favorite Robert Mondavi Cabernet Sauvignon. I poured a glass in one of my Rosetta wine glasses, and that was it. No trumpets, no parades, just a glass of wine that I leisurely sipped.

Corey set me up for book sales on Amazon and on his website; our next task was to find venues for book signings and talks about my work. With doors opening for me as a professional author, time passed quickly. I did not get back to Florida until July.

Since Dad was having issues with his legs, he was not at his assisted living home but in a nursing home for rehabilitation. My visit was a surprise, and when he saw me, he gave me that smile that I so wanted to see—the smile that made me know he was okay. I was so happy to see my dad sitting and laughing, looking every bit like the man I knew and loved.

"Ah, sweetheart! What are you doing here?" He reached his arms out from his sitting position in the wheelchair and hugged me as if tomorrow did not exist.

My brother kept taking pictures, and my sister-in-law laughed with us. "Wow, Dad, you don't smile like that for me," she teased through her laughter.

"Let me look at you!" said Dad.

I stood back and gazed at him in return. He was dressed in a white t-shirt and his favorite black pants. Despite his energy and good spirit, my heart sank knowing that the wheelchair was now a permanent fixture for him; his hip had given out after his illness in December.

Adam wheeled him out of the room, and we went out to the garden. It was beautiful, with trees, other foliage, and a fountain in the center. I was in awe at how peaceful it felt.

"Hey, Dad, you know what this reminds me of?" I asked, smiling.

He looked at me questioningly. "No, what?"

"The courtyard of King Arthur. The one we built in book three, the one where the knights practice before battle."

Dad glanced around, and his eyes lit up the way they had when we'd written in all those doctors' offices in Manhattan. "Yeah," he said, "it does."

That week, my dad and I enjoyed our time together, and my brother, his wife, and I toured Winter Garden, Florida. We shopped, talked in the nursing home garden with Dad, and even enjoyed a lunch together in the cafeteria. I savored every minute of being with my family.

On my last day in Florida, Dad was already out enjoying the garden when my brother, sister-in-law, and I arrived at the hospital.

"Hey, Dad," I said, leaning to kiss him.

"Hey, sweetheart, how are ya?" he asked with his great big grin.

I looked at my watch. I had only two hours left before I needed to be at the airport. If I could, I would have stayed and never left. The sun, the trees, and that fountain were mesmerizing to me and let me know that there was a God and that he was looking down at us, right then and there.

Dad asked all three of us for a special favor. "Please, can we say some prayers together?"

I smiled. "Yeah, Dad, just like we did when we were kids."

Dad pulled his rosary from his shirt pocket, where it was permanent fixture of his wardrobe. "In the name of the Father and of the Son and of the Holy Ghost..."

We all blessed ourselves and Dad led the prayers.

"Our Father, who art in heaven, hallowed be thy name ..."

We joined him. "Thy kingdom come, thy will be done, on earth as it is in heaven. Give us this day our daily bread and forgive us our trespasses, as we forgive those who trespass against us. And lead us not into temptation and deliver us from evil. Amen."

I sat there, no longer the child who hated praying with her parents, no longer the girl with a fanatical mother, but the woman who now enjoyed praying with her family. In those moments, I found some form of solace among the trees and water, as though Jesus was there in his living form, sitting and washing us—his children—in his peace.

In the year that followed, I worked so hard to promote my books that I maxed out my credit card and couldn't afford to book another ticket to see my dad. Instead, I spent a good amount of time calling him while I made dinner. We talked about his health, the kids, and my work.

"So are your books in the stores yet?" Dad asked for the thousandth time. He wanted to see my books on the shelves of Barnes and Noble more than I did.

While he sat in his room in Florida and I prepared meals in my kitchen, we exchanged ideas about a fantasy book I'd started writing about a dragon named Eryke who saved kids from being bullied. Dad and I went back and forth discussing characters, plots, and setting, and every phone call ended with, "Write it down—lest you forget!"

I had planned to visit dad for Father's Day 2010, and spoke to my brother about coming down by myself. He was ecstatic and so was his wife, as we had not seen each other in eleven months, but Adam had a better idea.

"Ang, I have the first two weeks of July for vacation. Why don't you surprise Dad again? I think he needs a lift."

I beamed, loving the idea. "I'll send you my plane schedule and see you then."

June ended, and I began packing. Toward the end of the month, however, Adam called again.

"Ang, listen. Dad is very low," he said. "I think it's best we tell him you're coming."

My heart sank at the news of Dad's health.

"Talk to him," Adam said. Moments later, he passed the phone to my dad.

"Honey?" Dad's voice was so low that I lost my appetite.

"Dad, what is going on?" I asked.

"Angela, come home," he said softly.

My heart skipped a beat—or two or a hundred. This was not good.

"Ang." It was my brother on the phone again.

"Adam, I am getting on a plane tonight."

Two weeks earlier, on Father's Day weekend, Dad had been hospitalized for an infection on his foot, but he'd remained in good spirits and was enjoying life again. What had changed in the last seventy-two hours?

"No, don't come yet," Adam said. "Let me see what gives, okay?"

"Okay, but keep me posted."

In the early hours of the morning, Adam called again. I jolted from sleep to answer.

"It's not good," he said. "Dad is very lethargic and confused. Talk to him."

I braced myself. "Hi, Dad, can you hear me?"

"Huh?" he said.

"Dad, it's me, your daughter—can you hear me?"

"Ang ... ela." His voice was garbled.

"Yes, Dad. It's me. I'm coming home."

Twenty-four hours and lots of prayers later, my daughter Andrea and I left for Florida. We landed with bags in tow, grabbed a cab, and met my brother, who was waiting for us outside the hospital. I couldn't get out of the cab fast enough. Adam and I hugged each other hard.

Adam placed our luggage in his car, which was in the lot, and we went up to see Dad. My father lay in a bed with tubes shooting out of him like he was an octopus. Pumps going, he was breathing hard, and his face told me all I needed to know at that moment: *I am dying. Please call a priest.*

I grabbed for his hand. It was ice cold.

"Dad, do you know who this is?" Adam asked loudly.

Dad looked at me and smiled. He squeezed my hand with the grip he'd had all his life, took one more look at me, and said, "You are my daughter."

"You better believe it, Dad." I kissed him. His face was clammy and pale, but his touch reminded me of my grandmother just before she passed. He was not going to make it this time.

For the next three days, my brother, sister-in-law, and Andrea sat watch at his bed, talking to the doctors about test results. We already knew he had pneumonia, both lungs were filled with fluid, and he had a urinary tract infection that was playing games with his toxins, but we did not know that Dad had an acute bacterial infection that was not responding to antibiotics. Adam was at Dad's side nonstop, addressing every need, not backing down once. I was impressed and proud of him, but I also needed my little brother—not the nurse he was while on duty—with me, at least for a while.

The end of the week was hard for both of us. We knew we were losing the fight. Dad was dying a bit each day, and we finally ordered that his pacemaker be shut down but that he continue to receive food and liquids.

The following Tuesday, we all went to Collison-Carey Hand Funeral Home to pick Dad's casket from a catalogue. We chose one called Golden Autumn, a royal black casket fully open with gold handles. Dad liked black and gold. Then we decided what Dad would wear: his navy suit, which Adam and I had bought him for his eightieth birthday, his white ribbed shirt, and red tie. Dad always looked great in his suit and black dress shoes. On the lapel, he would wear his Sacred Heart pin and a freshly ironed handkerchief in his suit pocket.

The funeral directors were kind and helped us plan every detail so that Dad could come home to New York for a wake at Roth Funeral Home in Woodside, where he lived and was respected by many.

Dad's prognosis kept getting more and more grim. My daughter and I shared a bed at my brother's house, and one night, Andrea told me, "Mom, I know Grandpa is not going to make it." She looked at me, eyes wracked with concern for both her grandfather and me.

"I know, honey," I said. "I'm worried, too."

Strange how the tides had turned. My dad had helped me understand my grandmother's passing, and now I was filling that role for my own child, though she was already a grown woman herself.

A few days later, Adam and I had but one more thing to do. We spoke to his doctors and ordered all medications stopped and tubes removed, except the feeding tube. We would not let Dad starve to death.

"How long do you give him?" Adam asked his friend and my dad's doctor.

"Adam, he could last days, weeks, even months like this," the doctor said. "It is up to God now."

We went into the room, but we had to wear isolation gowns to protect Dad and ourselves from infection. Dad was sleeping, and I looked up to heaven. *God take him now—please!* I silently begged. He was suffering. He could hardly breathe; even with the oxygen mask, his mouth was wide open, struggling for air. His face was dark gray, and bags hung under his eyes. This was not my strong, tear-the-house-down dad.

My brother went over to him and said, "Dad, we are here."

"Adam, let him sleep," I said.

"No, I want him to fight, damn it, fight back!" My brother was having a hard time backing down.

"There is nothing we can do, Adam. You have to be his son now, not his nurse."

"Leave me alone!" Adam yelled.

"Uncle Adam, stop fighting with Mom. Please." Andrea's voice was strong. "There is nothing we can do. You have to face it."

"What do you know?" he shot back.

"He's my grandfather, too, you know," Andrea said softly.

A few beats of silence passed, and Adam went to Andrea and held her tight. I joined in, and we held one another tightly, years of arguments and differences melting away for Dad's sake.

A fter I'd been there for eight days, I finally got a chance to be alone with Dad. It did not take long for me to break down and sob at his side. I was shaking and did not know if I would even make it out of the hospital, much less the less the airport that afternoon.

I was wearing a mask and hideous blue plastic full body gown, with blue gloves on my hands. I took one glove off and held my father's hand. I knew it might be the very last time I would hold him.

"Dad, pray with me," I said, though I knew he could hardly speak. "Hail Mary, full of grace, the Lord is with thee. Blessed art thou among women and blessed is the fruit of thy womb, Jesus …"

"Sweetheart …"

"Dad, can you hear me?" I gripped his hand and held it to my chest. "Dad, I love you. I love you so very much!"

His mouth wide open, he coughed out sputum and blood. His face was dark and gray. I let go of his hand and held his face in my two hands. "Dad, if you cannot fight this anymore, then go to Mom. Go to Mom, Dad. Hear me?"

I drew on my courage and said through tears, "You always wanted to know what God looks like. Go to him, go see him." My voice was garbled as I drew another hard breath. "Dad, I love you. I'm a big girl. I can take care of myself now. Go to Mom."

He raised his hand and grabbed for my arm. "You are my Angela," he said, his voice clear. "My daughter, Angela."

I took off my mask and kissed my father on his cheek, his forehead, and on his hands. I didn't care about infection. My father was leaving soon. I knew it.

The door opened, and it was the nurse coming to change the bag on Dad's catheter. She took one look at me and left. At three p.m. on July 14, 2010, I kissed my father and held him for the last time.

"I love you, Dad," I said. "I love you with all my heart."

CHAPTER 38:
GOODBYE
AND
HELLO

My father, Anthony Michael Marquise, passed from this earth at 12:05 on a Saturday afternoon—July 24, 2010—with a hospice nurse at his side. I wished I had been with him, but I believe he spared my brother and me the pain of those final moments.

Adam received the call at home that Dad passed away. Minutes later, he called me, and I braced myself at the sound of his voice. I nearly dropped to the floor when he said, "Angela, Dad passed away."

Adam and his wife would have Dad's body prepared in Florida and hold a wake there for his new friends and for my brother's. Meanwhile, I had to prepare my family and the funeral home in Woodside, where Dad lived, for his arrival. My heart ached for the week I waited for them to arrive. I wanted Dad home, safe again with me.

On Friday, July 30, 2011, I walked into Roth Funeral Home with my kids and husband. My brother and his wife waited for us on a white couch. The minute I set eyes on Adam, we jumped into each other's arms. We needed to be together. It was only us now.

"I love you, Angela," he said, and we were engulfed in each other's embrace. We were shaking, yet neither of us had really cried yet.

"I love you, too."

My sister-in-law greeted me with a warm embrace, but I pushed from her though I knew it seemed rude. All I wanted to do was see my dad.

"Do you want to be alone?" Adam asked.

"No, we'll go together."

I braced myself. The child in me was afraid, but the woman in me made me say, "Open the chapel door."

Dad looked so handsome lying there in his suit. Even at eighty-seven years old, he was one of the most handsome men in New York. I thought I would be afraid, but I bent down and kissed his face, stroked his full head of hair, and held his hand. I was not prepared for him to be so cold. It shocked me, but I was not afraid. I shook, weeping inside, but he was home and with me. That was all I cared about.

Three days later, my family and I buried my dad. After the morning ceremony, my children—Dad's grandchildren—filed in front of Dad's remains to say a brief silent prayer and final goodbye. Then they were led out of the chapel, and the doors were closed. Adam and I remained behind to bid our private goodbyes to our dad.

We approached the casket together. Holding each other for support, we said a prayer and repeated, "I love you, Dad." My heart was pounding, and my chest felt as though it would explode. A great cry wanted to be expressed, but for some reason it would not break.

We stayed behind to witness the closing of the casket. My children had given their grandfather a rosary created with red tea roses, and the flowers were wrapped around Dad's neck to be with him for all time. Adam and I had created memory posters of our lives with Dad, and the posters were folded and placed on the side. My hands bore a cold sweat, watching the funeral directors prepare my Dad. Then it was our turn. We were given the white funerary blanket, and my brother and I covered Dad's remains as though we were tucking him into bed. We backed away as his body was lowered in the casket and the lid closed, his nameplate fashioned to the foot of the casket.

We then proceeded to St. Sebastian's Church in Woodside, where Mass was held in Dad's honor. Our immediate family served as pallbearers, and my brother and I read from the Old and New Testaments. The priest spoke of Dad as a good Catholic man and active member of the church. At the end of Mass, we briefly eulogized our dad. The chapel was full of family and old friends. It was great to see that so many people had come out to say farewell to him.

At the cemetery, we were directed to the ceremonial canopy, where two soldiers stood guard over my dad. The immediate family was seated along with my elderly aunts and uncles; the rest stood behind us. The awning was gray and white marble, and the tabernacle where the coffin rested was black. "Taps" began to play, and I silently sung the words to the hymn. As the last note of the chant faded to a soft hush, the soldiers—stoic and reverent—folded an American flag into the ceremonial tri-fold, slid it from the casket, and creased the colors from the red and white striped end until it reached the indigo blue with the white stars. When all was done, one of the soldiers, flag in hand, pivoted on his heel and took three steps toward me. I was about to stand, but he knelt in front of me and placed the flag on my lap.

"On behalf of a grateful nation," he said, "I give you this flag in honor of your father."

On behalf of a grateful nation, I repeated inside. My heart soared with bittersweet pride for Dad, as both my hands rested on the blue of the flag. I could feel the embroidered pentagram under my right hand and caressed the rough-hewn cloth with the other. Unshed tears blurred my vision as the soldiers left the area and the priest began the prayers of burial.

I barely heard the priest's words. I held the flag tightly, clutching it to my chest, feeling my heart race through the thickness of the layers. *Yes, Dad,* I thought, *on behalf of a grateful nation, and on behalf of a grateful daughter, thank you, and I love you with all my heart.*

AFTERWORD

I will always remember and cherish my dad for all the wonderful things he gave to me. But the memory I hold most dear is the one by the fountain, where my family was whole and healthy for the last time. When we prayed together, I finally found some semblance of solace. And I know that it came, in part, because of the journey I dared to make through my books.

The Quest for Excalibur came to me at a time when I thought nothing was left—not even my faith. My world was constantly shredded and re-sewn as I tried to keep my family together. Writing gave me the key to unlocking doors of hurt so that I could move through them into what has become an amazing journey.

I remember how excited I was to have my first book signing at Barnes and Noble. Autographing my books for people who wanted to read them felt like a dream! The experience was as surreal and exciting as winning an Oscar. From there, I was invited to the Meet the Writers Book Fair at Southampton College, private signings at fairs, and interviews for newspapers, radio, and magazines. Writing about Arianna's adventures helped me become her, a journey that has spanned fifteen years and the shedding of one hundred pounds, making me a proud lifetime member of Weight Watchers. Losing the weight was like casting aside the bricks I'd hidden behind for so long—bricks I never want to be imprisoned by again.

After my third book, *Excalibur Reclaims Her King,* was published, a friend of mine asked me to lead a storytelling session in her children's store. I called my program "The Excalibur Reading Program." Soon, with my skills for writing and my knowledge of networking with politicians and educators, I found a meaning for my program: it wasn't just about storytelling. It was a way to help special needs and abused children dream and learn how to achieve those dreams.

At a book sale, I met Joe Aiello, who was then president of the Glendale Kiwanis Club. Joe invited me to the Kiwanis meeting to talk about my work and then invited me to join Kiwanis. I began to attend meetings on Thursdays, as well as going to as other Kiwanis functions. At a Christmas fundraiser, I met Council Member Elizabeth Crowley, and I gave her a flyer about my reading program. She asked me a few questions and then encouraged me to make an appointment at her office. There, Elizabeth suggested I make my reading program not-for-profit so that I could reach more kids with her help. She even printed out the paperwork for me.

I found a great lawyer through Corey, by now a good friend as well as my publisher, and then another lawyer in my area, Fred Haller. During the months of waiting for my papers to come in, my friend, Frankie Janello, and I planned events in her store. Two were safety days held in conjunction with our local police and fire departments; together, we helped three hundred children receive photo identifications so that if they were lost or, God forbid, abducted, the police had a tangible tool to help find them. Immersing myself in this new kind of work was an amazing feeling, and I threw myself into growing the program and involving myself in my community.

Sixteen months after applying for non-profit status, I received my state certificate and my 501(c)(3). I cannot describe the pride I felt and still feel, knowing I can help kids like my son, as well as those who grew up like me.

As my program evolved, something else was changing, too. In the fabric of my fantasy novels, I had woven aspects of my own life. In *The Quest for Excalibur*, in particular, I wrote, through Arianna, that I was raped. The revelation was not lost on my readers. To my surprise, they were beginning to relate to me as a person who was not only a writer but also a victim of a crime and abuse. Without fully realizing it, I eventually stopped talking about Arianna and started talking about myself—my own experiences, my own history with domestic violence and sexual assault.

In 2008, I began to work with a woman named Jennifer Geronimo, a consultant who helped me find speaking engagements. During our work together, she introduced me to some people from Amnesty International. At the organization's Human Rights Art Festival in April 2009, I presented a speech called "Living with Rage." In the speech, I told the tale of a young woman—me—who was molested, emotionally abused, beaten, and raped. I had only spoken once about my rape at a "Girls' Night Out" business dinner in my area. This was the first real public speaking engagement where I told the story of my life. After that, I found a new journey, a new purpose: sharing my story in hopes that it would move others to share theirs. Jennifer helped me start my own Blog Talk Radio show, through which I have become an advocate for children with special needs and also people like me—survivors of domestic violence and sexual abuse.

As I began to talk more about my experiences, Corey encouraged me to take the bravest step yet: write my memoir. At the beginning of the project, Corey introduced me to my new editor, Katie Gutierrez Painter. With Corey's encouragement and Katie's constant support and wisdom, I embarked on the task of writing this book. There were days when the words flowed on the page and other days when I could not even face the keyboard. I'd go for long walks instead, trying to escape the painful memories the writing process was conjuring for me. Katie supported me through e-mails and calls, and my friends from Amnesty would tell me to "go for it, break the silence." But the fear and shame haunted me, and I would close my laptop and walk away. Yet, in walking away, I discovered my words and the conviction that it was okay to speak, to share my truth without anyone judging me. I found myself at my desk until the wee hours of the morning, quietly writing, and there was peace.

Between my memoir and my radio show, speaking engagements and community work, and after decades of being silenced, I have found my voice. And, through it, my solace. It is my deepest hope that this book can help others find theirs.

RESOURCES FOR HELP WITH
DOMESTIC VIOLENCE

I f you or someone you love is a victim of domestic violence and/or sexual
abuse, the best thing you can do is reach out for help. Below are some
organizations that would welcome your call or e-mail.

National Hotline for Domestic Violence
24-Hour Hotline: 1-800-799-SAFE

New York State Coalition Against Domestic Violence
350 New Scotland Avenues
Albany, NY 12054
Phone: 518 482-55464
Fax: 518-482-3807
Toll-free (English): 800-942-6906
Toll-free (Spanish): 800-942-6908
www.nyscadv.org
nyxcadv@nyscadv.org

Institute on Violence, Abuse &Trauma
Alliant International University
10065 Old Grove Road, Suite 101
San Diego, CA 92131
Phone: (858) 527-1860 x 4410
Fax: (858)-527-1743
www.ivatcenters.org

Amnesty International Against Domestic Violence
www.amnestyinternaional.org
www.amnestyhumanrightsfestival.org

Office for Victims of Crime

OVC Recourse Center

www.ojp.usdoj.gov/ove/ovces/welcome.html

The National Center for Victims of Crime

www.ncvc.org/ncvc/main.aspx?dbID=DB_VictimAssistance207

National Organization for Victim Assistance (NOVA)

Victim Assistance

www.trynova.org

RAINN – Rape, Abuse, and Incest National Network

www.rainn.org

UNICEF – The United Nations Children's Fund

www.unicef.org

ABOUT
ANGELICA HARRIS

Angelica Harris is a successful author, entrepreneur, advocate, and speaker. She is using her personal story to build a community of conquerors that will together fight domestic violence and help others—and one another—find healing.

Angelica was born to a diverse European family in New York City. Her love for writing was ignited in high school, when she used the written word to escape the domestic violence and sexual abuse she was hiding from family and friends. She pursued creative arts at Hunter College, where she majored in history and theatre before leaving school to help financially support her family.

With a lifelong passion for medieval history, especially Arthurian lore, Angelica is the author of three fantasy novels: *The Quest for Excalibur, Excalibur and the Holy Grail,* and *Excalibur Reclaims Her King.* From these books was born the Excalibur Reading Program, a non-profit program that brings the importance of reading, writing, and the arts to all children, as well as to organizations dedicated to children with special needs. The Excalibur Reading Program is the new pilot program in designated public schools in Queens, New York, and Angelica continues to work with community leaders to better her program and community.

Writing *Living With Rage* has opened a new chapter in Angelica's life. She is partnering with organizations such as Amnesty International and the Institute on Violence, Abuse, and Trauma (IVAT) to raise awareness of domestic violence and support healing through story. She is also leading talks and writing workshops in a New York women's prison to help inmates—many of whom have been victims of domestic violence and sexual assault—return to the workforce and overcome past trauma or abuse. Angelica is actively seeking speaking engagements, guest blogging, and other ventures that will allow her to work with victims of domestic violence and sexual abuse. Together, she believes, we can all become conquerors.